GNU Coreutils

A catalogue record for this book is available from the Hong Kong Public Libraries.

Published in Hong Kong by Samurai Media Limited.

Email: info@samuraimedia.org

ISBN 978-988-8381-40-1

Short Contents

Table of Contents

1 Introduction

This manual is a work in progress: many sections make no attempt to explain basic concepts in a way suitable for novices. Thus, if you are interested, please get involved in improving this manual. The entire GNU community will benefit.

The GNU utilities documented here are mostly compatible with the POSIX standard. Please report bugs to `bug-coreutils@gnu.org`. Remember to include the version number, machine architecture, input files, and any other information needed to reproduce the bug: your input, what you expected, what you got, and why it is wrong. Diffs are welcome, but please include a description of the problem as well, since this is sometimes difficult to infer. See Section "Bugs" in *Using and Porting GNU CC*.

This manual was originally derived from the Unix man pages in the distributions, which were written by David MacKenzie and updated by Jim Meyering. What you are reading now is the authoritative documentation for these utilities; the man pages are no longer being maintained. The original `fmt` man page was written by Ross Paterson. François Pinard did the initial conversion to Texinfo format. Karl Berry did the indexing, some reorganization, and editing of the results. Brian Youmans of the Free Software Foundation office staff combined the manuals for textutils, fileutils, and sh-utils to produce the present omnibus manual. Richard Stallman contributed his usual invaluable insights to the overall process.

2 Common options

Certain options are available in all of these programs. Rather than writing identical descriptions for each of the programs, they are described here. (In fact, every GNU program accepts (or should accept) these options.)

Normally options and operands can appear in any order, and programs act as if all the options appear before any operands. For example, 'sort -r passwd -t :' acts like 'sort -r -t : passwd', since ':' is an option-argument of -t. However, if the POSIXLY_CORRECT environment variable is set, options must appear before operands, unless otherwise specified for a particular command.

A few programs can usefully have trailing operands with leading '-'. With such a program, options must precede operands even if POSIXLY_CORRECT is not set, and this fact is noted in the program description. For example, the env command's options must appear before its operands, since in some cases the operands specify a command that itself contains options.

Most programs that accept long options recognize unambiguous abbreviations of those options. For example, 'rmdir --ignore-fail-on-non-empty' can be invoked as 'rmdir --ignore-fail' or even 'rmdir --i'. Ambiguous options, such as 'ls --h', are identified as such.

Some of these programs recognize the --help and --version options only when one of them is the sole command line argument. For these programs, abbreviations of the long options are not always recognized.

'--help'   Print a usage message listing all available options, then exit successfully.

'--version'
             Print the version number, then exit successfully.

'--'   Delimit the option list. Later arguments, if any, are treated as operands even if they begin with '-'. For example, 'sort -- -r' reads from the file named -r.

A single '-' operand is not really an option, though it looks like one. It stands for a file operand, and some tools treat it as standard input, or as standard output if that is clear from the context. For example, 'sort -' reads from standard input, and is equivalent to plain 'sort'. Unless otherwise specified, a '-' can appear as any operand that requires a file name.

2.1 Exit status

Nearly every command invocation yields an integral *exit status* that can be used to change how other commands work. For the vast majority of commands, an exit status of zero indicates success. Failure is indicated by a nonzero value—typically '1', though it may differ on unusual platforms as POSIX requires only that it be nonzero.

However, some of the programs documented here do produce other exit status values and a few associate different meanings with the values '0' and '1'. Here are some of the exceptions: chroot, env, expr, nice, nohup, numfmt, printenv, sort, stdbuf, test, timeout, tty.

2.2 Backup options

Some GNU programs (at least cp, install, ln, and mv) optionally make backups of files before writing new versions. These options control the details of these backups. The options are also briefly mentioned in the descriptions of the particular programs.

'-b'

'--backup[=method]'

> Make a backup of each file that would otherwise be overwritten or removed. Without this option, the original versions are destroyed. Use *method* to determine the type of backups to make. When this option is used but *method* is not specified, then the value of the VERSION_CONTROL environment variable is used. And if VERSION_CONTROL is not set, the default backup type is 'existing'.
>
> Note that the short form of this option, -b does not accept any argument. Using -b is equivalent to using --backup=existing.
>
> This option corresponds to the Emacs variable 'version-control'; the values for *method* are the same as those used in Emacs. This option also accepts more descriptive names. The valid *method*s are (unique abbreviations are accepted):

> 'none'
>
> 'off'   Never make backups.

> 'numbered'
>
> 't'   Always make numbered backups.

> 'existing'
>
> 'nil'   Make numbered backups of files that already have them, simple backups of the others.

> 'simple'
>
> 'never'   Always make simple backups. Please note 'never' is not to be confused with 'none'.

'-S suffix'

'--suffix=suffix'

> Append *suffix* to each backup file made with -b. If this option is not specified, the value of the SIMPLE_BACKUP_SUFFIX environment variable is used. And if SIMPLE_BACKUP_SUFFIX is not set, the default is '~', just as in Emacs.

2.3 Block size

Some GNU programs (at least df, du, and ls) display sizes in "blocks". You can adjust the block size and method of display to make sizes easier to read. The block size used for display is independent of any file system block size. Fractional block counts are rounded up to the nearest integer.

The default block size is chosen by examining the following environment variables in turn; the first one that is set determines the block size.

DF_BLOCK_SIZE

> This specifies the default block size for the df command. Similarly, DU_BLOCK_SIZE specifies the default for du and LS_BLOCK_SIZE for ls.

BLOCK_SIZE

>This specifies the default block size for all three commands, if the above command-specific environment variables are not set.

BLOCKSIZE

>This specifies the default block size for all values that are normally printed as blocks, if neither `BLOCK_SIZE` nor the above command-specific environment variables are set. Unlike the other environment variables, `BLOCKSIZE` does not affect values that are normally printed as byte counts, e.g., the file sizes contained in `ls -l` output.

POSIXLY_CORRECT

>If neither *command*_`BLOCK_SIZE`, nor `BLOCK_SIZE`, nor `BLOCKSIZE` is set, but this variable is set, the block size defaults to 512.

If none of the above environment variables are set, the block size currently defaults to 1024 bytes in most contexts, but this number may change in the future. For `ls` file sizes, the block size defaults to 1 byte.

A block size specification can be a positive integer specifying the number of bytes per block, or it can be `human-readable` or `si` to select a human-readable format. Integers may be followed by suffixes that are upward compatible with the SI prefixes for decimal multiples and with the ISO/IEC 80000-13 (formerly IEC 60027-2) prefixes for binary multiples.

With human-readable formats, output sizes are followed by a size letter such as 'M' for megabytes. `BLOCK_SIZE=human-readable` uses powers of 1024; 'M' stands for 1,048,576 bytes. `BLOCK_SIZE=si` is similar, but uses powers of 1000 and appends 'B'; 'MB' stands for 1,000,000 bytes.

A block size specification preceded by '' causes output sizes to be displayed with thousands separators. The `LC_NUMERIC` locale specifies the thousands separator and grouping. For example, in an American English locale, '`--block-size="'1kB"`' would cause a size of 1234000 bytes to be displayed as '1,234'. In the default C locale, there is no thousands separator so a leading '' has no effect.

An integer block size can be followed by a suffix to specify a multiple of that size. A bare size letter, or one followed by 'iB', specifies a multiple using powers of 1024. A size letter followed by 'B' specifies powers of 1000 instead. For example, '1M' and '1MiB' are equivalent to '1048576', whereas '1MB' is equivalent to '1000000'.

A plain suffix without a preceding integer acts as if '1' were prepended, except that it causes a size indication to be appended to the output. For example, '`--block-size="kB"`' displays 3000 as '3kB'.

The following suffixes are defined. Large sizes like `1Y` may be rejected by your computer due to limitations of its arithmetic.

'kB'   kilobyte: $10^3 = 1000$.

'k'
'K'
'KiB'   kibibyte: $2^{10} = 1024$. 'K' is special: the SI prefix is 'k' and the ISO/IEC 80000-13 prefix is 'Ki', but tradition and POSIX use 'k' to mean 'KiB'.

'MB'   megabyte: $10^6 = 1,000,000$.

'M'
'MiB'   mebibyte: $2^{20} = 1,048,576$.

'GB'   gigabyte: $10^9 = 1,000,000,000$.

'G'
'GiB'   gibibyte: $2^{30} = 1,073,741,824$.

'TB'   terabyte: $10^{12} = 1,000,000,000,000$.

'T'
'TiB'   tebibyte: $2^{40} = 1,099,511,627,776$.

'PB'   petabyte: $10^{15} = 1,000,000,000,000,000$.

'P'
'PiB'   pebibyte: $2^{50} = 1,125,899,906,842,624$.

'EB'   exabyte: $10^{18} = 1,000,000,000,000,000,000$.

'E'
'EiB'   exbibyte: $2^{60} = 1,152,921,504,606,846,976$.

'ZB'   zettabyte: $10^{21} = 1,000,000,000,000,000,000,000$

'Z'
'ZiB' $2^{70} = 1,180,591,620,717,411,303,424$.

'YB'   yottabyte: $10^{24} = 1,000,000,000,000,000,000,000,000$.

'Y'
'YiB' $2^{80} = 1,208,925,819,614,629,174,706,176$.

Block size defaults can be overridden by an explicit `--block-size=`*size* option. The `-k` option is equivalent to `--block-size=1K`, which is the default unless the `POSIXLY_CORRECT` environment variable is set. The `-h` or `--human-readable` option is equivalent to `--block-size=human-readable`. The `--si` option is equivalent to `--block-size=si`. Note for `ls` the `-k` option does not control the display of the apparent file sizes, whereas the `--block-size` option does.

2.4 Floating point numbers

Commands that accept or produce floating point numbers employ the floating point representation of the underlying system, and suffer from rounding error, overflow, and similar floating-point issues. Almost all modern systems use IEEE-754 floating point, and it is typically portable to assume IEEE-754 behavior these days. IEEE-754 has positive and negative infinity, distinguishes positive from negative zero, and uses special values called NaNs to represent invalid computations such as dividing zero by itself. For more information, please see David Goldberg's paper What Every Computer Scientist Should Know About Floating-Point Arithmetic.

Commands that accept floating point numbers as options, operands or input use the standard C functions `strtod` and `strtold` to convert from text to floating point numbers. These floating point numbers therefore can use scientific notation like `1.0e-34` and `-10e100`. Commands that parse floating point also understand case-insensitive `inf`, `infinity`, and

NaN, although whether such values are useful depends on the command in question. Modern C implementations also accept hexadecimal floating point numbers such as `-0x.ep-3`, which stands for $-14/16$ times 2^-3, which equals -0.109375. The `LC_NUMERIC` locale determines the decimal-point character. See Section "Parsing of Floats" in *The GNU C Library Reference Manual*.

2.5 Signal specifications

A *signal* may be a signal name like 'HUP', or a signal number like '1', or an exit status of a process terminated by the signal. A signal name can be given in canonical form or prefixed by 'SIG'. The case of the letters is ignored. The following signal names and numbers are supported on all POSIX compliant systems:

'HUP'   1. Hangup.

'INT'   2. Terminal interrupt.

'QUIT'   3. Terminal quit.

'ABRT'   6. Process abort.

'KILL'   9. Kill (cannot be caught or ignored).

'ALRM'   14. Alarm Clock.

'TERM'   15. Termination.

Other supported signal names have system-dependent corresponding numbers. All systems conforming to POSIX 1003.1-2001 also support the following signals:

'BUS'   Access to an undefined portion of a memory object.

'CHLD'   Child process terminated, stopped, or continued.

'CONT'   Continue executing, if stopped.

'FPE'   Erroneous arithmetic operation.

'ILL'   Illegal Instruction.

'PIPE'   Write on a pipe with no one to read it.

'SEGV'   Invalid memory reference.

'STOP'   Stop executing (cannot be caught or ignored).

'TSTP'   Terminal stop.

'TTIN'   Background process attempting read.

'TTOU'   Background process attempting write.

'URG'   High bandwidth data is available at a socket.

'USR1'   User-defined signal 1.

'USR2'   User-defined signal 2.

POSIX 1003.1-2001 systems that support the XSI extension also support the following signals:

'POLL'   Pollable event.

'PROF'   Profiling timer expired.

'SYS'   Bad system call.

'TRAP'   Trace/breakpoint trap.

'VTALRM'   Virtual timer expired.

'XCPU'   CPU time limit exceeded.

'XFSZ'   File size limit exceeded.

POSIX 1003.1-2001 systems that support the XRT extension also support at least eight real-time signals called 'RTMIN', 'RTMIN+1', ..., 'RTMAX-1', 'RTMAX'.

2.6 chown, chgrp, chroot, id: Disambiguating user names and IDs

Since the *user* and *group* arguments to these commands may be specified as names or numeric IDs, there is an apparent ambiguity. What if a user or group *name* is a string of digits?[1] Should the command interpret it as a user name or as an ID? POSIX requires that these commands first attempt to resolve the specified string as a name, and only once that fails, then try to interpret it as an ID. This is troublesome when you want to specify a numeric ID, say 42, and it must work even in a pathological situation where '42' is a user name that maps to some other user ID, say 1000. Simply invoking chown 42 F, will set Fs owner ID to 1000—not what you intended.

GNU chown, chgrp, chroot, and id provide a way to work around this, that at the same time may result in a significant performance improvement by eliminating a database look-up. Simply precede each numeric user ID and/or group ID with a '+', in order to force its interpretation as an integer:

```
chown +42 F
chgrp +$numeric_group_id another-file
chown +0:+0 /
```

The name look-up process is skipped for each '+'-prefixed string, because a string containing '+' is never a valid user or group name. This syntax is accepted on most common Unix systems, but not on Solaris 10.

2.7 Sources of random data

The shuf, shred, and sort commands sometimes need random data to do their work. For example, 'sort -R' must choose a hash function at random, and it needs random data to make this selection.

By default these commands use an internal pseudo-random generator initialized by a small amount of entropy, but can be directed to use an external source with the --random-source=*file* option. An error is reported if *file* does not contain enough bytes.

For example, the device file /dev/urandom could be used as the source of random data. Typically, this device gathers environmental noise from device drivers and other sources

---

[1] Using a number as a user name is common in some environments.

into an entropy pool, and uses the pool to generate random bits. If the pool is short of data, the device reuses the internal pool to produce more bits, using a cryptographically secure pseudo-random number generator. But be aware that this device is not designed for bulk random data generation and is relatively slow.

`/dev/urandom` suffices for most practical uses, but applications requiring high-value or long-term protection of private data may require an alternate data source like `/dev/random` or `/dev/arandom`. The set of available sources depends on your operating system.

To reproduce the results of an earlier invocation of a command, you can save some random data into a file and then use that file as the random source in earlier and later invocations of the command. Rather than depending on a file, one can generate a reproducible arbitrary amount of pseudo-random data given a seed value, using for example:

```
get_seeded_random()
{
  seed="$1"
  openssl enc -aes-256-ctr -pass pass:"$seed" -nosalt \
    </dev/zero 2>/dev/null
}

shuf -i1-100 --random-source=<(get_seeded_random 42)
```

2.8 Target directory

The `cp`, `install`, `ln`, and `mv` commands normally treat the last operand specially when it is a directory or a symbolic link to a directory. For example, 'cp source dest' is equivalent to 'cp source dest/source' if dest is a directory. Sometimes this behavior is not exactly what is wanted, so these commands support the following options to allow more fine-grained control:

'`-T`'
'`--no-target-directory`'
>   Do not treat the last operand specially when it is a directory or a symbolic link to a directory. This can help avoid race conditions in programs that operate in a shared area. For example, when the command 'mv /tmp/source /tmp/dest' succeeds, there is no guarantee that `/tmp/source` was renamed to `/tmp/dest`: it could have been renamed to `/tmp/dest/source` instead, if some other process created `/tmp/dest` as a directory. However, if mv -T /tmp/source /tmp/dest succeeds, there is no question that `/tmp/source` was renamed to `/tmp/dest`.
>
>   In the opposite situation, where you want the last operand to be treated as a directory and want a diagnostic otherwise, you can use the `--target-directory` (`-t`) option.

'`-t directory`'
'`--target-directory=directory`'
>   Use *directory* as the directory component of each destination file name.
>
>   The interface for most programs is that after processing options and a finite (possibly zero) number of fixed-position arguments, the remaining argument list is either expected to be empty, or is a list of items (usually files) that will

all be handled identically. The `xargs` program is designed to work well with this convention.

The commands in the `mv`-family are unusual in that they take a variable number of arguments with a special case at the *end* (namely, the target directory). This makes it nontrivial to perform some operations, e.g., "move all files from here to ../d/", because `mv * ../d/` might exhaust the argument space, and `ls | xargs ...` doesn't have a clean way to specify an extra final argument for each invocation of the subject command. (It can be done by going through a shell command, but that requires more human labor and brain power than it should.)

The `--target-directory` (`-t`) option allows the `cp`, `install`, `ln`, and `mv` programs to be used conveniently with `xargs`. For example, you can move the files from the current directory to a sibling directory, `d` like this:

```
ls | xargs mv -t ../d --
```

However, this doesn't move files whose names begin with '.'. If you use the GNU `find` program, you can move those files too, with this command:

```
find . -mindepth 1 -maxdepth 1 \
    | xargs mv -t ../d
```

But both of the above approaches fail if there are no files in the current directory, or if any file has a name containing a blank or some other special characters. The following example removes those limitations and requires both GNU `find` and GNU `xargs`:

```
find . -mindepth 1 -maxdepth 1 -print0 \
    | xargs --null --no-run-if-empty \
        mv -t ../d
```

The `--target-directory` (`-t`) and `--no-target-directory` (`-T`) options cannot be combined.

2.9 Trailing slashes

Some GNU programs (at least `cp` and `mv`) allow you to remove any trailing slashes from each *source* argument before operating on it. The `--strip-trailing-slashes` option enables this behavior.

This is useful when a *source* argument may have a trailing slash and specify a symbolic link to a directory. This scenario is in fact rather common because some shells can automatically append a trailing slash when performing file name completion on such symbolic links. Without this option, `mv`, for example, (via the system's rename function) must interpret a trailing slash as a request to dereference the symbolic link and so must rename the indirectly referenced *directory* and not the symbolic link. Although it may seem surprising that such behavior be the default, it is required by POSIX and is consistent with other parts of that standard.

2.10 Traversing symlinks

The following options modify how `chown` and `chgrp` traverse a hierarchy when the `--recursive` (`-R`) option is also specified. If more than one of the following options is specified, only the final one takes effect. These options specify whether processing a symbolic link to a directory entails operating on just the symbolic link or on all files in the hierarchy rooted at that directory.

These options are independent of `--dereference` and `--no-dereference` (`-h`), which control whether to modify a symlink or its referent.

'-H'   If `--recursive` (`-R`) is specified and a command line argument is a symbolic link to a directory, traverse it.

'-L'   In a recursive traversal, traverse every symbolic link to a directory that is encountered.

'-P'   Do not traverse any symbolic links. This is the default if none of `-H`, `-L`, or `-P` is specified.

2.11 Treating / specially

Certain commands can operate destructively on entire hierarchies. For example, if a user with appropriate privileges mistakenly runs '`rm -rf / tmp/junk`', that may remove all files on the entire system. Since there are so few legitimate uses for such a command, GNU `rm` normally declines to operate on any directory that resolves to /. If you really want to try to remove all the files on your system, you can use the `--no-preserve-root` option, but the default behavior, specified by the `--preserve-root` option, is safer for most purposes.

The commands `chgrp`, `chmod` and `chown` can also operate destructively on entire hierarchies, so they too support these options. Although, unlike `rm`, they don't actually unlink files, these commands are arguably more dangerous when operating recursively on /, since they often work much more quickly, and hence damage more files before an alert user can interrupt them. Tradition and POSIX require these commands to operate recursively on /, so they default to `--no-preserve-root`, but using the `--preserve-root` option makes them safer for most purposes. For convenience you can specify `--preserve-root` in an alias or in a shell function.

Note that the `--preserve-root` option also ensures that `chgrp` and `chown` do not modify / even when dereferencing a symlink pointing to /.

2.12 Special built-in utilities

Some programs like `nice` can invoke other programs; for example, the command '`nice cat file`' invokes the program `cat` by executing the command '`cat file`'. However, *special built-in utilities* like `exit` cannot be invoked this way. For example, the command '`nice exit`' does not have a well-defined behavior: it may generate an error message instead of exiting.

Here is a list of the special built-in utilities that are standardized by POSIX 1003.1-2004.

```
. : break continue eval exec exit export readonly return set
shift times trap unset
```

For example, because '`.`', '`:`', and '`exec`' are special, the commands '`nice . foo.sh`', '`nice :`', and '`nice exec pwd`' do not work as you might expect.

Many shells extend this list. For example, Bash has several extra special built-in utilities like `history`, and `suspend`, and with Bash the command '`nice suspend`' generates an error message instead of suspending.

2.13 Standards conformance

In a few cases, the GNU utilities' default behavior is incompatible with the POSIX standard. To suppress these incompatibilities, define the `POSIXLY_CORRECT` environment variable. Unless you are checking for POSIX conformance, you probably do not need to define `POSIXLY_CORRECT`.

Newer versions of POSIX are occasionally incompatible with older versions. For example, older versions of POSIX required the command 'sort +1' to sort based on the second and succeeding fields in each input line, but starting with POSIX 1003.1 2001 the same command is required to sort the file named +1, and you must instead use the command 'sort -k 2' to get the field-based sort.

The GNU utilities normally conform to the version of POSIX that is standard for your system. To cause them to conform to a different version of POSIX, define the `_POSIX2_VERSION` environment variable to a value of the form *yyyymm* specifying the year and month the standard was adopted. Three values are currently supported for `_POSIX2_VERSION`: '199209' stands for POSIX 1003.2-1992, '200112' stands for POSIX 1003.1-2001, and '200809' stands for POSIX 1003.1-2008. For example, if you have a newer system but are running software that assumes an older version of POSIX and uses 'sort +1' or 'tail +10', you can work around any compatibility problems by setting '_POSIX2_VERSION=199209' in your environment.

2.14 coreutils: Multi-call program

The `coreutils` command invokes an individual utility, either implicitly selected by the last component of the name used to invoke `coreutils`, or explicitly with the `--coreutils-prog` option. Synopsis:

```
coreutils --coreutils-prog=PROGRAM ...
```

The `coreutils` command is not installed by default, so portable scripts should not rely on its existence.

3 Output of entire files

These commands read and write entire files, possibly transforming them in some way.

3.1 `cat`: Concatenate and write files

`cat` copies each *file* ('-' means standard input), or standard input if none are given, to standard output. Synopsis:

        cat [option] [file]...

The program accepts the following options. Also see Chapter 2 [Common options], page 2.

'-A'
'--show-all'
        Equivalent to -vET.

'-b'
'--number-nonblank'
        Number all nonempty output lines, starting with 1.

'-e'   Equivalent to -vE.

'-E'
'--show-ends'
        Display a '$' after the end of each line.

'-n'
'--number'
        Number all output lines, starting with 1. This option is ignored if -b is in effect.

'-s'
'--squeeze-blank'
        Suppress repeated adjacent empty lines; output just one empty line instead of several.

'-t'   Equivalent to -vT.

'-T'
'--show-tabs'
        Display TAB characters as '^I'.

'-u'   Ignored; for POSIX compatibility.

'-v'
'--show-nonprinting'
        Display control characters except for LFD and TAB using '^' notation and precede characters that have the high bit set with 'M-'.

On systems like MS-DOS that distinguish between text and binary files, `cat` normally reads and writes in binary mode. However, `cat` reads in text mode if one of the options -bensAE is used or if `cat` is reading from standard input and standard input is a terminal. Similarly, `cat` writes in text mode if one of the options -bensAE is used or if standard output is a terminal.

An exit status of zero indicates success, and a nonzero value indicates failure.

Examples:

```
# Output f's contents, then standard input, then g's contents.
cat f - g

# Copy standard input to standard output.
cat
```

3.2 tac: Concatenate and write files in reverse

tac copies each *file* ('-' means standard input), or standard input if none are given, to standard output, reversing the records (lines by default) in each separately. Synopsis:

```
tac [option]... [file]...
```

Records are separated by instances of a string (newline by default). By default, this separator string is attached to the end of the record that it follows in the file.

The program accepts the following options. Also see Chapter 2 [Common options], page 2.

'-b'
'--before'

> The separator is attached to the beginning of the record that it precedes in the file.

'-r'
'--regex'   Treat the separator string as a regular expression.

'-s separator'
'--separator=separator'

> Use *separator* as the record separator, instead of newline.

On systems like MS-DOS that distinguish between text and binary files, tac reads and writes in binary mode.

An exit status of zero indicates success, and a nonzero value indicates failure.

Example:

```
# Reverse a file character by character.
tac -r -s 'x\|[^x]'
```

3.3 nl: Number lines and write files

nl writes each *file* ('-' means standard input), or standard input if none are given, to standard output, with line numbers added to some or all of the lines. Synopsis:

```
nl [option]... [file]...
```

nl decomposes its input into (logical) pages; by default, the line number is reset to 1 at the top of each logical page. nl treats all of the input files as a single document; it does not reset line numbers or logical pages between files.

A logical page consists of three sections: header, body, and footer. Any of the sections can be empty. Each can be numbered in a different style from the others.

The beginnings of the sections of logical pages are indicated in the input file by a line containing exactly one of these delimiter strings:

'\:\:\:'   start of header;

'\:\:'   start of body;

'\:'   start of footer.

The two characters from which these strings are made can be changed from '\' and ':' via options (see below), but the pattern and length of each string cannot be changed.

A section delimiter is replaced by an empty line on output. Any text that comes before the first section delimiter string in the input file is considered to be part of a body section, so nl treats a file that contains no section delimiters as a single body section.

The program accepts the following options. Also see Chapter 2 [Common options], page 2.

'-b *style*'
'--body-numbering=*style*'
> Select the numbering style for lines in the body section of each logical page. When a line is not numbered, the current line number is not incremented, but the line number separator character is still prepended to the line. The styles are:
>
> 'a'   number all lines,
>
> 't'   number only nonempty lines (default for body),
>
> 'n'   do not number lines (default for header and footer),
>
> 'p*bre*'   number only lines that contain a match for the basic regular expression *bre*. See Section "Regular Expressions" in *The GNU Grep Manual*.

'-d *cd*'
'--section-delimiter=*cd*'
> Set the section delimiter characters to *cd*; default is '\:'. If only *c* is given, the second remains ':'. (Remember to protect '\' or other metacharacters from shell expansion with quotes or extra backslashes.)

'-f *style*'
'--footer-numbering=*style*'
> Analogous to --body-numbering.

'-h *style*'
'--header-numbering=*style*'
> Analogous to --body-numbering.

'-i *number*'
'--line-increment=*number*'
> Increment line numbers by *number* (default 1).

'-l *number*'
'--join-blank-lines=*number*'
> Consider *number* (default 1) consecutive empty lines to be one logical line for numbering, and only number the last one. Where fewer than *number* consecutive empty lines occur, do not number them. An empty line is one that contains no characters, not even spaces or tabs.

'-n *format*'
'--number-format=*format*'

> Select the line numbering format (default is **rn**):

> > '**ln**' left justified, no leading zeros;

> > '**rn**' right justified, no leading zeros;

> > '**rz**' right justified, leading zeros.

'-p'
'--no-renumber'

> Do not reset the line number at the start of a logical page.

'-s *string*'
'--number-separator=*string*'

> Separate the line number from the text line in the output with *string* (default is the TAB character).

'-v *number*'
'--starting-line-number=*number*'

> Set the initial line number on each logical page to *number* (default 1).

'-w *number*'
'--number-width=*number*'

> Use *number* characters for line numbers (default 6).

An exit status of zero indicates success, and a nonzero value indicates failure.

3.4 od: Write files in octal or other formats

od writes an unambiguous representation of each *file* ('-' means standard input), or standard input if none are given. Synopses:

```
od [option]... [file]...
od [-abcdfilosx]... [file] [[+]offset[.][b]]
od [option]... --traditional [file] [[+]offset[.][b] [[+]label[.][b]]]
```

Each line of output consists of the offset in the input, followed by groups of data from the file. By default, od prints the offset in octal, and each group of file data is a C **short int**'s worth of input printed as a single octal number.

If *offset* is given, it specifies how many input bytes to skip before formatting and writing. By default, it is interpreted as an octal number, but the optional trailing decimal point causes it to be interpreted as decimal. If no decimal is specified and the offset begins with '0x' or '0X' it is interpreted as a hexadecimal number. If there is a trailing 'b', the number of bytes skipped will be *offset* multiplied by 512.

If a command is of both the first and second forms, the second form is assumed if the last operand begins with '+' or (if there are two operands) a digit. For example, in 'od foo 10' and 'od +10' the '10' is an offset, whereas in 'od 10' the '10' is a file name.

The program accepts the following options. Also see Chapter 2 [Common options], page 2.

'-A *radix*'
'--address-radix=*radix*'

> Select the base in which file offsets are printed. *radix* can be one of the following:

'd'   decimal;

'o'   octal;

'x'   hexadecimal;

'n'   none (do not print offsets).

The default is octal.

'--endian=*order*'

Reorder input bytes, to handle inputs with differing byte orders, or to provide consistent output independent of the endian convention of the current system. Swapping is performed according to the specified --type size and endian *order*, which can be 'little' or 'big'.

'-j *bytes*'
'--skip-bytes=*bytes*'

Skip *bytes* input bytes before formatting and writing. If *bytes* begins with '0x' or '0X', it is interpreted in hexadecimal; otherwise, if it begins with '0', in octal; otherwise, in decimal. *bytes* may be, or may be an integer optionally followed by, one of the following multiplicative suffixes:

```
'b'  => 512 ("blocks")
'KB' => 1000 (KiloBytes)
'K'  => 1024 (KibiBytes)
'MB' => 1000*1000 (MegaBytes)
'M'  => 1024*1024 (MebiBytes)
'GB' => 1000*1000*1000 (GigaBytes)
'G'  => 1024*1024*1024 (GibiBytes)
```

and so on for 'T', 'P', 'E', 'Z', and 'Y'.

'-N *bytes*'
'--read-bytes=*bytes*'

Output at most *bytes* bytes of the input. Prefixes and suffixes on bytes are interpreted as for the -j option.

'-S *bytes*'
'--strings[=*bytes*]'

Instead of the normal output, output only *string constants*: at least *bytes* consecutive ASCII graphic characters, followed by a zero byte (ASCII NUL). Prefixes and suffixes on *bytes* are interpreted as for the -j option.

If *bytes* is omitted with --strings, the default is 3.

'-t *type*'
'--format=*type*'

Select the format in which to output the file data. *type* is a string of one or more of the below type indicator characters. If you include more than one type indicator character in a single *type* string, or use this option more than once, od writes one copy of each output line using each of the data types that you specified, in the order that you specified.

Adding a trailing "z" to any type specification appends a display of the single byte character representation of the printable characters to the output line generated by the type specification.

'a'   named character, ignoring high-order bit

'c'   printable single byte character, C backslash escape or a 3 digit octal sequence

'd'   signed decimal

'f'   floating point (see Section 2.4 [Floating point], page 5)

'o'   octal

'u'   unsigned decimal

'x'   hexadecimal

The type **a** outputs things like 'sp' for space, 'nl' for newline, and 'nul' for a zero byte. Only the least significant seven bits of each byte is used; the high-order bit is ignored. Type **c** outputs ' ', '\n', and \0, respectively.

Except for types 'a' and 'c', you can specify the number of bytes to use in interpreting each number in the given data type by following the type indicator character with a decimal integer. Alternately, you can specify the size of one of the C compiler's built-in data types by following the type indicator character with one of the following characters. For integers ('d', 'o', 'u', 'x'):

'C'   char

'S'   short

'I'   int

'L'   long

For floating point (**f**):

F   float

D   double

L   long double

'-v'

'--output-duplicates'

Output consecutive lines that are identical. By default, when two or more consecutive output lines would be identical, **od** outputs only the first line, and puts just an asterisk on the following line to indicate the elision.

'-w[n]'

'--width[=n]'

Dump n input bytes per output line. This must be a multiple of the least common multiple of the sizes associated with the specified output types.

If this option is not given at all, the default is 16. If n is omitted, the default is 32.

The next several options are shorthands for format specifications. GNU od accepts any combination of shorthands and format specification options. These options accumulate.

'-a'   Output as named characters. Equivalent to '-t a'.

'-b'   Output as octal bytes. Equivalent to '-t o1'.

'-c'   Output as printable single byte characters, C backslash escapes or 3 digit octal sequences. Equivalent to '-t c'.

'-d'   Output as unsigned decimal two-byte units. Equivalent to '-t u2'.

'-f'   Output as floats. Equivalent to '-t fF'.

'-i'   Output as decimal ints. Equivalent to '-t dI'.

'-l'   Output as decimal long ints. Equivalent to '-t dL'.

'-o'   Output as octal two-byte units. Equivalent to -t o2.

'-s'   Output as decimal two-byte units. Equivalent to -t d2.

'-x'   Output as hexadecimal two-byte units. Equivalent to '-t x2'.

'--traditional'
            Recognize the non-option label argument that traditional od accepted. The following syntax:

                od --traditional [*file*] [[+]*offset*[.][b] [[+]*label*[.][b]]]

            can be used to specify at most one file and optional arguments specifying an offset and a pseudo-start address, *label*. The *label* argument is interpreted just like *offset*, but it specifies an initial pseudo-address. The pseudo-addresses are displayed in parentheses following any normal address.

An exit status of zero indicates success, and a nonzero value indicates failure.

3.5 base64: Transform data into printable data

base64 transforms data read from a file, or standard input, into (or from) base64 encoded form. The base64 encoded form uses printable ASCII characters to represent binary data. Synopses:

        base64 [*option*]... [*file*]
        base64 --decode [*option*]... [*file*]

The base64 encoding expands data to roughly 133% of the original. The format conforms to RFC 4648.

The program accepts the following options. Also see Chapter 2 [Common options], page 2.

'-w *cols*'
'--wrap=*cols*'
            During encoding, wrap lines after *cols* characters. This must be a positive number.

            The default is to wrap after 76 characters. Use the value 0 to disable line wrapping altogether.

'-d'

'--decode'

> Change the mode of operation, from the default of encoding data, to decoding data. Input is expected to be base64 encoded data, and the output will be the original data.

'-i'

'--ignore-garbage'

> When decoding, newlines are always accepted. During decoding, ignore unrecognized bytes, to permit distorted data to be decoded.

An exit status of zero indicates success, and a nonzero value indicates failure.

4 Formatting file contents

These commands reformat the contents of files.

4.1 `fmt`: Reformat paragraph text

`fmt` fills and joins lines to produce output lines of (at most) a given number of characters (75 by default). Synopsis:

```
fmt [option]... [file]...
```

`fmt` reads from the specified *file* arguments (or standard input if none are given), and writes to standard output.

By default, blank lines, spaces between words, and indentation are preserved in the output; successive input lines with different indentation are not joined; tabs are expanded on input and introduced on output.

`fmt` prefers breaking lines at the end of a sentence, and tries to avoid line breaks after the first word of a sentence or before the last word of a sentence. A *sentence break* is defined as either the end of a paragraph or a word ending in any of '.?!', followed by two spaces or end of line, ignoring any intervening parentheses or quotes. Like TEX, `fmt` reads entire "paragraphs" before choosing line breaks; the algorithm is a variant of that given by Donald E. Knuth and Michael F. Plass in "Breaking Paragraphs Into Lines", *Software—Practice & Experience* **11**, 11 (November 1981), 1119–1184.

The program accepts the following options. Also see Chapter 2 [Common options], page 2.

'`-c`'
'`--crown-margin`'

> *Crown margin* mode: preserve the indentation of the first two lines within a paragraph, and align the left margin of each subsequent line with that of the second line.

'`-t`'
'`--tagged-paragraph`'

> *Tagged paragraph* mode: like crown margin mode, except that if indentation of the first line of a paragraph is the same as the indentation of the second, the first line is treated as a one-line paragraph.

'`-s`'
'`--split-only`'

> Split lines only. Do not join short lines to form longer ones. This prevents sample lines of code, and other such "formatted" text from being unduly combined.

'`-u`'
'`--uniform-spacing`'

> Uniform spacing. Reduce spacing between words to one space, and spacing between sentences to two spaces.

'-width'
'-w width'
'--width=width'

> Fill output lines up to width characters (default 75 or goal plus 10, if goal is provided).

'-g goal'
'--goal=goal'

> fmt initially tries to make lines goal characters wide. By default, this is 7% shorter than width.

'-p prefix'
'--prefix=prefix'

> Only lines beginning with prefix (possibly preceded by whitespace) are subject to formatting. The prefix and any preceding whitespace are stripped for the formatting and then re-attached to each formatted output line. One use is to format certain kinds of program comments, while leaving the code unchanged.

An exit status of zero indicates success, and a nonzero value indicates failure.

4.2 pr: Paginate or columnate files for printing

pr writes each file ('-' means standard input), or standard input if none are given, to standard output, paginating and optionally outputting in multicolumn format; optionally merges all files, printing all in parallel, one per column. Synopsis:

> pr [option]... [file]...

By default, a 5-line header is printed at each page: two blank lines; a line with the date, the file name, and the page count; and two more blank lines. A footer of five blank lines is also printed. The default page_length is 66 lines. The default number of text lines is therefore 56. The text line of the header takes the form 'date string page', with spaces inserted around string so that the line takes up the full page_width. Here, date is the date (see the -D or --date-format option for details), string is the centered header string, and page identifies the page number. The LC_MESSAGES locale category affects the spelling of page; in the default C locale, it is 'Page number' where number is the decimal page number.

Form feeds in the input cause page breaks in the output. Multiple form feeds produce empty pages.

Columns are of equal width, separated by an optional string (default is 'space'). For multicolumn output, lines will always be truncated to page_width (default 72), unless you use the -J option. For single column output no line truncation occurs by default. Use -W option to truncate lines in that case.

The program accepts the following options. Also see Chapter 2 [Common options], page 2.

'+first_page[:last_page]'
'--pages=first_page[:last_page]'

> Begin printing with page first_page and stop with last_page. Missing ':last_page' implies end of file. While estimating the number of skipped pages each form feed in the input file results in a new page. Page counting

with and without '+*first_page*' is identical. By default, counting starts with the first page of input file (not first page printed). Line numbering may be altered by -N option.

'-*column*'
'--columns=*column*'

> With each single *file*, produce *column* columns of output (default is 1) and print columns down, unless -a is used. The column width is automatically decreased as *column* increases; unless you use the -W/-w option to increase *page_width* as well. This option might well cause some lines to be truncated. The number of lines in the columns on each page are balanced. The options -e and -i are on for multiple text-column output. Together with -J option column alignment and line truncation is turned off. Lines of full length are joined in a free field format and -S option may set field separators. -*column* may not be used with -m option.

'-a'
'--across'

> With each single *file*, print columns across rather than down. The -*column* option must be given with *column* greater than one. If a line is too long to fit in a column, it is truncated.

'-c'
'--show-control-chars'

> Print control characters using hat notation (e.g., '^G'); print other nonprinting characters in octal backslash notation. By default, nonprinting characters are not changed.

'-d'
'--double-space'

> Double space the output.

'-D *format*'
'--date-format=*format*'

> Format header dates using *format*, using the same conventions as for the command 'date +*format*'. See Section 21.1 [date invocation], page 175. Except for directives, which start with '%', characters in *format* are printed unchanged. You can use this option to specify an arbitrary string in place of the header date, e.g., --date-format="Monday morning".

> The default date format is '%Y-%m-%d %H:%M' (for example, '2001-12-04 23:59'); but if the POSIXLY_CORRECT environment variable is set and the LC_TIME locale category specifies the POSIX locale, the default is '%b %e %H:%M %Y' (for example, 'Dec   4 23:59 2001'.

> Time stamps are listed according to the time zone rules specified by the TZ environment variable, or by the system default rules if TZ is not set. See Section "Specifying the Time Zone with TZ" in *The GNU C Library Reference Manual*.

'-e[*in-tabchar*[*in-tabwidth*]]'
'--expand-tabs[=*in-tabchar*[*in-tabwidth*]]'

> Expand *tabs* to spaces on input. Optional argument *in-tabchar* is the input tab character (default is the TAB character). Second optional argument *in-tabwidth* is the input tab character's width (default is 8).

'-f'
'-F'
'--form-feed'

> Use a form feed instead of newlines to separate output pages. This does not alter the default page length of 66 lines.

'-h *header*'
'--header=*header*'

> Replace the file name in the header with the centered string *header*. When using the shell, *header* should be quoted and should be separated from -h by a space.

'-i[*out-tabchar*[*out-tabwidth*]]'
'--output-tabs[=*out-tabchar*[*out-tabwidth*]]'

> Replace spaces with *tabs* on output. Optional argument *out-tabchar* is the output tab character (default is the TAB character). Second optional argument *out-tabwidth* is the output tab character's width (default is 8).

'-J'
'--join-lines'

> Merge lines of full length. Used together with the column options -*column*, -a -*column* or -m. Turns off -W/-w line truncation; no column alignment used; may be used with --sep-string[=*string*]. -J has been introduced (together with -W and --sep-string) to disentangle the old (POSIX-compliant) options -w and -s along with the three column options.

'-l *page_length*'
'--length=*page_length*'

> Set the page length to *page_length* (default 66) lines, including the lines of the header [and the footer]. If *page_length* is less than or equal to 10, the header and footer are omitted, as if the -t option had been given.

'-m'
'--merge' Merge and print all *files* in parallel, one in each column. If a line is too long to fit in a column, it is truncated, unless the -J option is used. --sep-string[=*string*] may be used. Empty pages in some *files* (form feeds set) produce empty columns, still marked by *string*. The result is a continuous line numbering and column marking throughout the whole merged file. Completely empty merged pages show no separators or line numbers. The default header becomes '*date page*' with spaces inserted in the middle; this may be used with the -h or --header option to fill up the middle blank part.

'-n[*number-separator*[*digits*]]'
'--number-lines[=*number-separator*[*digits*]]'

> Provide *digits* digit line numbering (default for *digits* is 5). With multicolumn output the number occupies the first *digits* column positions of each text column or only each line of -m output. With single column output the number precedes each line just as -m does. Default counting of the line numbers starts with the first line of the input file (not the first line printed, compare the --page option and -N option). Optional argument *number-separator* is the character appended to the line number to separate it from the text followed. The default separator is the TAB character. In a strict sense a TAB is always printed with single column output only. The TAB width varies with the TAB position, e.g., with the left *margin* specified by -o option. With multicolumn output priority is given to 'equal width of output columns' (a POSIX specification). The TAB width is fixed to the value of the first column and does not change with different values of left *margin*. That means a fixed number of spaces is always printed in the place of the *number-separator* TAB. The tabification depends upon the output position.

'-N *line_number*'
'--first-line-number=*line_number*'

> Start line counting with the number *line_number* at first line of first page printed (in most cases not the first line of the input file).

'-o *margin*'
'--indent=*margin*'

> Indent each line with a margin *margin* spaces wide (default is zero). The total page width is the size of the margin plus the *page_width* set with the -W/-w option. A limited overflow may occur with numbered single column output (compare -n option).

'-r'
'--no-file-warnings'

> Do not print a warning message when an argument *file* cannot be opened. (The exit status will still be nonzero, however.)

'-s[*char*]'
'--separator[=*char*]'

> Separate columns by a single character *char*. The default for *char* is the TAB character without -w and 'no character' with -w. Without -s the default separator 'space' is set. -s[*char*] turns off line truncation of all three column options (-COLUMN|-a -COLUMN|-m) unless -w is set. This is a POSIX-compliant formulation.

'-S[*string*]'
'--sep-string[=*string*]'

> Use *string* to separate output columns. The -S option doesn't affect the -W/-w option, unlike the -s option which does. It does not affect line truncation or column alignment. Without -S, and with -J, pr uses the default output separator, TAB. Without -S or -J, pr uses a 'space' (same as -S" "). If no '*string*' argument is specified, '""' is assumed.

'-t'
'--omit-header'

> Do not print the usual header [and footer] on each page, and do not fill out the bottom of pages (with blank lines or a form feed). No page structure is produced, but form feeds set in the input files are retained. The predefined pagination is not changed. -t or -T may be useful together with other options; e.g.: -t -e4, expand TAB characters in the input file to 4 spaces but don't make any other changes. Use of -t overrides -h

'-T'
'--omit-pagination'

> Do not print header [and footer]. In addition eliminate all form feeds set in the input files.

'-v'
'--show-nonprinting'

> Print nonprinting characters in octal backslash notation.

'-w *page_width*'
'--width=*page_width*'

> Set page width to *page_width* characters for multiple text-column output only (default for *page_width* is 72). The specified *page_width* is rounded down so that columns have equal width. -s[CHAR] turns off the default page width and any line truncation and column alignment. Lines of full length are merged, regardless of the column options set. No *page_width* setting is possible with single column output. A POSIX-compliant formulation.

'-W *page_width*'
'--page_width=*page_width*'

> Set the page width to *page_width* characters, honored with and without a column option. With a column option, the specified *page_width* is rounded down so that columns have equal width. Text lines are truncated, unless -J is used. Together with one of the three column options (-*column*, -a -*column* or -m) column alignment is always used. The separator options -S or -s don't disable the -W option. Default is 72 characters. Without -W *page_width* and without any of the column options NO line truncation is used (defined to keep downward compatibility and to meet most frequent tasks). That's equivalent to -W 72 -J. The header line is never truncated.

An exit status of zero indicates success, and a nonzero value indicates failure.

4.3 `fold`: Wrap input lines to fit in specified width

`fold` writes each *file* (- means standard input), or standard input if none are given, to standard output, breaking long lines. Synopsis:

```
fold [option]... [file]...
```

By default, `fold` breaks lines wider than 80 columns. The output is split into as many lines as necessary.

`fold` counts screen columns by default; thus, a tab may count more than one column, backspace decreases the column count, and carriage return sets the column to zero.

The program accepts the following options. Also see Chapter 2 [Common options], page 2.

'-b'

'--bytes'   Count bytes rather than columns, so that tabs, backspaces, and carriage returns are each counted as taking up one column, just like other characters.

'-s'

'--spaces'

Break at word boundaries: the line is broken after the last blank before the maximum line length. If the line contains no such blanks, the line is broken at the maximum line length as usual.

'-w *width*'

'--width=*width*'

Use a maximum line length of *width* columns instead of 80.

For compatibility **fold** supports an obsolete option syntax -*width*. New scripts should use -w *width* instead.

An exit status of zero indicates success, and a nonzero value indicates failure.

5 Output of parts of files

These commands output pieces of the input.

5.1 head: Output the first part of files

head prints the first part (10 lines by default) of each file; it reads from standard input if no files are given or when given a file of -. Synopsis:

```
head [option]... [file]...
```

If more than one file is specified, head prints a one-line header consisting of:

```
==> file name <==
```

before the output for each file.

The program accepts the following options. Also see Chapter 2 [Common options], page 2.

'-c k'
'--bytes=k'

> Print the first k bytes, instead of initial lines. However, if k starts with a '-', print all but the last k bytes of each file. k may be, or may be an integer optionally followed by, one of the following multiplicative suffixes:
>
> > 'b' => 512 ("blocks")
> > 'KB' => 1000 (KiloBytes)
> > 'K' => 1024 (KibiBytes)
> > 'MB' => 1000*1000 (MegaBytes)
> > 'M' => 1024*1024 (MebiBytes)
> > 'GB' => 1000*1000*1000 (GigaBytes)
> > 'G' => 1024*1024*1024 (GibiBytes)
>
> and so on for 'T', 'P', 'E', 'Z', and 'Y'.

'-n k'
'--lines=k'

> Output the first k lines. However, if k starts with a '-', print all but the last k lines of each file. Size multiplier suffixes are the same as with the -c option.

'-q'
'--quiet'
'--silent'

> Never print file name headers.

'-v'
'--verbose'

> Always print file name headers.

For compatibility head also supports an obsolete option syntax -countoptions, which is recognized only if it is specified first. count is a decimal number optionally followed by a size letter ('b', 'k', 'm') as in -c, or 'l' to mean count by lines, or other option letters ('cqv'). Scripts intended for standard hosts should use -c count or -n count instead. If your script must also run on hosts that support only the obsolete syntax, it is usually simpler to avoid head, e.g., by using 'sed 5q' instead of 'head -5'.

An exit status of zero indicates success, and a nonzero value indicates failure.

5.2 `tail`: Output the last part of files

`tail` prints the last part (10 lines by default) of each *file*; it reads from standard input if no files are given or when given a *file* of '-'. Synopsis:

```
tail [option]... [file]...
```

If more than one *file* is specified, `tail` prints a one-line header consisting of:

```
==> file name <==
```

before the output for each *file*.

GNU `tail` can output any amount of data (some other versions of `tail` cannot). It also has no `-r` option (print in reverse), since reversing a file is really a different job from printing the end of a file; BSD `tail` (which is the one with `-r`) can only reverse files that are at most as large as its buffer, which is typically 32 KiB. A more reliable and versatile way to reverse files is the GNU `tac` command.

The program accepts the following options. Also see Chapter 2 [Common options], page 2.

'`-c k`'
'`--bytes=k`'

> Output the last *k* bytes, instead of final lines. However, if *k* starts with a '+', start printing with the *k*th byte from the start of each file, instead of from the end. *k* may be, or may be an integer optionally followed by, one of the following multiplicative suffixes:
>
> ```
> 'b'  => 512 ("blocks")
> 'KB' => 1000 (KiloBytes)
> 'K'  => 1024 (KibiBytes)
> 'MB' => 1000*1000 (MegaBytes)
> 'M'  => 1024*1024 (MebiBytes)
> 'GB' => 1000*1000*1000 (GigaBytes)
> 'G'  => 1024*1024*1024 (GibiBytes)
> ```
>
> and so on for 'T', 'P', 'E', 'Z', and 'Y'.

'`-f`'
'`--follow[=how]`'

> Loop forever trying to read more characters at the end of the file, presumably because the file is growing. If more than one file is given, `tail` prints a header whenever it gets output from a different file, to indicate which file that output is from.
>
> There are two ways to specify how you'd like to track files with this option, but that difference is noticeable only when a followed file is removed or renamed. If you'd like to continue to track the end of a growing file even after it has been unlinked, use `--follow=descriptor`. This is the default behavior, but it is not useful if you're tracking a log file that may be rotated (removed or renamed, then reopened). In that case, use `--follow=name` to track the named file, perhaps by reopening it periodically to see if it has been removed and recreated by some other program. Note that the inotify-based implementation handles this case without the need for any periodic reopening.

No matter which method you use, if the tracked file is determined to have shrunk, `tail` prints a message saying the file has been truncated and resumes tracking the end of the file from the newly-determined endpoint.

When a file is removed, `tail`'s behavior depends on whether it is following the name or the descriptor. When following by name, tail can detect that a file has been removed and gives a message to that effect, and if `--retry` has been specified it will continue checking periodically to see if the file reappears. When following a descriptor, tail does not detect that the file has been unlinked or renamed and issues no message; even though the file may no longer be accessible via its original name, it may still be growing.

The option values 'descriptor' and 'name' may be specified only with the long form of the option, not with `-f`.

The `-f` option is ignored if no *file* operand is specified and standard input is a FIFO or a pipe. Likewise, the `-f` option has no effect for any operand specified as '-', when standard input is a FIFO or a pipe.

With kernel inotify support, output is triggered by file changes and is generally very prompt. Otherwise, `tail` sleeps for one second between checks— use `--sleep-interval=n` to change that default—which can make the output appear slightly less responsive or bursty. When using tail without inotify support, you can make it more responsive by using a sub-second sleep interval, e.g., via an alias like this:

```
alias tail='tail -s.1'
```

'-F' This option is the same as `--follow=name --retry`. That is, tail will attempt to reopen a file when it is removed. Should this fail, tail will keep trying until it becomes accessible again.

'--retry' Indefinitely try to open the specified file. This option is useful mainly when following (and otherwise issues a warning).

When following by file descriptor (i.e., with `--follow=descriptor`), this option only affects the initial open of the file, as after a successful open, `tail` will start following the file descriptor.

When following by name (i.e., with `--follow=name`), `tail` infinitely retries to re-open the given files until killed.

Without this option, when `tail` encounters a file that doesn't exist or is otherwise inaccessible, it reports that fact and never checks it again.

'--sleep-interval=*number*'

Change the number of seconds to wait between iterations (the default is 1.0). During one iteration, every specified file is checked to see if it has changed size. Historical implementations of `tail` have required that *number* be an integer. However, GNU `tail` accepts an arbitrary floating point number. See Section 2.4 [Floating point], page 5. When `tail` uses inotify, this polling-related option is usually ignored. However, if you also specify `--pid=p`, `tail` checks whether process *p* is alive at least every *number* seconds.

'--pid=*pid*'

When following by name or by descriptor, you may specify the process ID, *pid*, of the sole writer of all *file* arguments. Then, shortly after that process terminates, tail will also terminate. This will work properly only if the writer and the tailing process are running on the same machine. For example, to save the output of a build in a file and to watch the file grow, if you invoke `make` and `tail` like this then the tail process will stop when your build completes. Without this option, you would have had to kill the `tail -f` process yourself.

```
$ make >& makerr & tail --pid=$! -f makerr
```

If you specify a *pid* that is not in use or that does not correspond to the process that is writing to the tailed files, then `tail` may terminate long before any *files* stop growing or it may not terminate until long after the real writer has terminated. Note that `--pid` cannot be supported on some systems; `tail` will print a warning if this is the case.

'--max-unchanged-stats=*n*'

When tailing a file by name, if there have been *n* (default n=5) consecutive iterations for which the file has not changed, then `open`/`fstat` the file to determine if that file name is still associated with the same device/inode-number pair as before. When following a log file that is rotated, this is approximately the number of seconds between when tail prints the last pre-rotation lines and when it prints the lines that have accumulated in the new log file. This option is meaningful only when polling (i.e., without inotify) and when following by name.

'-n *k*'
'--lines=*k*'

Output the last *k* lines. However, if *k* starts with a '+', start printing with the *k*th line from the start of each file, instead of from the end. Size multiplier suffixes are the same as with the -c option.

'-q'
'--quiet'
'--silent'

Never print file name headers.

'-v'
'--verbose'

Always print file name headers.

For compatibility `tail` also supports an obsolete usage 'tail -[*count*][bcl][f] [*file*]', which is recognized only if it does not conflict with the usage described above. This obsolete form uses exactly one option and at most one file. In the option, *count* is an optional decimal number optionally followed by a size letter ('b', 'c', 'l') to mean count by 512-byte blocks, bytes, or lines, optionally followed by 'f' which has the same meaning as -f.

On older systems, the leading '-' can be replaced by '+' in the obsolete option syntax with the same meaning as in counts, and obsolete usage overrides normal usage when the two conflict. This obsolete behavior can be enabled or disabled with the `_POSIX2_VERSION` environment variable (see Section 2.13 [Standards conformance], page 11).

Scripts intended for use on standard hosts should avoid obsolete syntax and should use `-c count[b]`, `-n count`, and/or `-f` instead. If your script must also run on hosts that support only the obsolete syntax, you can often rewrite it to avoid problematic usages, e.g., by using 'sed -n '$p'' rather than 'tail -1'. If that's not possible, the script can use a test like 'if tail -c +1 </dev/null >/dev/null 2>&1; then ...' to decide which syntax to use.

Even if your script assumes the standard behavior, you should still beware usages whose behaviors differ depending on the POSIX version. For example, avoid 'tail - main.c', since it might be interpreted as either 'tail main.c' or as 'tail -- - main.c'; avoid 'tail -c 4', since it might mean either 'tail -c4' or 'tail -c 10 4'; and avoid 'tail +4', since it might mean either 'tail ./+4' or 'tail -n +4'.

An exit status of zero indicates success, and a nonzero value indicates failure.

5.3 `split`: **Split a file into pieces.**

`split` creates output files containing consecutive or interleaved sections of *input* (standard input if none is given or *input* is '-'). Synopsis:

```
split [option] [input [prefix]]
```

By default, `split` puts 1000 lines of *input* (or whatever is left over for the last section), into each output file.

The output files' names consist of *prefix* ('x' by default) followed by a group of characters ('aa', 'ab', ... by default), such that concatenating the output files in traditional sorted order by file name produces the original input file (except `-nr/n`). By default split will initially create files with two generated suffix characters, and will increase this width by two when the next most significant position reaches the last character. ('yz', 'zaaa', 'zaab', ...). In this way an arbitrary number of output files are supported, which sort as described above, even in the presence of an `--additional-suffix` option. If the `-a` option is specified and the output file names are exhausted, `split` reports an error without deleting the output files that it did create.

The program accepts the following options. Also see Chapter 2 [Common options], page 2.

'`-l lines`'
'`--lines=lines`'

> Put *lines* lines of *input* into each output file. If `--separator` is specified, then *lines* determines the number of records.
>
> For compatibility `split` also supports an obsolete option syntax `-lines`. New scripts should use `-l lines` instead.

'`-b size`'
'`--bytes=size`'

> Put *size* bytes of *input* into each output file. *size* may be, or may be an integer optionally followed by, one of the following multiplicative suffixes:
>
> > '`b`' => 512 ("blocks")

```
'KB' => 1000 (KiloBytes)
'K' => 1024 (KibiBytes)
'MB' => 1000*1000 (MegaBytes)
'M' => 1024*1024 (MebiBytes)
'GB' => 1000*1000*1000 (GigaBytes)
'G' => 1024*1024*1024 (GibiBytes)
```

and so on for 'T', 'P', 'E', 'Z', and 'Y'.

'`-C size`'
'`--line-bytes=size`'

Put into each output file as many complete lines of *input* as possible without exceeding *size* bytes. Individual lines or records longer than *size* bytes are broken into multiple files. *size* has the same format as for the `--bytes` option. If `--separator` is specified, then *lines* determines the number of records.

'`--filter=command`'

With this option, rather than simply writing to each output file, write through a pipe to the specified shell *command* for each output file. *command* should use the $FILE environment variable, which is set to a different output file name for each invocation of the command. For example, imagine that you have a 1TiB compressed file that, if uncompressed, would be too large to reside on disk, yet you must split it into individually-compressed pieces of a more manageable size. To do that, you might run this command:

```
xz -dc BIG.xz | split -b200G --filter='xz > $FILE.xz' - big-
```

Assuming a 10:1 compression ratio, that would create about fifty 20GiB files with names **big-aa.xz**, **big-ab.xz**, **big-ac.xz**, etc.

'`-n chunks`'
'`--number=chunks`'

Split *input* to *chunks* output files where *chunks* may be:

```
n       generate n files based on current size of input
k/n     only output kth of n to stdout
l/n     generate n files without splitting lines or records
l/k/n   likewise but only output kth of n to stdout
r/n     like 'l' but use round robin distribution
r/k/n   likewise but only output kth of n to stdout
```

Any excess bytes remaining after dividing the *input* into *n* chunks, are assigned to the last chunk. Any excess bytes appearing after the initial calculation are discarded (except when using 'r' mode).

All *n* files are created even if there are fewer than *n* lines, or the *input* is truncated.

For 'l' mode, chunks are approximately *input* size / *n*. The *input* is partitioned into *n* equal sized portions, with the last assigned any excess. If a line *starts* within a partition it is written completely to the corresponding file. Since lines or records are not split even if they overlap a partition, the files written can be larger or smaller than the partition size, and even empty if a line/record is so long as to completely overlap the partition.

For 'r' mode, the size of *input* is irrelevant, and so can be a pipe for example.

'-a *length*'
'--suffix-length=*length*'

>Use suffixes of length *length*. If a *length* of 0 is specified, this is the same as if (any previous) -a was not specified, and thus enables the default behavior, which starts the suffix length at 2, and unless -n or --numeric-suffixes=*from* is specified, will auto increase the length by 2 as required.

'-d'
'--numeric-suffixes[=*from*]'

>Use digits in suffixes rather than lower-case letters. The numerical suffix counts from *from* if specified, 0 otherwise.

>*from* is used to either set the initial suffix for a single run, or to set the suffix offset for independently split inputs, and consequently the auto suffix length expansion described above is disabled. Therefore you may also want to use option -a to allow suffixes beyond '99'. Note if option --number is specified and the number of files is less than *from*, a single run is assumed and the minimum suffix length required is automatically determined.

'--additional-suffix=*suffix*'

>Append an additional *suffix* to output file names. *suffix* must not contain slash.

'-e'
'--elide-empty-files'

>Suppress the generation of zero-length output files. This can happen with the --number option if a file is (truncated to be) shorter than the number requested, or if a line is so long as to completely span a chunk. The output file sequence numbers, always run consecutively even when this option is specified.

'-t *separator*'
'--separator=*separator*'

>Use character *separator* as the record separator instead of the default newline character (ASCII LF). To specify ASCII NUL as the separator, use the two-character string '\0', e.g., 'split -t '\0''.

'-u'
'--unbuffered'

>Immediately copy input to output in --number r/... mode, which is a much slower mode of operation.

'--verbose'

>Write a diagnostic just before each output file is opened.

An exit status of zero indicates success, and a nonzero value indicates failure.

Here are a few examples to illustrate how the --number (-n) option works:

Notice how, by default, one line may be split onto two or more:

```
$ seq -w 6 10 > k; split -n3 k; head xa?
==> xaa <==
06
```

```
07
==> xab <==

08
0
==> xac <==
9
10
```

Use the "l/" modifier to suppress that:

```
$ seq -w 6 10 > k; split -nl/3 k; head xa?
==> xaa <==
06
07

==> xab <==
08
09

==> xac <==
10
```

Use the "r/" modifier to distribute lines in a round-robin fashion:

```
$ seq -w 6 10 > k; split -nr/3 k; head xa?
==> xaa <==
06
09

==> xab <==
07
10

==> xac <==
08
```

You can also extract just the Kth chunk. This extracts and prints just the 7th "chunk" of 33:

```
$ seq 100 > k; split -nl/7/33 k
20
21
22
```

5.4 `csplit`: Split a file into context-determined pieces

`csplit` creates zero or more output files containing sections of *input* (standard input if *input* is '-'). Synopsis:

```
csplit [option]... input pattern...
```

The contents of the output files are determined by the *pattern* arguments, as detailed below. An error occurs if a *pattern* argument refers to a nonexistent line of the input file (e.g., if no remaining line matches a given regular expression). After every *pattern* has been matched, any remaining input is copied into one last output file.

By default, `csplit` prints the number of bytes written to each output file after it has been created.

The types of pattern arguments are:

'**n**'   Create an output file containing the input up to but not including line *n* (a positive integer). If followed by a repeat count, also create an output file containing the next *n* lines of the input file once for each repeat.

'`/`*regexp*`/`[*offset*]'

Create an output file containing the current line up to (but not including) the next line of the input file that contains a match for *regexp*. The optional *offset* is an integer. If it is given, the input up to (but not including) the matching line plus or minus *offset* is put into the output file, and the line after that begins the next section of input.

'`%`*regexp*`%`[*offset*]'

Like the previous type, except that it does not create an output file, so that section of the input file is effectively ignored.

'`{`*repeat-count*`}`'

Repeat the previous pattern *repeat-count* additional times. The *repeat-count* can either be a positive integer or an asterisk, meaning repeat as many times as necessary until the input is exhausted.

The output files' names consist of a prefix ('xx' by default) followed by a suffix. By default, the suffix is an ascending sequence of two-digit decimal numbers from '00' to '99'. In any case, concatenating the output files in sorted order by file name produces the original input file.

By default, if `csplit` encounters an error or receives a hangup, interrupt, quit, or terminate signal, it removes any output files that it has created so far before it exits.

The program accepts the following options. Also see Chapter 2 [Common options], page 2.

'`-f `*prefix*'
'`--prefix=`*prefix*'

Use *prefix* as the output file name prefix.

'`-b `*suffix*'
'`--suffix=`*suffix*'

Use *suffix* as the output file name suffix. When this option is specified, the suffix string must include exactly one `printf(3)`-style conversion specification, possibly including format specification flags, a field width, a precision specifications, or all of these kinds of modifiers. The format letter must convert a binary unsigned integer argument to readable form. The format letters '`d`' and '`i`' are aliases for '`u`', and the '`u`', '`o`', '`x`', and '`X`' conversions are allowed. The entire *suffix* is given (with the current output file number) to `sprintf(3)` to form the file name suffixes for each of the individual output files in turn. If this option is used, the `--digits` option is ignored.

'-n *digits*'

'--digits=*digits*'

> Use output file names containing numbers that are *digits* digits long instead of the default 2.

'-k'

'--keep-files'

> Do not remove output files when errors are encountered.

'--suppress-matched'

> Do not output lines matching the specified *pattern*. I.e., suppress the boundary line from the start of the second and subsequent splits.

'-z'

'--elide-empty-files'

> Suppress the generation of zero-length output files. (In cases where the section delimiters of the input file are supposed to mark the first lines of each of the sections, the first output file will generally be a zero-length file unless you use this option.) The output file sequence numbers always run consecutively starting from 0, even when this option is specified.

'-s'

'-q'

'--silent'

'--quiet' Do not print counts of output file sizes.

An exit status of zero indicates success, and a nonzero value indicates failure.

Here is an example of its usage. First, create an empty directory for the exercise, and cd into it:

```
$ mkdir d && cd d
```

Now, split the sequence of 1..14 on lines that end with 0 or 5:

```
$ seq 14 | csplit - '/[05]$/' '{*}'
8
10
15
```

Each number printed above is the size of an output file that csplit has just created. List the names of those output files:

```
$ ls
xx00   xx01   xx02
```

Use head to show their contents:

```
$ head xx*
==> xx00 <==
1
2
3
4

==> xx01 <==
```

```
        5
        6
        7
        8
        9

        ==> xx02 <==
        10
        11
        12
        13
        14
```

Example of splitting input by empty lines:

```
$ csplit --suppress-matched input.txt '/^$/' '{*}'
```

6 Summarizing files

These commands generate just a few numbers representing entire contents of files.

6.1 `wc`: Print newline, word, and byte counts

`wc` counts the number of bytes, characters, whitespace-separated words, and newlines in each given *file*, or standard input if none are given or for a *file* of '-'. Synopsis:

        wc [option]... [file]...

`wc` prints one line of counts for each file, and if the file was given as an argument, it prints the file name following the counts. If more than one *file* is given, `wc` prints a final line containing the cumulative counts, with the file name `total`. The counts are printed in this order: newlines, words, characters, bytes, maximum line length. Each count is printed right-justified in a field with at least one space between fields so that the numbers and file names normally line up nicely in columns. The width of the count fields varies depending on the inputs, so you should not depend on a particular field width. However, as a GNU extension, if only one count is printed, it is guaranteed to be printed without leading spaces.

By default, `wc` prints three counts: the newline, words, and byte counts. Options can specify that only certain counts be printed. Options do not undo others previously given, so

        wc --bytes --words

prints both the byte counts and the word counts.

With the `--max-line-length` option, `wc` prints the length of the longest line per file, and if there is more than one file it prints the maximum (not the sum) of those lengths. The line lengths here are measured in screen columns, according to the current locale and assuming tab positions in every 8th column.

The program accepts the following options. Also see Chapter 2 [Common options], page 2.

'-c'
'--bytes'   Print only the byte counts.

'-m'
'--chars'   Print only the character counts.

'-w'
'--words'   Print only the word counts.

'-l'
'--lines'   Print only the newline counts.

'-L'
'--max-line-length'
             Print only the maximum display widths. Tabs are set at every 8th column.
             Display widths of wide characters are considered. Non-printable characters are
             given 0 width.

'--files0-from=*file*'
             Disallow processing files named on the command line, and instead process those
             named in file *file*; each name being terminated by a zero byte (ASCII NUL). This

is useful when the list of file names is so long that it may exceed a command line length limitation. In such cases, running `wc` via `xargs` is undesirable because it splits the list into pieces and makes `wc` print a total for each sublist rather than for the entire list. One way to produce a list of ASCII NUL terminated file names is with GNU `find`, using its `-print0` predicate. If *file* is '-' then the ASCII NUL terminated file names are read from standard input.

For example, to find the length of the longest line in any `.c` or `.h` file in the current hierarchy, do this:

```
find . -name '*.[ch]' -print0 |
  wc -L --files0-from=- | tail -n1
```

An exit status of zero indicates success, and a nonzero value indicates failure.

6.2 `sum`: Print checksum and block counts

`sum` computes a 16-bit checksum for each given *file*, or standard input if none are given or for a *file* of '-'. Synopsis:

```
sum [option]... [file]...
```

`sum` prints the checksum for each *file* followed by the number of blocks in the file (rounded up). If more than one *file* is given, file names are also printed (by default). (With the `--sysv` option, corresponding file names are printed when there is at least one file argument.)

By default, GNU `sum` computes checksums using an algorithm compatible with BSD `sum` and prints file sizes in units of 1024-byte blocks.

The program accepts the following options. Also see Chapter 2 [Common options], page 2.

'`-r`'   Use the default (BSD compatible) algorithm. This option is included for compatibility with the System V `sum`. Unless `-s` was also given, it has no effect.

'`-s`'
'`--sysv`' Compute checksums using an algorithm compatible with System V `sum`'s default, and print file sizes in units of 512-byte blocks.

`sum` is provided for compatibility; the `cksum` program (see next section) is preferable in new applications.

An exit status of zero indicates success, and a nonzero value indicates failure.

6.3 `cksum`: Print CRC checksum and byte counts

`cksum` computes a cyclic redundancy check (CRC) checksum for each given *file*, or standard input if none are given or for a *file* of '-'. Synopsis:

```
cksum [option]... [file]...
```

`cksum` prints the CRC checksum for each file along with the number of bytes in the file, and the file name unless no arguments were given.

`cksum` is typically used to ensure that files transferred by unreliable means (e.g., netnews) have not been corrupted, by comparing the `cksum` output for the received files with the `cksum` output for the original files (typically given in the distribution).

The CRC algorithm is specified by the POSIX standard. It is not compatible with the BSD or System V `sum` algorithms (see the previous section); it is more robust.

The only options are `--help` and `--version`. See Chapter 2 [Common options], page 2.

An exit status of zero indicates success, and a nonzero value indicates failure.

6.4 `md5sum`: Print or check MD5 digests

`md5sum` computes a 128-bit checksum (or *fingerprint* or *message-digest*) for each specified *file*.

Note: The MD5 digest is more reliable than a simple CRC (provided by the `cksum` command) for detecting accidental file corruption, as the chances of accidentally having two files with identical MD5 are vanishingly small. However, it should not be considered secure against malicious tampering: although finding a file with a given MD5 fingerprint is considered infeasible at the moment, it is known how to modify certain files, including digital certificates, so that they appear valid when signed with an MD5 digest. For more secure hashes, consider using SHA-2. See Section 6.6 [sha2 utilities], page 42.

If a *file* is specified as '-' or if no files are given `md5sum` computes the checksum for the standard input. `md5sum` can also determine whether a file and checksum are consistent. Synopsis:

    md5sum [option]... [file]...

For each *file*, 'md5sum' outputs by default, the MD5 checksum, a space, a flag indicating binary or text input mode, and the file name. Binary mode is indicated with '*', text mode with ' ' (space). Binary mode is the default on systems where it's significant, otherwise text mode is the default. If *file* contains a backslash or newline, the line is started with a backslash, and each problematic character in the file name is escaped with a backslash, making the output unambiguous even in the presence of arbitrary file names. If *file* is omitted or specified as '-', standard input is read.

The program accepts the following options. Also see Chapter 2 [Common options], page 2.

'-b'
'--binary'

> Treat each input file as binary, by reading it in binary mode and outputting a '*' flag. This is the inverse of `--text`. On systems like GNU that do not distinguish between binary and text files, this option merely flags each input mode as binary: the MD5 checksum is unaffected. This option is the default on systems like MS-DOS that distinguish between binary and text files, except for reading standard input when standard input is a terminal.

'-c'
'--check' Read file names and checksum information (not data) from each *file* (or from stdin if no *file* was specified) and report whether the checksums match the contents of the named files. The input to this mode of `md5sum` is usually the output of a prior, checksum-generating run of 'md5sum'. Three input formats are supported. Either the default output format described above, the `--tag` output format, or the BSD reversed mode format which is similar to the default mode, but doesn't use a character to distinguish binary and text modes.

For each such line, `md5sum` reads the named file and computes its MD5 checksum. Then, if the computed message digest does not match the one on the line with the file name, the file is noted as having failed the test. Otherwise, the file passes the test. By default, for each valid line, one line is written to standard output indicating whether the named file passed the test. After all checks have been performed, if there were any failures, a warning is issued to standard error. Use the `--status` option to inhibit that output. If any listed file cannot be opened or read, if any valid line has an MD5 checksum inconsistent with the associated file, or if no valid line is found, `md5sum` exits with nonzero status. Otherwise, it exits successfully.

'`--quiet`'   This option is useful only when verifying checksums. When verifying checksums, don't generate an 'OK' message per successfully checked file. Files that fail the verification are reported in the default one-line-per-file format. If there is any checksum mismatch, print a warning summarizing the failures to standard error.

'`--status`'

This option is useful only when verifying checksums. When verifying checksums, don't generate the default one-line-per-file diagnostic and don't output the warning summarizing any failures. Failures to open or read a file still evoke individual diagnostics to standard error. If all listed files are readable and are consistent with the associated MD5 checksums, exit successfully. Otherwise exit with a status code indicating there was a failure.

'`--tag`'   Output BSD style checksums, which indicate the checksum algorithm used. As a GNU extension, file names with problematic characters are escaped as described above, with the same escaping indicator of '\' at the start of the line, being used. The `--tag` option implies binary mode, and is disallowed with `--text` mode as supporting that would unnecessarily complicate the output format, while providing little benefit.

'`-t`'
'`--text`'   Treat each input file as text, by reading it in text mode and outputting a ' ' flag. This is the inverse of `--binary`. This option is the default on systems like GNU that do not distinguish between binary and text files. On other systems, it is the default for reading standard input when standard input is a terminal. This mode is never defaulted to if `--tag` is used.

'`-w`'
'`--warn`'   When verifying checksums, warn about improperly formatted MD5 checksum lines. This option is useful only if all but a few lines in the checked input are valid.

'`--strict`'

When verifying checksums, if one or more input line is invalid, exit nonzero after all warnings have been issued.

An exit status of zero indicates success, and a nonzero value indicates failure.

6.5 `sha1sum`: Print or check SHA-1 digests

`sha1sum` computes a 160-bit checksum for each specified *file*. The usage and options of this command are precisely the same as for `md5sum`. See Section 6.4 [md5sum invocation], page 40.

Note: The SHA-1 digest is more secure than MD5, and no collisions of it are known (different files having the same fingerprint). However, it is known that they can be produced with considerable, but not unreasonable, resources. For this reason, it is generally considered that SHA-1 should be gradually phased out in favor of the more secure SHA-2 hash algorithms. See Section 6.6 [sha2 utilities], page 42.

6.6 sha2 utilities: Print or check SHA-2 digests

The commands `sha224sum`, `sha256sum`, `sha384sum` and `sha512sum` compute checksums of various lengths (respectively 224, 256, 384 and 512 bits), collectively known as the SHA-2 hashes. The usage and options of these commands are precisely the same as for `md5sum` and `sha1sum`. See Section 6.4 [md5sum invocation], page 40.

Note: The SHA384 and SHA512 digests are considerably slower to compute, especially on 32-bit computers, than SHA224 or SHA256.

7 Operating on sorted files

These commands work with (or produce) sorted files.

7.1 sort: Sort text files

sort sorts, merges, or compares all the lines from the given files, or standard input if
none are given or for a *file* of '-'. By default, sort writes the results to standard output.
Synopsis:

    sort [option]... [file]...

sort has three modes of operation: sort (the default), merge, and check for sortedness.
The following options change the operation mode:

'-c'
'--check'
'--check=diagnose-first'

> Check whether the given file is already sorted: if it is not all sorted, print a
> diagnostic containing the first out-of-order line and exit with a status of 1.
> Otherwise, exit successfully. At most one input file can be given.

'-C'
'--check=quiet'
'--check=silent'

> Exit successfully if the given file is already sorted, and exit with status 1 oth-
> erwise. At most one input file can be given. This is like -c, except it does not
> print a diagnostic.

'-m'
'--merge'   Merge the given files by sorting them as a group. Each input file must always
> be individually sorted. It always works to sort instead of merge; merging is
> provided because it is faster, in the case where it works.

A pair of lines is compared as follows: sort compares each pair of fields, in the order
specified on the command line, according to the associated ordering options, until a difference is found or no fields are left. If no key fields are specified, sort uses a default key of
the entire line. Finally, as a last resort when all keys compare equal, sort compares entire
lines as if no ordering options other than --reverse (-r) were specified. The --stable
(-s) option disables this *last-resort comparison* so that lines in which all fields compare
equal are left in their original relative order. The --unique (-u) option also disables the
last-resort comparison.

Unless otherwise specified, all comparisons use the character collating sequence specified
by the LC_COLLATE locale.[1]

GNU sort (as specified for all GNU utilities) has no limit on input line length or restrictions on bytes allowed within lines. In addition, if the final byte of an input file is not

---

[1] If you use a non-POSIX locale (e.g., by setting LC_ALL to 'en_US'), then sort may produce output that
is sorted differently than you're accustomed to. In that case, set the LC_ALL environment variable to 'C'.
Note that setting only LC_COLLATE has two problems. First, it is ineffective if LC_ALL is also set. Second,
it has undefined behavior if LC_CTYPE (or LANG, if LC_CTYPE is unset) is set to an incompatible value. For
example, you get undefined behavior if LC_CTYPE is ja_JP.PCK but LC_COLLATE is en_US.UTF-8.

a newline, GNU `sort` silently supplies one. A line's trailing newline is not part of the line for comparison purposes.

Exit status:

> 0 if no error occurred
> 1 if invoked with -c or -C and the input is not sorted
> 2 if an error occurred

If the environment variable `TMPDIR` is set, `sort` uses its value as the directory for temporary files instead of `/tmp`. The `--temporary-directory` (-T) option in turn overrides the environment variable.

The following options affect the ordering of output lines. They may be specified globally or as part of a specific key field. If no key fields are specified, global options apply to comparison of entire lines; otherwise the global options are inherited by key fields that do not specify any special options of their own. In pre-POSIX versions of `sort`, global options affect only later key fields, so portable shell scripts should specify global options first.

'-b'
'--ignore-leading-blanks'

> Ignore leading blanks when finding sort keys in each line. By default a blank is a space or a tab, but the `LC_CTYPE` locale can change this. Note blanks may be ignored by your locale's collating rules, but without this option they will be significant for character positions specified in keys with the -k option.

'-d'
'--dictionary-order'

> Sort in *phone directory* order: ignore all characters except letters, digits and blanks when sorting. By default letters and digits are those of ASCII and a blank is a space or a tab, but the `LC_CTYPE` locale can change this.

'-f'
'--ignore-case'

> Fold lowercase characters into the equivalent uppercase characters when comparing so that, for example, 'b' and 'B' sort as equal. The `LC_CTYPE` locale determines character types. When used with `--unique` those lower case equivalent lines are thrown away. (There is currently no way to throw away the upper case equivalent instead. (Any `--reverse` given would only affect the final result, after the throwing away.))

'-g'
'--general-numeric-sort'
'--sort=general-numeric'

> Sort numerically, converting a prefix of each line to a long double-precision floating point number. See Section 2.4 [Floating point], page 5. Do not report overflow, underflow, or conversion errors. Use the following collating sequence:
>
> - Lines that do not start with numbers (all considered to be equal).
> - NaNs ("Not a Number" values, in IEEE floating point arithmetic) in a consistent but machine-dependent order.
> - Minus infinity.

- Finite numbers in ascending numeric order (with −0 and +0 equal).
- Plus infinity.

Use this option only if there is no alternative; it is much slower than `--numeric-sort` (`-n`) and it can lose information when converting to floating point.

'`-h`'
'`--human-numeric-sort`'
'`--sort=human-numeric`'

Sort numerically, first by numeric sign (negative, zero, or positive); then by SI suffix (either empty, or '`k`' or '`K`', or one of '`MGTPEZY`', in that order; see Section 2.3 [Block size], page 3); and finally by numeric value. For example, '`1023M`' sorts before '`1G`' because '`M`' (mega) precedes '`G`' (giga) as an SI suffix. This option sorts values that are consistently scaled to the nearest suffix, regardless of whether suffixes denote powers of 1000 or 1024, and it therefore sorts the output of any single invocation of the `df`, `du`, or `ls` commands that are invoked with their `--human-readable` or `--si` options. The syntax for numbers is the same as for the `--numeric-sort` option; the SI suffix must immediately follow the number. Note also the `numfmt` command, which can be used to reformat numbers to human format *after* the sort, thus often allowing sort to operate on more accurate numbers.

'`-i`'
'`--ignore-nonprinting`'

Ignore nonprinting characters. The `LC_CTYPE` locale determines character types. This option has no effect if the stronger `--dictionary-order` (`-d`) option is also given.

'`-M`'
'`--month-sort`'
'`--sort=month`'

An initial string, consisting of any amount of blanks, followed by a month name abbreviation, is folded to UPPER case and compared in the order '`JAN`' < '`FEB`' < . . . < '`DEC`'. Invalid names compare low to valid names. The `LC_TIME` locale category determines the month spellings. By default a blank is a space or a tab, but the `LC_CTYPE` locale can change this.

'`-n`'
'`--numeric-sort`'
'`--sort=numeric`'

Sort numerically. The number begins each line and consists of optional blanks, an optional '`-`' sign, and zero or more digits possibly separated by thousands separators, optionally followed by a decimal-point character and zero or more digits. An empty number is treated as '`0`'. The `LC_NUMERIC` locale specifies the decimal-point character and thousands separator. By default a blank is a space or a tab, but the `LC_CTYPE` locale can change this.

Comparison is exact; there is no rounding error.

Neither a leading '`+`' nor exponential notation is recognized. To compare such strings numerically, use the `--general-numeric-sort` (`-g`) option.

'-V'
'--version-sort'

> Sort by version name and number. It behaves like a standard sort, except that each sequence of decimal digits is treated numerically as an index/version number. (See Section 10.1.4 [Details about version sort], page 84.)

'-r'
'--reverse'

> Reverse the result of comparison, so that lines with greater key values appear earlier in the output instead of later.

'-R'
'--random-sort'
'--sort=random'

> Sort by hashing the input keys and then sorting the hash values. Choose the hash function at random, ensuring that it is free of collisions so that differing keys have differing hash values. This is like a random permutation of the inputs (see Section 7.2 [shuf invocation], page 51), except that keys with the same value sort together.

> If multiple random sort fields are specified, the same random hash function is used for all fields. To use different random hash functions for different fields, you can invoke **sort** more than once.

> The choice of hash function is affected by the --random-source option.

Other options are:

'--compress-program=*prog*'

> Compress any temporary files with the program *prog*.

> With no arguments, *prog* must compress standard input to standard output, and when given the -d option it must decompress standard input to standard output.

> Terminate with an error if *prog* exits with nonzero status.

> White space and the backslash character should not appear in *prog*; they are reserved for future use.

'--files0-from=*file*'

> Disallow processing files named on the command line, and instead process those named in file *file*; each name being terminated by a zero byte (ASCII NUL). This is useful when the list of file names is so long that it may exceed a command line length limitation. In such cases, running **sort** via **xargs** is undesirable because it splits the list into pieces and makes **sort** print sorted output for each sublist rather than for the entire list. One way to produce a list of ASCII NUL terminated file names is with GNU **find**, using its -print0 predicate. If *file* is '-' then the ASCII NUL terminated file names are read from standard input.

'-k *pos1*[,*pos2*]'
'--key=*pos1*[,*pos2*]'

> Specify a sort field that consists of the part of the line between *pos1* and *pos2* (or the end of the line, if *pos2* is omitted), *inclusive*.

Each *pos* has the form '`f[.c][opts]`', where *f* is the number of the field to use, and *c* is the number of the first character from the beginning of the field. Fields and character positions are numbered starting with 1; a character position of zero in *pos2* indicates the field's last character. If '`.c`' is omitted from *pos1*, it defaults to 1 (the beginning of the field); if omitted from *pos2*, it defaults to 0 (the end of the field). *opts* are ordering options, allowing individual keys to be sorted according to different rules; see below for details. Keys can span multiple fields.

Example: To sort on the second field, use `--key=2,2` (`-k 2,2`). See below for more notes on keys and more examples. See also the `--debug` option to help determine the part of the line being used in the sort.

'`--debug`'   Highlight the portion of each line used for sorting. Also issue warnings about questionable usage to stderr.

'`--batch-size=nmerge`'

Merge at most *nmerge* inputs at once.

When **sort** has to merge more than *nmerge* inputs, it merges them in groups of *nmerge*, saving the result in a temporary file, which is then used as an input in a subsequent merge.

A large value of *nmerge* may improve merge performance and decrease temporary storage utilization at the expense of increased memory usage and I/O. Conversely a small value of *nmerge* may reduce memory requirements and I/O at the expense of temporary storage consumption and merge performance.

The value of *nmerge* must be at least 2. The default value is currently 16, but this is implementation-dependent and may change in the future.

The value of *nmerge* may be bounded by a resource limit for open file descriptors. The commands '`ulimit -n`' or '`getconf OPEN_MAX`' may display limits for your systems; these limits may be modified further if your program already has some files open, or if the operating system has other limits on the number of open files. If the value of *nmerge* exceeds the resource limit, **sort** silently uses a smaller value.

'`-o output-file`'
'`--output=output-file`'

Write output to *output-file* instead of standard output. Normally, **sort** reads all input before opening *output-file*, so you can safely sort a file in place by using commands like `sort -o F F` and `cat F | sort -o F`. However, **sort** with `--merge` (`-m`) can open the output file before reading all input, so a command like `cat F | sort -m -o F - G` is not safe as **sort** might start writing F before **cat** is done reading it.

On newer systems, `-o` cannot appear after an input file if `POSIXLY_CORRECT` is set, e.g., '`sort F -o F`'. Portable scripts should specify `-o output-file` before any input files.

'`--random-source=file`'

Use *file* as a source of random data used to determine which random hash function to use with the `-R` option. See Section 2.7 [Random sources], page 7.

'`-s`'

'`--stable`'

> Make `sort` stable by disabling its last-resort comparison. This option has no effect if no fields or global ordering options other than `--reverse` (`-r`) are specified.

'`-S size`'

'`--buffer-size=size`'

> Use a main-memory sort buffer of the given *size*. By default, *size* is in units of 1024 bytes. Appending '%' causes *size* to be interpreted as a percentage of physical memory. Appending 'K' multiplies *size* by 1024 (the default), 'M' by 1,048,576, 'G' by 1,073,741,824, and so on for 'T', 'P', 'E', 'Z', and 'Y'. Appending 'b' causes *size* to be interpreted as a byte count, with no multiplication.

> This option can improve the performance of `sort` by causing it to start with a larger or smaller sort buffer than the default. However, this option affects only the initial buffer size. The buffer grows beyond *size* if `sort` encounters input lines larger than *size*.

'`-t separator`'

'`--field-separator=separator`'

> Use character *separator* as the field separator when finding the sort keys in each line. By default, fields are separated by the empty string between a non-blank character and a blank character. By default a blank is a space or a tab, but the `LC_CTYPE` locale can change this.

> That is, given the input line ' foo bar', `sort` breaks it into fields ' foo' and ' bar'. The field separator is not considered to be part of either the field preceding or the field following, so with '`sort -t " "`' the same input line has three fields: an empty field, '`foo`', and '`bar`'. However, fields that extend to the end of the line, as `-k 2`, or fields consisting of a range, as `-k 2,3`, retain the field separators present between the endpoints of the range.

> To specify ASCII NUL as the field separator, use the two-character string '`\0`', e.g., '`sort -t '\0''`'.

'`-T tempdir`'

'`--temporary-directory=tempdir`'

> Use directory *tempdir* to store temporary files, overriding the `TMPDIR` environment variable. If this option is given more than once, temporary files are stored in all the directories given. If you have a large sort or merge that is I/O-bound, you can often improve performance by using this option to specify directories on different disks and controllers.

'`--parallel=n`'

> Set the number of sorts run in parallel to *n*. By default, *n* is set to the number of available processors, but limited to 8, as there are diminishing performance gains after that. Note also that using *n* threads increases the memory usage by a factor of log *n*. Also see Section 21.3 [nproc invocation], page 183.

'-u'

'--unique'

>   Normally, output only the first of a sequence of lines that compare equal. For the --check (-c or -C) option, check that no pair of consecutive lines compares equal.
>
>   This option also disables the default last-resort comparison.
>
>   The commands sort -u and sort | uniq are equivalent, but this equivalence does not extend to arbitrary sort options. For example, sort -n -u inspects only the value of the initial numeric string when checking for uniqueness, whereas sort -n | uniq inspects the entire line. See Section 7.3 [uniq invocation], page 53.

'-z'

'--zero-terminated'

>   Delimit items with a zero byte rather than a newline (ASCII LF). I.e., treat input as items separated by ASCII NUL and terminate output items with ASCII NUL. This option can be useful in conjunction with 'perl -0' or 'find -print0' and 'xargs -0' which do the same in order to reliably handle arbitrary file names (even those containing blanks or other special characters).

Historical (BSD and System V) implementations of sort have differed in their interpretation of some options, particularly -b, -f, and -n. GNU sort follows the POSIX behavior, which is usually (but not always!) like the System V behavior. According to POSIX, -n no longer implies -b. For consistency, -M has been changed in the same way. This may affect the meaning of character positions in field specifications in obscure cases. The only fix is to add an explicit -b.

A position in a sort field specified with -k may have any of the option letters 'MbdfghinRrV' appended to it, in which case no global ordering options are inherited by that particular field. The -b option may be independently attached to either or both of the start and end positions of a field specification, and if it is inherited from the global options it will be attached to both. If input lines can contain leading or adjacent blanks and -t is not used, then -k is typically combined with -b or an option that implicitly ignores leading blanks ('Mghn') as otherwise the varying numbers of leading blanks in fields can cause confusing results.

If the start position in a sort field specifier falls after the end of the line or after the end field, the field is empty. If the -b option was specified, the '.c' part of a field specification is counted from the first nonblank character of the field.

On older systems, sort supports an obsolete origin-zero syntax '+pos1 [-pos2]' for specifying sort keys. The obsolete sequence 'sort +a.x -b.y' is equivalent to 'sort -k a+1.x+1,b' if y is '0' or absent, otherwise it is equivalent to 'sort -k a+1.x+1,b+1.y'.

This obsolete behavior can be enabled or disabled with the _POSIX2_VERSION environment variable (see Section 2.13 [Standards conformance], page 11); it can also be enabled when POSIXLY_CORRECT is not set by using the obsolete syntax with '-pos2' present.

Scripts intended for use on standard hosts should avoid obsolete syntax and should use -k instead. For example, avoid 'sort +2', since it might be interpreted as either 'sort ./+2' or 'sort -k 3'. If your script must also run on hosts that support only the obsolete syntax, it can use a test like 'if sort -k 1 </dev/null >/dev/null 2>&1; then ...' to decide which syntax to use.

Here are some examples to illustrate various combinations of options.

- Sort in descending (reverse) numeric order.

  ```
  sort -n -r
  ```

- Run no more than 4 sorts concurrently, using a buffer size of 10M.

  ```
  sort --parallel=4 -S 10M
  ```

- Sort alphabetically, omitting the first and second fields and the blanks at the start of the third field. This uses a single key composed of the characters beginning at the start of the first nonblank character in field three and extending to the end of each line.

  ```
  sort -k 3b
  ```

- Sort numerically on the second field and resolve ties by sorting alphabetically on the third and fourth characters of field five. Use ':' as the field delimiter.

  ```
  sort -t : -k 2,2n -k 5.3,5.4
  ```

Note that if you had written -k 2n instead of -k 2,2n sort would have used all characters beginning in the second field and extending to the end of the line as the primary *numeric* key. For the large majority of applications, treating keys spanning more than one field as numeric will not do what you expect.

Also note that the 'n' modifier was applied to the field-end specifier for the first key. It would have been equivalent to specify -k 2n,2 or -k 2n,2n. All modifiers except 'b' apply to the associated *field*, regardless of whether the modifier character is attached to the field-start and/or the field-end part of the key specifier.

- Sort the password file on the fifth field and ignore any leading blanks. Sort lines with equal values in field five on the numeric user ID in field three. Fields are separated by ':'.

  ```
  sort -t : -k 5b,5 -k 3,3n /etc/passwd
  sort -t : -n -k 5b,5 -k 3,3 /etc/passwd
  sort -t : -b -k 5,5 -k 3,3n /etc/passwd
  ```

These three commands have equivalent effect. The first specifies that the first key's start position ignores leading blanks and the second key is sorted numerically. The other two commands rely on global options being inherited by sort keys that lack modifiers. The inheritance works in this case because -k 5b,5b and -k 5b,5 are equivalent, as the location of a field-end lacking a '.c' character position is not affected by whether initial blanks are skipped.

- Sort a set of log files, primarily by IPv4 address and secondarily by time stamp. If two lines' primary and secondary keys are identical, output the lines in the same order that they were input. The log files contain lines that look like this:

  ```
  4.150.156.3 - - [01/Apr/2004:06:31:51 +0000] message 1
  211.24.3.231 - - [24/Apr/2004:20:17:39 +0000] message 2
  ```

Fields are separated by exactly one space. Sort IPv4 addresses lexicographically, e.g., 212.61.52.2 sorts before 212.129.233.201 because 61 is less than 129.

  ```
  sort -s -t ' ' -k 4.9n -k 4.5M -k 4.2n -k 4.14,4.21 file*.log |
  sort -s -t '.' -k 1,1n -k 2,2n -k 3,3n -k 4,4n
  ```

This example cannot be done with a single **sort** invocation, since IPv4 address components are separated by '.' while dates come just after a space. So it is broken down into two invocations of **sort**: the first sorts by time stamp and the second by IPv4 address. The time stamp is sorted by year, then month, then day, and finally by hour-minute-second field, using -k to isolate each field. Except for hour-minute-second there's no need to specify the end of each key field, since the 'n' and 'M' modifiers sort based on leading prefixes that cannot cross field boundaries. The IPv4 addresses are sorted lexicographically. The second sort uses '-s' so that ties in the primary key are broken by the secondary key; the first sort uses '-s' so that the combination of the two sorts is stable.

- Generate a tags file in case-insensitive sorted order.

```
find src -type f -print0 | sort -z -f | xargs -0 etags --append
```

The use of -print0, -z, and -0 in this case means that file names that contain blanks or other special characters are not broken up by the sort operation.

- Use the common DSU, Decorate Sort Undecorate idiom to sort lines according to their length.

```
awk '{print length, $0}' /etc/passwd | sort -n | cut -f2- -d' '
```

In general this technique can be used to sort data that the **sort** command does not support, or is inefficient at, sorting directly.

- Shuffle a list of directories, but preserve the order of files within each directory. For instance, one could use this to generate a music playlist in which albums are shuffled but the songs of each album are played in order.

```
ls */* | sort -t / -k 1,1R -k 2,2
```

7.2 shuf: Shuffling text

shuf shuffles its input by outputting a random permutation of its input lines. Each output permutation is equally likely. Synopses:

```
shuf [option]... [file]
shuf -e [option]... [arg]...
shuf -i lo-hi [option]...
```

shuf has three modes of operation that affect where it obtains its input lines. By default, it reads lines from standard input. The following options change the operation mode:

'-e'
'--echo'   Treat each command-line operand as an input line.

'-i lo-hi'
'--input-range=lo-hi'
                Act as if input came from a file containing the range of unsigned decimal integers lo...hi, one per line.

shuf's other options can affect its behavior in all operation modes:

'-n lines'
'--head-count=count'
                Output at most *count* lines. By default, all input lines are output.

'-o output-file'
'--output=output-file'

> Write output to *output-file* instead of standard output. shuf reads all input
> before opening *output-file*, so you can safely shuffle a file in place by using
> commands like shuf -o F <F and cat F | shuf -o F.

'--random-source=file'

> Use *file* as a source of random data used to determine which permutation to
> generate. See Section 2.7 [Random sources], page 7.

'-r'
'--repeat'

> Repeat output values, that is, select with replacement. With this option the
> output is not a permutation of the input; instead, each output line is ran-
> domly chosen from all the inputs. This option is typically combined with
> --head-count; if --head-count is not given, shuf repeats indefinitely.

'-z'
'--zero-terminated'

> Delimit items with a zero byte rather than a newline (ASCII LF). I.e., treat
> input as items separated by ASCII NUL and terminate output items with ASCII
> NUL. This option can be useful in conjunction with 'perl -0' or 'find -print0'
> and 'xargs -0' which do the same in order to reliably handle arbitrary file names
> (even those containing blanks or other special characters).

For example:

```
shuf <<EOF
A man,
a plan,
a canal:
Panama!
EOF
```

might produce the output

```
Panama!
A man,
a canal:
a plan,
```

Similarly, the command:

```
shuf -e clubs hearts diamonds spades
```

might output:

```
clubs
diamonds
spades
hearts
```

and the command 'shuf -i 1-4' might output:

```
4
2
```

```
1
3
```

The above examples all have four input lines, so `shuf` might produce any of the twenty-four possible permutations of the input. In general, if there are n input lines, there are $n!$ (i.e., n factorial, or $n * (n - 1) * \ldots * 1$) possible output permutations.

To output 50 random numbers each in the range 0 through 9, use:

```
shuf -r -n 50 -i 0-9
```

To simulate 100 coin flips, use:

```
shuf -r -n 100 -e Head Tail
```

An exit status of zero indicates success, and a nonzero value indicates failure.

7.3 uniq: Uniquify files

`uniq` writes the unique lines in the given `input`, or standard input if nothing is given or for an *input* name of '-'. Synopsis:

```
uniq [option]... [input [output]]
```

By default, `uniq` prints its input lines, except that it discards all but the first of adjacent repeated lines, so that no output lines are repeated. Optionally, it can instead discard lines that are not repeated, or all repeated lines.

The input need not be sorted, but repeated input lines are detected only if they are adjacent. If you want to discard non-adjacent duplicate lines, perhaps you want to use `sort -u`. See Section 7.1 [sort invocation], page 43.

Comparisons honor the rules specified by the `LC_COLLATE` locale category.

If no *output* file is specified, `uniq` writes to standard output.

The program accepts the following options. Also see Chapter 2 [Common options], page 2.

'-f n'
'--skip-fields=n'

> Skip n fields on each line before checking for uniqueness. Use a null string for comparison if a line has fewer than n fields. Fields are sequences of non-space non-tab characters that are separated from each other by at least one space or tab.
>
> For compatibility `uniq` supports an obsolete option syntax `-n`. New scripts should use `-f n` instead.

'-s n'
'--skip-chars=n'

> Skip n characters before checking for uniqueness. Use a null string for comparison if a line has fewer than n characters. If you use both the field and character skipping options, fields are skipped over first.
>
> On older systems, `uniq` supports an obsolete option syntax `+n`. This obsolete behavior can be enabled or disabled with the `_POSIX2_VERSION` environment variable (see Section 2.13 [Standards conformance], page 11), but portable scripts should avoid commands whose behavior depends on this variable. For

example, use 'uniq ./+10' or 'uniq -s 10' rather than the ambiguous 'uniq +10'.

'-c'

'--count'   Print the number of times each line occurred along with the line.

'-i'

'--ignore-case'

Ignore differences in case when comparing lines.

'-d'

'--repeated'

Discard lines that are not repeated. When used by itself, this option causes uniq to print the first copy of each repeated line, and nothing else.

'-D'

'--all-repeated[=*delimit-method*]'

Do not discard the second and subsequent repeated input lines, but discard lines that are not repeated. This option is useful mainly in conjunction with other options e.g., to ignore case or to compare only selected fields. The optional *delimit-method* specifies how to delimit groups of repeated lines, and must be one of the following:

'none'   Do not delimit groups of repeated lines. This is equivalent to --all-repeated (-D).

'prepend'   Output a newline before each group of repeated lines. With --zero-terminated (-z), use a zero byte (ASCII NUL) instead of a newline as the delimiter.

'separate'

Separate groups of repeated lines with a single newline. This is the same as using 'prepend', except that no delimiter is inserted before the first group, and hence may be better suited for output direct to users. With --zero-terminated (-z), use a zero byte (ASCII NUL) instead of a newline as the delimiter.

Note that when groups are delimited and the input stream contains two or more consecutive blank lines, then the output is ambiguous. To avoid that, filter the input through 'tr -s '\n'' to replace each sequence of consecutive newlines with a single newline.

This is a GNU extension.

'--group[=*delimit-method*]'

Output all lines, and delimit each unique group. With --zero-terminated (-z), use a zero byte (ASCII NUL) instead of a newline as the delimiter.The optional *delimit-method* specifies how to delimit groups, and must be one of the following:

'separate'

Separate unique groups with a single delimiter. This is the default delimiting method if none is specified, and better suited for output direct to users.

'prepend'   Output a delimiter before each group of unique items.

'append'   Output a delimiter after each group of unique items.

'both'   Output a delimiter around each group of unique items.

Note that when groups are delimited and the input stream contains two or more consecutive blank lines, then the output is ambiguous. To avoid that, filter the input through 'tr -s '\n'' to replace each sequence of consecutive newlines with a single newline.

This is a GNU extension.

'-u'

'--unique'

Discard the last line that would be output for a repeated input group. When used by itself, this option causes uniq to print unique lines, and nothing else.

'-w n'

'--check-chars=n'

Compare at most n characters on each line (after skipping any specified fields and characters). By default the entire rest of the lines are compared.

'-z'

'--zero-terminated'

Delimit items with a zero byte rather than a newline (ASCII LF). I.e., treat input as items separated by ASCII NUL and terminate output items with ASCII NUL. This option can be useful in conjunction with 'perl -0' or 'find -print0' and 'xargs -0' which do the same in order to reliably handle arbitrary file names (even those containing blanks or other special characters).

An exit status of zero indicates success, and a nonzero value indicates failure.

7.4 comm: Compare two sorted files line by line

comm writes to standard output lines that are common, and lines that are unique, to two input files; a file name of '-' means standard input. Synopsis:

```
comm [option]... file1 file2
```

Before comm can be used, the input files must be sorted using the collating sequence specified by the LC_COLLATE locale. If an input file ends in a non-newline character, a newline is silently appended. The sort command with no options always outputs a file that is suitable input to comm.

With no options, comm produces three-column output. Column one contains lines unique to file1, column two contains lines unique to file2, and column three contains lines common to both files. Columns are separated by a single TAB character.

The options -1, -2, and -3 suppress printing of the corresponding columns (and separators). Also see Chapter 2 [Common options], page 2.

Unlike some other comparison utilities, comm has an exit status that does not depend on the result of the comparison. Upon normal completion comm produces an exit code of zero. If there is an error it exits with nonzero status.

If the `--check-order` option is given, unsorted inputs will cause a fatal error message. If the option `--nocheck-order` is given, unsorted inputs will never cause an error message. If neither of these options is given, wrongly sorted inputs are diagnosed only if an input file is found to contain unpairable lines. If an input file is diagnosed as being unsorted, the `comm` command will exit with a nonzero status (and the output should not be used).

Forcing `comm` to process wrongly sorted input files containing unpairable lines by specifying `--nocheck-order` is not guaranteed to produce any particular output. The output will probably not correspond with whatever you hoped it would be.

'`--check-order`'

> Fail with an error message if either input file is wrongly ordered.

'`--nocheck-order`'

> Do not check that both input files are in sorted order.

> Other options are:

'`--output-delimiter=str`'

> Print *str* between adjacent output columns, rather than the default of a single TAB character.

> The delimiter *str* may not be empty.

7.5 `ptx`: Produce permuted indexes

`ptx` reads a text file and essentially produces a permuted index, with each keyword in its context. The calling sketch is either one of:

```
ptx [option ...] [file ...]
ptx -G [option ...] [input [output]]
```

The `-G` (or its equivalent: `--traditional`) option disables all GNU extensions and reverts to traditional mode, thus introducing some limitations and changing several of the program's default option values. When `-G` is not specified, GNU extensions are always enabled. GNU extensions to `ptx` are documented wherever appropriate in this document. See Section 7.5.5 [Compatibility in ptx], page 61, for the full list.

Individual options are explained in the following sections.

When GNU extensions are enabled, there may be zero, one or several *files* after the options. If there is no *file*, the program reads the standard input. If there is one or several *files*, they give the name of input files which are all read in turn, as if all the input files were concatenated. However, there is a full contextual break between each file and, when automatic referencing is requested, file names and line numbers refer to individual text input files. In all cases, the program outputs the permuted index to the standard output.

When GNU extensions are *not* enabled, that is, when the program operates in traditional mode, there may be zero, one or two parameters besides the options. If there are no parameters, the program reads the standard input and outputs the permuted index to the standard output. If there is only one parameter, it names the text *input* to be read instead of the standard input. If two parameters are given, they give respectively the name of the *input* file to read and the name of the *output* file to produce. *Be very careful* to note that, in this case, the contents of file given by the second parameter is destroyed. This behavior is dictated by System V `ptx` compatibility; GNU Standards normally discourage output parameters not introduced by an option.

Note that for *any* file named as the value of an option or as an input text file, a single dash '-' may be used, in which case standard input is assumed. However, it would not make sense to use this convention more than once per program invocation.

7.5.1 General options

'-G'

'--traditional'

>   As already explained, this option disables all GNU extensions to `ptx` and switches to traditional mode.

'--help'   Print a short help on standard output, then exit without further processing.

'--version'

>   Print the program version on standard output, then exit without further processing.

An exit status of zero indicates success, and a nonzero value indicates failure.

7.5.2 Charset selection

As it is set up now, the program assumes that the input file is coded using 8-bit ISO 8859-1 code, also known as Latin-1 character set, *unless* it is compiled for MS-DOS, in which case it uses the character set of the IBM-PC. (GNU `ptx` is not known to work on smaller MS-DOS machines anymore.) Compared to 7-bit ASCII, the set of characters which are letters is different; this alters the behavior of regular expression matching. Thus, the default regular expression for a keyword allows foreign or diacriticized letters. Keyword sorting, however, is still crude; it obeys the underlying character set ordering quite blindly.

'-f'

'--ignore-case'

>   Fold lower case letters to upper case for sorting.

7.5.3 Word selection and input processing

'-b *file*'

'--break-file=*file*'

>   This option provides an alternative (to -W) method of describing which characters make up words. It introduces the name of a file which contains a list of characters which can*not* be part of one word; this file is called the *Break file*. Any character which is not part of the Break file is a word constituent. If both options -b and -W are specified, then -W has precedence and -b is ignored.
>
>   When GNU extensions are enabled, the only way to avoid newline as a break character is to write all the break characters in the file with no newline at all, not even at the end of the file. When GNU extensions are disabled, spaces, tabs and newlines are always considered as break characters even if not included in the Break file.

'-i *file*'

'--ignore-file=*file*'

>   The file associated with this option contains a list of words which will never be taken as keywords in concordance output. It is called the *Ignore file*. The file

contains exactly one word in each line; the end of line separation of words is not subject to the value of the -S option.

'-o *file*'

'--only-file=*file*'

The file associated with this option contains a list of words which will be retained in concordance output; any word not mentioned in this file is ignored. The file is called the *Only file*. The file contains exactly one word in each line; the end of line separation of words is not subject to the value of the -S option.

There is no default for the Only file. When both an Only file and an Ignore file are specified, a word is considered a keyword only if it is listed in the Only file and not in the Ignore file.

'-r'

'--references'

On each input line, the leading sequence of non-white space characters will be taken to be a reference that has the purpose of identifying this input line in the resulting permuted index. See Section 7.5.4 [Output formatting in ptx], page 59, for more information about reference production. Using this option changes the default value for option -S.

Using this option, the program does not try very hard to remove references from contexts in output, but it succeeds in doing so *when* the context ends exactly at the newline. If option -r is used with -S default value, or when GNU extensions are disabled, this condition is always met and references are completely excluded from the output contexts.

'-S *regexp*'

'--sentence-regexp=*regexp*'

This option selects which regular expression will describe the end of a line or the end of a sentence. In fact, this regular expression is not the only distinction between end of lines or end of sentences, and input line boundaries have no special significance outside this option. By default, when GNU extensions are enabled and if -r option is not used, end of sentences are used. In this case, this *regex* is imported from GNU Emacs:

        [.?!][]\"')}]*\\($\\|\t\\| \\)[\t\n]*

Whenever GNU extensions are disabled or if -r option is used, end of lines are used; in this case, the default *regexp* is just:

        \n

Using an empty *regexp* is equivalent to completely disabling end of line or end of sentence recognition. In this case, the whole file is considered to be a single big line or sentence. The user might want to disallow all truncation flag generation as well, through option -F "". See Section "Syntax of Regular Expressions" in *The GNU Emacs Manual*.

When the keywords happen to be near the beginning of the input line or sentence, this often creates an unused area at the beginning of the output context line; when the keywords happen to be near the end of the input line or sentence, this often creates an unused area at the end of the output context line. The program tries to fill those unused areas by wrapping around context in them; the tail of the input line or sentence is used to fill the unused area on the left of the output line; the head of the input line or sentence is used to fill the unused area on the right of the output line.

As a matter of convenience to the user, many usual backslashed escape sequences from the C language are recognized and converted to the corresponding characters by `ptx` itself.

'`-W regexp`'
'`--word-regexp=regexp`'

This option selects which regular expression will describe each keyword. By default, if GNU extensions are enabled, a word is a sequence of letters; the *regexp* used is '`\w+`'. When GNU extensions are disabled, a word is by default anything which ends with a space, a tab or a newline; the *regexp* used is '`[^ \t\n]+`'.

An empty *regexp* is equivalent to not using this option. See Section "Syntax of Regular Expressions" in *The GNU Emacs Manual*.

As a matter of convenience to the user, many usual backslashed escape sequences, as found in the C language, are recognized and converted to the corresponding characters by `ptx` itself.

7.5.4 Output formatting

Output format is mainly controlled by the `-O` and `-T` options described in the table below. When neither `-O` nor `-T` are selected, and if GNU extensions are enabled, the program chooses an output format suitable for a dumb terminal. Each keyword occurrence is output to the center of one line, surrounded by its left and right contexts. Each field is properly justified, so the concordance output can be readily observed. As a special feature, if automatic references are selected by option `-A` and are output before the left context, that is, if option `-R` is *not* selected, then a colon is added after the reference; this nicely interfaces with GNU Emacs `next-error` processing. In this default output format, each white space character, like newline and tab, is merely changed to exactly one space, with no special attempt to compress consecutive spaces. This might change in the future. Except for those white space characters, every other character of the underlying set of 256 characters is transmitted verbatim.

Output format is further controlled by the following options.

'`-g number`'
'`--gap-size=number`'

Select the size of the minimum white space gap between the fields on the output line.

'`-w number`'
'`--width=number`'

Select the maximum output width of each final line. If references are used, they are included or excluded from the maximum output width depending on the value of option `-R`. If this option is not selected, that is, when references are output before the left context, the maximum output width takes into account the maximum length of all references. If this option is selected, that is, when references are output after the right context, the maximum output width does not take into account the space taken by references, nor the gap that precedes them.

'-A'
'--auto-reference'

Select automatic references. Each input line will have an automatic reference made up of the file name and the line ordinal, with a single colon between them. However, the file name will be empty when standard input is being read. If both -A and -r are selected, then the input reference is still read and skipped, but the automatic reference is used at output time, overriding the input reference.

'-R'
'--right-side-refs'

In the default output format, when option -R is not used, any references produced by the effect of options -r or -A are placed to the far right of output lines, after the right context. With default output format, when the -R option is specified, references are rather placed at the beginning of each output line, before the left context. For any other output format, option -R is ignored, with one exception: with -R the width of references is *not* taken into account in total output width given by -w.

This option is automatically selected whenever GNU extensions are disabled.

'-F *string*'
'--flac-truncation=*string*'

This option will request that any truncation in the output be reported using the string *string*. Most output fields theoretically extend towards the beginning or the end of the current line, or current sentence, as selected with option -S. But there is a maximum allowed output line width, changeable through option -w, which is further divided into space for various output fields. When a field has to be truncated because it cannot extend beyond the beginning or the end of the current line to fit in, then a truncation occurs. By default, the string used is a single slash, as in -F /.

string may have more than one character, as in -F .... Also, in the particular case when *string* is empty (-F ""), truncation flagging is disabled, and no truncation marks are appended in this case.

As a matter of convenience to the user, many usual backslashed escape sequences, as found in the C language, are recognized and converted to the corresponding characters by ptx itself.

'-M *string*'
'--macro-name=*string*'

Select another *string* to be used instead of 'xx', while generating output suitable for nroff, troff or TEX.

'-O'
'--format=roff'

Choose an output format suitable for nroff or troff processing. Each output line will look like:

> .xx "tail" "before" "keyword_and_after" "head" "ref"

so it will be possible to write a '.xx' roff macro to take care of the output type-setting. This is the default output format when GNU extensions are disabled. Option -M can be used to change 'xx' to another macro name.

In this output format, each non-graphical character, like newline and tab, is merely changed to exactly one space, with no special attempt to compress consecutive spaces. Each quote character '"' is doubled so it will be correctly processed by **nroff** or **troff**.

'-T'

'--format=tex'

Choose an output format suitable for TeX processing. Each output line will look like:

> \xx {tail}{before}{keyword}{after}{head}{ref}

so it will be possible to write a \xx definition to take care of the output typeset-ting. Note that when references are not being produced, that is, neither option -A nor option -r is selected, the last parameter of each \xx call is inhibited. Option -M can be used to change 'xx' to another macro name.

In this output format, some special characters, like '$', '%', '&', '#' and '_' are automatically protected with a backslash. Curly brackets '{', '}' are protected with a backslash and a pair of dollar signs (to force mathematical mode). The backslash itself produces the sequence \backslash{}. Circumflex and tilde diacritical marks produce the sequence ^\{ } and ~\{ } respectively. Other diacriticized characters of the underlying character set produce an appropriate TeX sequence as far as possible. The other non-graphical characters, like new-line and tab, and all other characters which are not part of ASCII, are merely changed to exactly one space, with no special attempt to compress consecutive spaces. Let me know how to improve this special character processing for TeX.

7.5.5 The GNU extensions to ptx

This version of **ptx** contains a few features which do not exist in System V **ptx**. These extra features are suppressed by using the -G command line option, unless overridden by other command line options. Some GNU extensions cannot be recovered by overriding, so the simple rule is to avoid -G if you care about GNU extensions. Here are the differences between this program and System V **ptx**.

- This program can read many input files at once, it always writes the resulting concordance on standard output. On the other hand, System V **ptx** reads only one file and sends the result to standard output or, if a second *file* parameter is given on the command, to that *file*.

  Having output parameters not introduced by options is a dangerous practice which GNU avoids as far as possible. So, for using **ptx** portably between GNU and System V, you should always use it with a single input file, and always expect the result on standard output. You might also want to automatically configure in a -G option to **ptx** calls in products using **ptx**, if the configurator finds that the installed **ptx** accepts -G.

- The only options available in System V **ptx** are options -b, -f, -g, -i, -o, -r, -t and -w. All other options are GNU extensions and are not repeated in this enumeration.

Moreover, some options have a slightly different meaning when GNU extensions are enabled, as explained below.

- By default, concordance output is not formatted for `troff` or `nroff`. It is rather formatted for a dumb terminal. `troff` or `nroff` output may still be selected through option `-O`.

- Unless `-R` option is used, the maximum reference width is subtracted from the total output line width. With GNU extensions disabled, width of references is not taken into account in the output line width computations.

- All 256 bytes, even ASCII NUL bytes, are always read and processed from input file with no adverse effect, even if GNU extensions are disabled. However, System V `ptx` does not accept 8-bit characters, a few control characters are rejected, and the tilde '~' is also rejected.

- Input line length is only limited by available memory, even if GNU extensions are disabled. However, System V `ptx` processes only the first 200 characters in each line.

- The break (non-word) characters default to be every character except all letters of the underlying character set, diacriticized or not. When GNU extensions are disabled, the break characters default to space, tab and newline only.

- The program makes better use of output line width. If GNU extensions are disabled, the program rather tries to imitate System V `ptx`, but still, there are some slight disposition glitches this program does not completely reproduce.

- The user can specify both an Ignore file and an Only file. This is not allowed with System V `ptx`.

7.6 `tsort`: Topological sort

`tsort` performs a topological sort on the given *file*, or standard input if no input file is given or for a *file* of '-'. For more details and some history, see Section 7.6.1 [tsort background], page 64. Synopsis:

```
tsort [option] [file]
```

`tsort` reads its input as pairs of strings, separated by blanks, indicating a partial ordering. The output is a total ordering that corresponds to the given partial ordering.

For example

```
tsort <<EOF
a b c
d
e f
b c d e
EOF
```

will produce the output

```
a
b
c
d
e
```

f

Consider a more realistic example. You have a large set of functions all in one file, and they may all be declared static except one. Currently that one (say `main`) is the first function defined in the file, and the ones it calls directly follow it, followed by those they call, etc. Let's say that you are determined to take advantage of prototypes, so you have to choose between declaring all of those functions (which means duplicating a lot of information from the definitions) and rearranging the functions so that as many as possible are defined before they are used. One way to automate the latter process is to get a list for each function of the functions it calls directly. Many programs can generate such lists. They describe a call graph. Consider the following list, in which a given line indicates that the function on the left calls the one on the right directly.

```
main parse_options
main tail_file
main tail_forever
tail_file pretty_name
tail_file write_header
tail_file tail
tail_forever recheck
tail_forever pretty_name
tail_forever write_header
tail_forever dump_remainder
tail tail_lines
tail tail_bytes
tail_lines start_lines
tail_lines dump_remainder
tail_lines file_lines
tail_lines pipe_lines
tail_bytes xlseek
tail_bytes start_bytes
tail_bytes dump_remainder
tail_bytes pipe_bytes
file_lines dump_remainder
recheck pretty_name
```

then you can use `tsort` to produce an ordering of those functions that satisfies your requirement.

```
example$ tsort call-graph | tac
dump_remainder
start_lines
file_lines
pipe_lines
xlseek
start_bytes
pipe_bytes
tail_lines
tail_bytes
pretty_name
```

```
write_header
tail
recheck
parse_options
tail_file
tail_forever
main
```

tsort detects any cycles in the input and writes the first cycle encountered to standard error.

Note that for a given partial ordering, generally there is no unique total ordering. In the context of the call graph above, the function **parse_options** may be placed anywhere in the list as long as it precedes **main**.

The only options are **--help** and **--version**. See Chapter 2 [Common options], page 2.

An exit status of zero indicates success, and a nonzero value indicates failure.

7.6.1 tsort: Background

tsort exists because very early versions of the Unix linker processed an archive file exactly once, and in order. As **ld** read each object in the archive, it decided whether it was needed in the program based on whether it defined any symbols which were undefined at that point in the link.

This meant that dependencies within the archive had to be handled specially. For example, scanf probably calls **read**. That means that in a single pass through an archive, it was important for scanf.o to appear before read.o, because otherwise a program which calls **scanf** but not **read** might end up with an unexpected unresolved reference to **read**.

The way to address this problem was to first generate a set of dependencies of one object file on another. This was done by a shell script called **lorder**. The GNU tools don't provide a version of lorder, as far as I know, but you can still find it in BSD distributions.

Then you ran **tsort** over the **lorder** output, and you used the resulting sort to define the order in which you added objects to the archive.

This whole procedure has been obsolete since about 1980, because Unix archives now contain a symbol table (traditionally built by **ranlib**, now generally built by **ar** itself), and the Unix linker uses the symbol table to effectively make multiple passes over an archive file.

Anyhow, that's where tsort came from. To solve an old problem with the way the linker handled archive files, which has since been solved in different ways.

8 Operating on fields

8.1 cut: Print selected parts of lines

cut writes to standard output selected parts of each line of each input file, or standard
input if no files are given or for a file name of '-'. Synopsis:

        cut option... [file]...

In the table which follows, the *byte-list*, *character-list*, and *field-list* are one or more
numbers or ranges (two numbers separated by a dash) separated by commas. Bytes, characters, and fields are numbered starting at 1. Incomplete ranges may be given: -*m* means
'1-*m*'; '*n*-' means '*n*' through end of line or last field. The list elements can be repeated,
can overlap, and can be specified in any order; but the selected input is written in the same
order that it is read, and is written exactly once.

The program accepts the following options. Also see Chapter 2 [Common options],
page 2.

'-b *byte-list*'
'--bytes=*byte-list*'
> Select for printing only the bytes in positions listed in *byte-list*. Tabs and
> backspaces are treated like any other character; they take up 1 byte. If an
> output delimiter is specified, (see the description of --output-delimiter), then
> output that string between ranges of selected bytes.

'-c *character-list*'
'--characters=*character-list*'
> Select for printing only the characters in positions listed in *character-list*.
> The same as -b for now, but internationalization will change that. Tabs and
> backspaces are treated like any other character; they take up 1 character. If
> an output delimiter is specified, (see the description of --output-delimiter),
> then output that string between ranges of selected bytes.

'-f *field-list*'
'--fields=*field-list*'
> Select for printing only the fields listed in *field-list*. Fields are separated by
> a TAB character by default. Also print any line that contains no delimiter
> character, unless the --only-delimited (-s) option is specified.

> Note awk supports more sophisticated field processing, and by default will use
> (and discard) runs of blank characters to separate fields, and ignore leading and
> trailing blanks.

```
awk '{print $2}'    # print the second field
awk '{print $NF-1}' # print the penultimate field
awk '{print $2,$1}' # reorder the first two fields
```

> In the unlikely event that awk is unavailable, one can use the join command,
> to process blank characters as awk does above.

```
join -a1 -o 1.2    - /dev/null # print the second field
join -a1 -o 1.2,1.1 - /dev/null # reorder the first two fields
```

'-d *input_delim_byte*'
'--delimiter=*input_delim_byte*'

> With -f, use the first byte of *input_delim_byte* as the input fields separator (default is TAB).

'-n'   Do not split multi-byte characters (no-op for now).

'-s'
'--only-delimited'

> For -f, do not print lines that do not contain the field separator character. Normally, any line without a field separator is printed verbatim.

'--output-delimiter=*output_delim_string*'

> With -f, output fields are separated by *output_delim_string*. The default with -f is to use the input delimiter. When using -b or -c to select ranges of byte or character offsets (as opposed to ranges of fields), output *output_delim_string* between non-overlapping ranges of selected bytes.

'--complement'

> This option is a GNU extension. Select for printing the complement of the bytes, characters or fields selected with the -b, -c or -f options. In other words, do *not* print the bytes, characters or fields specified via those options. This option is useful when you have many fields and want to print all but a few of them.

An exit status of zero indicates success, and a nonzero value indicates failure.

8.2 paste: Merge lines of files

paste writes to standard output lines consisting of sequentially corresponding lines of each given file, separated by a TAB character. Standard input is used for a file name of '-' or if no input files are given.

Synopsis:

```
paste [option]... [file]...
```

For example, with:

```
$ cat num2
1
2
$ cat let3
a
b
c
```

Take lines sequentially from each file:

```
$ paste num2 let3
1       a
2       b
        c
```

Duplicate lines from a file:

```
$ paste num2 let3 num2
1       a       1
2       b       2
        c
```

Intermix lines from stdin:

```
$ paste - let3 - < num2
1       a       2
        b
        c
```

Join consecutive lines with a space:

```
$ seq 4 | paste -d ' ' - -
1 2
3 4
```

The program accepts the following options. Also see Chapter 2 [Common options], page 2.

'-s'
'--serial'

> Paste the lines of one file at a time rather than one line from each file. Using the above example data:

```
$ paste -s num2 let3
1       2
a       b       c
```

'-d delim-list'
'--delimiters=delim-list'

> Consecutively use the characters in delim-list instead of TAB to separate merged lines. When delim-list is exhausted, start again at its beginning. Using the above example data:

```
$ paste -d '%_' num2 let3 num2
1%a_1
2%b_2
%c_
```

An exit status of zero indicates success, and a nonzero value indicates failure.

8.3 join: Join lines on a common field

join writes to standard output a line for each pair of input lines that have identical join fields. Synopsis:

```
join [option]... file1 file2
```

Either file1 or file2 (but not both) can be '-', meaning standard input. file1 and file2 should be sorted on the join fields.

Normally, the sort order is that of the collating sequence specified by the LC_COLLATE locale. Unless the -t option is given, the sort comparison ignores blanks at the start of the join field, as in sort -b. If the --ignore-case option is given, the sort comparison ignores the case of characters in the join field, as in sort -f.

The `sort` and `join` commands should use consistent locales and options if the output of `sort` is fed to `join`. You can use a command like 'sort -k 1b,1' to sort a file on its default join field, but if you select a non-default locale, join field, separator, or comparison options, then you should do so consistently between `join` and `sort`. If 'join -t '' ' is specified then the whole line is considered which matches the default operation of sort.

If the input has no unpairable lines, a GNU extension is available; the sort order can be any order that considers two fields to be equal if and only if the sort comparison described above considers them to be equal. For example:

```
$ cat file1
a a1
c c1
b b1
$ cat file2
a a2
c c2
b b2
$ join file1 file2
a a1 a2
c c1 c2
b b1 b2
```

If the `--check-order` option is given, unsorted inputs will cause a fatal error message. If the option `--nocheck-order` is given, unsorted inputs will never cause an error message. If neither of these options is given, wrongly sorted inputs are diagnosed only if an input file is found to contain unpairable lines, and when both input files are non empty. If an input file is diagnosed as being unsorted, the `join` command will exit with a nonzero status (and the output should not be used).

Forcing `join` to process wrongly sorted input files containing unpairable lines by specifying `--nocheck-order` is not guaranteed to produce any particular output. The output will probably not correspond with whatever you hoped it would be.

The defaults are:

- the join field is the first field in each line;
- fields in the input are separated by one or more blanks, with leading blanks on the line ignored;
- fields in the output are separated by a space;
- each output line consists of the join field, the remaining fields from *file1*, then the remaining fields from *file2*.

The program accepts the following options. Also see Chapter 2 [Common options], page 2.

'-a *file-number*'
> Print a line for each unpairable line in file *file-number* (either '1' or '2'), in addition to the normal output.

'--check-order'
> Fail with an error message if either input file is wrongly ordered.

'--nocheck-order'

> Do not check that both input files are in sorted order. This is the default.

'-e string'

> Replace those output fields that are missing in the input with *string*. I.e.,
> missing fields specified with the -12jo options.

'--header'

> Treat the first line of each input file as a header line. The header lines will
> be joined and printed as the first output line. If -o is used to specify output
> format, the header line will be printed according to the specified format. The
> header lines will not be checked for ordering even if --check-order is specified.
> Also if the header lines from each file do not match, the heading fields from the
> first file will be used.

'-i'
'--ignore-case'

> Ignore differences in case when comparing keys. With this option, the lines of
> the input files must be ordered in the same way. Use 'sort -f' to produce this
> ordering.

'-1 field' Join on field *field* (a positive integer) of file 1.

'-2 field' Join on field *field* (a positive integer) of file 2.

'-j field' Equivalent to -1 *field* -2 *field*.

'-o field-list'
'-o auto'   If the keyword 'auto' is specified, infer the output format from the first line in
> each file. This is the same as the default output format but also ensures the
> same number of fields are output for each line. Missing fields are replaced with
> the -e option and extra fields are discarded.

> Otherwise, construct each output line according to the format in *field-list*. Each
> element in *field-list* is either the single character '0' or has the form *m.n* where
> the file number, *m*, is '1' or '2' and *n* is a positive field number.

> A field specification of '0' denotes the join field. In most cases, the functionality
> of the '0' field spec may be reproduced using the explicit *m.n* that corresponds
> to the join field. However, when printing unpairable lines (using either of the -a
> or -v options), there is no way to specify the join field using *m.n* in *field-list* if
> there are unpairable lines in both files. To give join that functionality, POSIX
> invented the '0' field specification notation.

> The elements in *field-list* are separated by commas or blanks. Blank separators
> typically need to be quoted for the shell. For example, the commands 'join -o
> 1.2,2.2' and 'join -o '1.2 2.2'' are equivalent.

> All output lines—including those printed because of any -a or -v option—are
> subject to the specified *field-list*.

'-t char'   Use character *char* as the input and output field separator. Treat as significant
> each occurrence of *char* in the input file. Use 'sort -t char', without the -b
> option of 'sort', to produce this ordering. If 'join -t ''' is specified, the

whole line is considered, matching the default operation of sort. If '`-t '\0'`' is specified then the ASCII NUL character is used to delimit the fields.

'`-v file-number`'

> Print a line for each unpairable line in file *file-number* (either '1' or '2'), instead of the normal output.

'`-z`'
'`--zero-terminated`'

> Delimit items with a zero byte rather than a newline (ASCII LF). I.e., treat input as items separated by ASCII NUL and terminate output items with ASCII NUL. This option can be useful in conjunction with '`perl -0`' or '`find -print0`' and '`xargs -0`' which do the same in order to reliably handle arbitrary file names (even those containing blanks or other special characters).

An exit status of zero indicates success, and a nonzero value indicates failure.

9 Operating on characters

These commands operate on individual characters.

9.1 tr: Translate, squeeze, and/or delete characters

Synopsis:

    tr [option]... set1 [set2]

tr copies standard input to standard output, performing one of the following operations:

- translate, and optionally squeeze repeated characters in the result,
- squeeze repeated characters,
- delete characters,
- delete characters, then squeeze repeated characters from the result.

The *set1* and (if given) *set2* arguments define ordered sets of characters, referred to below as *set1* and *set2*. These sets are the characters of the input that **tr** operates on. The **--complement** (**-c**, **-C**) option replaces *set1* with its complement (all of the characters that are not in *set1*).

Currently **tr** fully supports only single-byte characters. Eventually it will support multibyte characters; when it does, the **-C** option will cause it to complement the set of characters, whereas **-c** will cause it to complement the set of values. This distinction will matter only when some values are not characters, and this is possible only in locales using multibyte encodings when the input contains encoding errors.

The program accepts the **--help** and **--version** options. See Chapter 2 [Common options], page 2. Options must precede operands.

An exit status of zero indicates success, and a nonzero value indicates failure.

9.1.1 Specifying sets of characters

The format of the *set1* and *set2* arguments resembles the format of regular expressions; however, they are not regular expressions, only lists of characters. Most characters simply represent themselves in these strings, but the strings can contain the shorthands listed below, for convenience. Some of them can be used only in *set1* or *set2*, as noted below.

Backslash escapes

The following backslash escape sequences are recognized:

'\a'   Control-G.

'\b'   Control-H.

'\f'   Control-L.

'\n'   Control-J.

'\r'   Control-M.

'\t'   Control-I.

'\v'   Control-K.

'\ooo' The 8-bit character with the value given by *ooo*, which is 1 to 3 octal digits. Note that '\400' is interpreted as the two-byte sequence, '\040' '0'.

'\\' A backslash.

While a backslash followed by a character not listed above is interpreted as that character, the backslash also effectively removes any special significance, so it is useful to escape '[', ']', '*', and '-'.

Ranges

The notation '*m-n*' expands to all of the characters from *m* through *n*, in ascending order. *m* should collate before *n*; if it doesn't, an error results. As an example, '0-9' is the same as '0123456789'.

GNU `tr` does not support the System V syntax that uses square brackets to enclose ranges. Translations specified in that format sometimes work as expected, since the brackets are often transliterated to themselves. However, they should be avoided because they sometimes behave unexpectedly. For example, '`tr -d ’[0-9]’`' deletes brackets as well as digits.

Many historically common and even accepted uses of ranges are not portable. For example, on EBCDIC hosts using the 'A-Z' range will not do what most would expect because 'A' through 'Z' are not contiguous as they are in ASCII. If you can rely on a POSIX compliant version of `tr`, then the best way to work around this is to use character classes (see below). Otherwise, it is most portable (and most ugly) to enumerate the members of the ranges.

Repeated characters

The notation '[c*n]' in *set2* expands to *n* copies of character *c*. Thus, '[y*6]' is the same as 'yyyyyy'. The notation '[c*]' in *string2* expands to as many copies of *c* as are needed to make *set2* as long as *set1*. If *n* begins with '0', it is interpreted in octal, otherwise in decimal.

Character classes

The notation '[:*class*:]' expands to all of the characters in the (predefined) class *class*. The characters expand in no particular order, except for the **upper** and **lower** classes, which expand in ascending order. When the `--delete` (`-d`) and `--squeeze-repeats` (`-s`) options are both given, any character class can be used in *set2*. Otherwise, only the character classes **lower** and **upper** are accepted in *set2*, and then only if the corresponding character class (**upper** and **lower**, respectively) is specified in the same relative position in *set1*. Doing this specifies case conversion. The class names are given below; an error results when an invalid class name is given.

alnum Letters and digits.

alpha Letters.

blank Horizontal whitespace.

cntrl Control characters.

digit Digits.

graph	Printable characters, not including space.
lower	Lowercase letters.
print	Printable characters, including space.
punct	Punctuation characters.
space	Horizontal or vertical whitespace.
upper	Uppercase letters
xdigit	Hexadecimal digits.

Equivalence classes

The syntax '[=c=]' expands to all of the characters that are equivalent to c, in no particular order. Equivalence classes are a relatively recent invention intended to support non-English alphabets. But there seems to be no standard way to define them or determine their contents. Therefore, they are not fully implemented in GNU tr; each character's equivalence class consists only of that character, which is of no particular use.

9.1.2 Translating

tr performs translation when *set1* and *set2* are both given and the --delete (-d) option is not given. tr translates each character of its input that is in *set1* to the corresponding character in *set2*. Characters not in *set1* are passed through unchanged. When a character appears more than once in *set1* and the corresponding characters in *set2* are not all the same, only the final one is used. For example, these two commands are equivalent:

```
tr aaa xyz
tr a z
```

A common use of tr is to convert lowercase characters to uppercase. This can be done in many ways. Here are three of them:

```
tr abcdefghijklmnopqrstuvwxyz ABCDEFGHIJKLMNOPQRSTUVWXYZ
tr a-z A-Z
tr '[:lower:]' '[:upper:]'
```

But note that using ranges like a-z above is not portable.

When tr is performing translation, *set1* and *set2* typically have the same length. If *set1* is shorter than *set2*, the extra characters at the end of *set2* are ignored.

On the other hand, making *set1* longer than *set2* is not portable; POSIX says that the result is undefined. In this situation, BSD tr pads *set2* to the length of *set1* by repeating the last character of *set2* as many times as necessary. System V tr truncates *set1* to the length of *set2*.

By default, GNU tr handles this case like BSD tr. When the --truncate-set1 (-t) option is given, GNU tr handles this case like the System V tr instead. This option is ignored for operations other than translation.

Acting like System V tr in this case breaks the relatively common BSD idiom:

```
tr -cs A-Za-z0-9 '\012'
```

because it converts only zero bytes (the first element in the complement of *set1*), rather than all non-alphanumerics, to newlines.

By the way, the above idiom is not portable because it uses ranges, and it assumes that the octal code for newline is 012. Assuming a POSIX compliant `tr`, here is a better way to write it:

```
tr -cs '[:alnum:]' '[\n*]'
```

9.1.3 Squeezing repeats and deleting

When given just the `--delete` (`-d`) option, `tr` removes any input characters that are in *set1*.

When given just the `--squeeze-repeats` (`-s`) option, `tr` replaces each input sequence of a repeated character that is in *set1* with a single occurrence of that character.

When given both `--delete` and `--squeeze-repeats`, `tr` first performs any deletions using *set1*, then squeezes repeats from any remaining characters using *set2*.

The `--squeeze-repeats` option may also be used when translating, in which case `tr` first performs translation, then squeezes repeats from any remaining characters using *set2*.

Here are some examples to illustrate various combinations of options:

- Remove all zero bytes:

  ```
  tr -d '\0'
  ```

- Put all words on lines by themselves. This converts all non-alphanumeric characters to newlines, then squeezes each string of repeated newlines into a single newline:

  ```
  tr -cs '[:alnum:]' '[\n*]'
  ```

- Convert each sequence of repeated newlines to a single newline:

  ```
  tr -s '\n'
  ```

- Find doubled occurrences of words in a document. For example, people often write "the the" with the repeated words separated by a newline. The Bourne shell script below works first by converting each sequence of punctuation and blank characters to a single newline. That puts each "word" on a line by itself. Next it maps all uppercase characters to lower case, and finally it runs `uniq` with the `-d` option to print out only the words that were repeated.

  ```
  #!/bin/sh
  cat -- "$@" \
    | tr -s '[:punct:][:blank:]' '[\n*]' \
    | tr '[:upper:]' '[:lower:]' \
    | uniq -d
  ```

- Deleting a small set of characters is usually straightforward. For example, to remove all 'a's, 'x's, and 'M's you would do this:

  ```
  tr -d axM
  ```

However, when '-' is one of those characters, it can be tricky because '-' has special meanings. Performing the same task as above but also removing all '-' characters, we might try `tr -d -axM`, but that would fail because `tr` would try to interpret `-a` as a command-line option. Alternatively, we could try putting the hyphen inside the string, `tr -d a-xM`, but that wouldn't work either because it would make `tr` interpret `a-x` as the range of characters 'a'…'x' rather than the three. One way to solve the problem is to put the hyphen at the end of the list of characters:

```
tr -d axM-
```

Or you can use '--' to terminate option processing:

```
tr -d -- -axM
```

More generally, use the character class notation [=c=] with '-' (or any other character) in place of the 'c':

```
tr -d '[=-=]axM'
```

Note how single quotes are used in the above example to protect the square brackets from interpretation by a shell.

9.2 expand: Convert tabs to spaces

expand writes the contents of each given *file*, or standard input if none are given or for a *file* of '-', to standard output, with tab characters converted to the appropriate number of spaces. Synopsis:

```
expand [option]... [file]...
```

By default, expand converts all tabs to spaces. It preserves backspace characters in the output; they decrement the column count for tab calculations. The default action is equivalent to -t 8 (set tabs every 8 columns).

The program accepts the following options. Also see Chapter 2 [Common options], page 2.

'-t *tab1*[,*tab2*]...'
'--tabs=*tab1*[,*tab2*]...'

> If only one tab stop is given, set the tabs *tab1* spaces apart (default is 8). Otherwise, set the tabs at columns *tab1*, *tab2*, ... (numbered from 0), and replace any tabs beyond the last tab stop given with single spaces. Tab stops can be separated by blanks as well as by commas.
>
> For compatibility, GNU expand also accepts the obsolete option syntax, -t*1*[,*t2*].... New scripts should use -t *t1*[,*t2*]... instead.

'-i'
'--initial'

> Only convert initial tabs (those that precede all non-space or non-tab characters) on each line to spaces.

An exit status of zero indicates success, and a nonzero value indicates failure.

9.3 unexpand: Convert spaces to tabs

unexpand writes the contents of each given *file*, or standard input if none are given or for a *file* of '-', to standard output, converting blanks at the beginning of each line into as many tab characters as needed. In the default POSIX locale, a *blank* is a space or a tab; other locales may specify additional blank characters. Synopsis:

```
unexpand [option]... [file]...
```

By default, unexpand converts only initial blanks (those that precede all non-blank characters) on each line. It preserves backspace characters in the output; they decrement the column count for tab calculations. By default, tabs are set at every 8th column.

The program accepts the following options. Also see Chapter 2 [Common options], page 2.

'-t *tab1*[,*tab2*] ...'
'--tabs=*tab1*[,*tab2*] ...'

> If only one tab stop is given, set the tabs *tab1* columns apart instead of the default 8. Otherwise, set the tabs at columns *tab1*, *tab2*, ... (numbered from 0), and leave blanks beyond the tab stops given unchanged. Tab stops can be separated by blanks as well as by commas. This option implies the -a option.

> For compatibility, GNU unexpand supports the obsolete option syntax, -*tab1*[,*tab2*] ..., where tab stops must be separated by commas. (Unlike -t, this obsolete option does not imply -a.) New scripts should use --first-only -t *tab1*[,*tab2*] ... instead.

'-a'
'--all' Also convert all sequences of two or more blanks just before a tab stop, even if they occur after non-blank characters in a line.

An exit status of zero indicates success, and a nonzero value indicates failure.

10 Directory listing

This chapter describes the `ls` command and its variants `dir` and `vdir`, which list information about files.

10.1 `ls`: List directory contents

The `ls` program lists information about files (of any type, including directories). Options and file arguments can be intermixed arbitrarily, as usual.

For non-option command-line arguments that are directories, by default `ls` lists the contents of directories, not recursively, and omitting files with names beginning with '.'. For other non-option arguments, by default `ls` lists just the file name. If no non-option argument is specified, `ls` operates on the current directory, acting as if it had been invoked with a single argument of '.'.

By default, the output is sorted alphabetically, according to the locale settings in effect.[1] If standard output is a terminal, the output is in columns (sorted vertically) and control characters are output as question marks; otherwise, the output is listed one per line and control characters are output as-is.

Because `ls` is such a fundamental program, it has accumulated many options over the years. They are described in the subsections below; within each section, options are listed alphabetically (ignoring case). The division of options into the subsections is not absolute, since some options affect more than one aspect of `ls`'s operation.

Exit status:

    0 success
    1 minor problems (e.g., failure to access a file or directory not
       specified as a command line argument. This happens when listing a
       directory in which entries are actively being removed or renamed.)
    2 serious trouble (e.g., memory exhausted, invalid option, failure
       to access a file or directory specified as a command line argument
       or a directory loop)

Also see Chapter 2 [Common options], page 2.

10.1.1 Which files are listed

These options determine which files `ls` lists information for. By default, `ls` lists files and the contents of any directories on the command line, except that in directories it ignores files whose names start with '.'.

'`-a`'
'`--all`'   In directories, do not ignore file names that start with '.'.

'`-A`'
'`--almost-all`'

        In directories, do not ignore all file names that start with '.'; ignore only . and
        ... The `--all` (`-a`) option overrides this option.

---

[1] If you use a non-POSIX locale (e.g., by setting `LC_ALL` to '`en_US`'), then `ls` may produce output that is sorted differently than you're accustomed to. In that case, set the `LC_ALL` environment variable to '`C`'.

'-B'
'--ignore-backups'
> In directories, ignore files that end with '~'. This option is equivalent to
> '--ignore='*~' --ignore='.*~''.

'-d'
'--directory'
> List just the names of directories, as with other types of files, rather than
> listing their contents. Do not follow symbolic links listed on the command
> line unless the --dereference-command-line (-H), --dereference (-L), or
> --dereference-command-line-symlink-to-dir options are specified.

'-H'
'--dereference-command-line'
> If a command line argument specifies a symbolic link, show information for the
> file the link references rather than for the link itself.

'--dereference-command-line-symlink-to-dir'
> Do not dereference symbolic links, with one exception: if a command
> line argument specifies a symbolic link that refers to a directory, show
> information for that directory rather than for the link itself. This is the
> default behavior when no other dereferencing-related option has been
> specified (--classify (-F), --directory (-d), (-1), --dereference (-L), or
> --dereference-command-line (-H)).

'--group-directories-first'
> Group all the directories before the files and then sort the directories and the
> files separately using the selected sort key (see –sort option). That is, this
> option specifies a primary sort key, and the –sort option specifies a secondary
> key. However, any use of --sort=none (-U) disables this option altogether.

'--hide=PATTERN'
> In directories, ignore files whose names match the shell pattern *pattern*, un-
> less the --all (-a) or --almost-all (-A) is also given. This option acts like
> --ignore=*pattern* except that it has no effect if --all (-a) or --almost-all
> (-A) is also given.
>
> This option can be useful in shell aliases. For example, if 1x is an alias for '1s
> --hide='*~'' and 1y is an alias for '1s --ignore='*~'', then the command
> '1x -A' lists the file README~ even though '1y -A' would not.

'-I *pattern*'
'--ignore=*pattern*'
> In directories, ignore files whose names match the shell pattern (not regular
> expression) *pattern*. As in the shell, an initial '.' in a file name does not match
> a wildcard at the start of *pattern*. Sometimes it is useful to give this option
> several times. For example,
>
> $ ls --ignore='.??*' --ignore='.[^.]' --ignore='#*'
>
> The first option ignores names of length 3 or more that start with '.', the second
> ignores all two-character names that start with '.' except '..', and the third
> ignores names that start with '#'.

'-L'

'--dereference'

> When showing file information for a symbolic link, show information for the file the link references rather than the link itself. However, even with this option, ls still prints the name of the link itself, not the name of the file that the link points to.

'-R'

' recursive'

> List the contents of all directories recursively.

10.1.2 What information is listed

These options affect the information that ls displays. By default, only file names are shown.

'--author'

> List each file's author when producing long format directory listings. In GNU/Hurd, file authors can differ from their owners, but in other operating systems the two are the same.

'-D'

'--dired'   With the long listing (-1) format, print an additional line after the main output:

> //DIRED// *beg1 end1 beg2 end2* ...

> The *begn* and *endn* are unsigned integers that record the byte position of the beginning and end of each file name in the output. This makes it easy for Emacs to find the names, even when they contain unusual characters such as space or newline, without fancy searching.

> If directories are being listed recursively (-R), output a similar line with offsets for each subdirectory name:

> //SUBDIRED// *beg1 end1* ...

> Finally, output a line of the form:

> //DIRED-OPTIONS// --quoting-style=*word*

> where *word* is the quoting style (see Section 10.1.7 [Formatting the file names], page 89).

> Here is an actual example:

```
$ mkdir -p a/sub/deeper a/sub2
$ touch a/f1 a/f2
$ touch a/sub/deeper/file
$ ls -gloRF --dired a
  a:
  total 8
  -rw-r--r-- 1    0 Jun 10 12:27 f1
  -rw-r--r-- 1    0 Jun 10 12:27 f2
  drwxr-xr-x 3 4096 Jun 10 12:27 sub/
  drwxr-xr-x 2 4096 Jun 10 12:27 sub2/

  a/sub:
```

```
total 4
drwxr-xr-x 2 4096 Jun 10 12:27 deeper/

a/sub/deeper:
total 0
-rw-r--r-- 1 0 Jun 10 12:27 file

a/sub2:
total 0
//DIRED// 48 50 84 86 120 123 158 162 217 223 282 286
//SUBDIRED// 2 3 167 172 228 240 290 296
//DIRED-OPTIONS// --quoting-style=literal
```

Note that the pairs of offsets on the '//DIRED//' line above delimit these names: f1, f2, sub, sub2, deeper, file. The offsets on the '//SUBDIRED//' line delimit the following directory names: a, a/sub, a/sub/deeper, a/sub2.

Here is an example of how to extract the fifth entry name, 'deeper', corresponding to the pair of offsets, 222 and 228:

```
$ ls -gloRF --dired a > out
$ dd bs=1 skip=222 count=6 < out 2>/dev/null; echo
deeper
```

Note that although the listing above includes a trailing slash for the 'deeper' entry, the offsets select the name without the trailing slash. However, if you invoke ls with --dired along with an option like --escape (aka -b) and operate on a file whose name contains special characters, notice that the backslash *is* included:

```
$ touch 'a b'
$ ls -blog --dired 'a b'
  -rw-r--r-- 1 0 Jun 10 12:28 a\ b
//DIRED// 30 34
//DIRED-OPTIONS// --quoting-style=escape
```

If you use a quoting style that adds quote marks (e.g., --quoting-style=c), then the offsets include the quote marks. So beware that the user may select the quoting style via the environment variable QUOTING_STYLE. Hence, applications using --dired should either specify an explicit --quoting-style=literal option (aka -N or --literal) on the command line, or else be prepared to parse the escaped names.

'--full-time'

Produce long format directory listings, and list times in full. It is equivalent to using --format=long with --time-style=full-iso (see Section 10.1.6 [Formatting file timestamps], page 87).

'-g'   Produce long format directory listings, but don't display owner information.

'-G'

'--no-group'

> Inhibit display of group information in a long format directory listing. (This is the default in some non-GNU versions of ls, so we provide this option for compatibility.)

'-h'

'--human-readable'

> Append a size letter to each size, such as 'M' for mebibytes. Powers of 1024 are used, not 1000; 'M' stands for 1,048,576 bytes. This option is equivalent to --block-size=human-readable. Use the --si option if you prefer powers of 1000.

'-i'

'--inode' Print the inode number (also called the file serial number and index number) of each file to the left of the file name. (This number uniquely identifies each file within a particular file system.)

'-l'

'--format=long'

'--format=verbose'

> In addition to the name of each file, print the file type, file mode bits, number of hard links, owner name, group name, size, and timestamp (see Section 10.1.6 [Formatting file timestamps], page 87), normally the modification time. Print question marks for information that cannot be determined.

> Normally the size is printed as a byte count without punctuation, but this can be overridden (see Section 2.3 [Block size], page 3). For example, -h prints an abbreviated, human-readable count, and '--block-size="'1"' prints a byte count with the thousands separator of the current locale.

> For each directory that is listed, preface the files with a line 'total blocks', where blocks is the total disk allocation for all files in that directory. The block size currently defaults to 1024 bytes, but this can be overridden (see Section 2.3 [Block size], page 3). The blocks computed counts each hard link separately; this is arguably a deficiency.

> The file type is one of the following characters:

> | '-' | regular file |
> |-----|--------------|
> | 'b' | block special file |
> | 'c' | character special file |
> | 'C' | high performance ("contiguous data") file |
> | 'd' | directory |
> | 'D' | door (Solaris 2.5 and up) |
> | 'l' | symbolic link |
> | 'M' | off-line ("migrated") file (Cray DMF) |
> | 'n' | network special file (HP-UX) |

'p'   FIFO (named pipe)

'P'   port (Solaris 10 and up)

's'   socket

'?'   some other file type

The file mode bits listed are similar to symbolic mode specifications (see Section 27.2 [Symbolic Modes], page 207). But `ls` combines multiple bits into the third character of each set of permissions as follows:

's'   If the set-user-ID or set-group-ID bit and the corresponding executable bit are both set.

'S'   If the set-user-ID or set-group-ID bit is set but the corresponding executable bit is not set.

't'   If the restricted deletion flag or sticky bit, and the other-executable bit, are both set. The restricted deletion flag is another name for the sticky bit. See Section 27.1 [Mode Structure], page 206.

'T'   If the restricted deletion flag or sticky bit is set but the other-executable bit is not set.

'x'   If the executable bit is set and none of the above apply.

'-'   Otherwise.

Following the file mode bits is a single character that specifies whether an alternate access method such as an access control list applies to the file. When the character following the file mode bits is a space, there is no alternate access method. When it is a printing character, then there is such a method.

GNU `ls` uses a '.' character to indicate a file with a security context, but no other alternate access method.

A file with any other combination of alternate access methods is marked with a '+' character.

'-n'
'--numeric-uid-gid'
                 Produce long format directory listings, but display numeric user and group IDs instead of the owner and group names.

'-o'   Produce long format directory listings, but don't display group information. It is equivalent to using `--format=long` with `--no-group` .

'-s'
'--size'   Print the disk allocation of each file to the left of the file name. This is the amount of disk space used by the file, which is usually a bit more than the file's size, but it can be less if the file has holes.

                 Normally the disk allocation is printed in units of 1024 bytes, but this can be overridden (see Section 2.3 [Block size], page 3).

                 For files that are NFS-mounted from an HP-UX system to a BSD system, this option reports sizes that are half the correct values. On HP-UX systems, it reports sizes that are twice the correct values for files that are NFS-mounted from BSD systems. This is due to a flaw in HP-UX; it also affects the HP-UX `ls` program.

'--si' Append an SI-style abbreviation to each size, such as 'M' for megabytes. Powers of 1000 are used, not 1024; 'M' stands for 1,000,000 bytes. This option is equivalent to `--block-size=si`. Use the `-h` or `--human-readable` option if you prefer powers of 1024.

'-Z'
'--context'

Display the SELinux security context or '?' if none is found. When used with the `-l` option, print the security context to the left of the size column.

10.1.3 Sorting the output

These options change the order in which `ls` sorts the information it outputs. By default, sorting is done by character code (e.g., ASCII order).

'-c'
'--time=ctime'
'--time=status'

If the long listing format (e.g., `-l`, `-o`) is being used, print the status change time (the 'ctime' in the inode) instead of the modification time. When explicitly sorting by time (`--sort=time` or `-t`) or when not using a long listing format, sort according to the status change time.

'-f' Primarily, like -U—do not sort; list the files in whatever order they are stored in the directory. But also enable `-a` (list all files) and disable `-l`, `--color`, and `-s` (if they were specified before the `-f`).

'-r'
'--reverse'

Reverse whatever the sorting method is—e.g., list files in reverse alphabetical order, youngest first, smallest first, or whatever.

'-S'
'--sort=size'

Sort by file size, largest first.

'-t'
'--sort=time'

Sort by modification time (the 'mtime' in the inode), newest first.

'-u'
'--time=atime'
'--time=access'
'--time=use'

If the long listing format (e.g., `--format=long`) is being used, print the last access time (the 'atime' in the inode). When explicitly sorting by time (`--sort=time` or `-t`) or when not using a long listing format, sort according to the access time.

'-U'

'--sort=none'

> Do not sort; list the files in whatever order they are stored in the directory. (Do not do any of the other unrelated things that -f does.) This is especially useful when listing very large directories, since not doing any sorting can be noticeably faster.

'-v'

'--sort=version'

> Sort by version name and number, lowest first. It behaves like a default sort, except that each sequence of decimal digits is treated numerically as an index/version number. (See Section 10.1.4 [Details about version sort], page 84.)

'-X'

'--sort=extension'

> Sort directory contents alphabetically by file extension (characters after the last '.'); files with no extension are sorted first.

10.1.4 Details about version sort

Version sorting handles the fact that file names frequently include indices or version numbers. Standard sorting usually does not produce the order that one expects because comparisons are made on a character-by-character basis. Version sorting is especially useful when browsing directories that contain many files with indices/version numbers in their names:

```
$ ls -1          $ ls -1v
abc.zml-1.gz     abc.zml-1.gz
abc.zml-12.gz    abc.zml-2.gz
abc.zml-2.gz     abc.zml-12.gz
```

Version-sorted strings are compared such that if *ver1* and *ver2* are version numbers and *prefix* and *suffix* (*suffix* matching the regular expression '(\.[A-Za-z~][A-Za-z0-9~]*)*') are strings then *ver1* < *ver2* implies that the name composed of "*prefix ver1 suffix*" sorts before "*prefix ver2 suffix*".

Note also that leading zeros of numeric parts are ignored:

```
$ ls -1           $ ls -1v
abc-1.007.tgz     abc-1.01a.tgz
abc-1.012b.tgz    abc-1.007.tgz
abc-1.01a.tgz     abc-1.012b.tgz
```

This functionality is implemented using gnulib's `filevercmp` function, which has some caveats worth noting.

- LC_COLLATE is ignored, which means 'ls -v' and 'sort -V' will sort non-numeric prefixes as if the LC_COLLATE locale category was set to 'C'.

- Some suffixes will not be matched by the regular expression mentioned above. Consequently these examples may not sort as you expect:

    ```
    abc-1.2.3.4.7z
    abc-1.2.3.7z
    ```

```
abc-1.2.3.4.x86_64.rpm
abc-1.2.3.x86_64.rpm
```

10.1.5 General output formatting

These options affect the appearance of the overall output.

'-1'
'--format=single-column'

> List one file per line. This is the default for ls when standard output is not a terminal. See also the -b and -q options to suppress direct output of newline characters within a file name.

'-C'
'--format=vertical'

> List files in columns, sorted vertically. This is the default for ls if standard output is a terminal. It is always the default for the dir program. GNU ls uses variable width columns to display as many files as possible in the fewest lines.

'--color [=*when*]'

> Specify whether to use color for distinguishing file types. *when* may be omitted, or one of:

> - none - Do not use color at all. This is the default.
> - auto - Only use color if standard output is a terminal.
> - always - Always use color.

> Specifying --color and no *when* is equivalent to --color=always. Piping a colorized listing through a pager like more or less usually produces unreadable results. However, using more -f does seem to work.

> Note that using the --color option may incur a noticeable performance penalty when run in a directory with very many entries, because the default settings require that ls stat every single file it lists. However, if you would like most of the file-type coloring but can live without the other coloring options (e.g., executable, orphan, sticky, other-writable, capability), use dircolors to set the LS_COLORS environment variable like this,

```
eval $(dircolors -p | perl -pe \
  's/^((CAP|S[ET]|O[TR]|M|E)\w+).*/$1 00/' | dircolors -)
```

> and on a dirent.d_type-capable file system, ls will perform only one stat call per command line argument.

'-F'
'--classify'
'--indicator-style=classify'

> Append a character to each file name indicating the file type. Also, for regular files that are executable, append '*'. The file type indicators are '/' for directories, '@' for symbolic links, '|' for FIFOs, '=' for sockets, '>' for doors, and nothing for regular files. Do not follow symbolic links listed on the command line unless the --dereference-command-line (-H), --dereference (-L), or --dereference-command-line-symlink-to-dir options are specified.

'--file-type'
'--indicator-style=file-type'

        Append a character to each file name indicating the file type. This is like -F, except that executables are not marked.

'--indicator-style=*word*'

        Append a character indicator with style *word* to entry names, as follows:

        'none'   Do not append any character indicator; this is the default.

        'slash'   Append '/' for directories. This is the same as the -p option.

        'file-type'

                Append '/' for directories, '@' for symbolic links, '|' for FIFOs, '=' for sockets, and nothing for regular files. This is the same as the --file-type option.

        'classify'

                Append '*' for executable regular files, otherwise behave as for 'file-type'. This is the same as the -F or --classify option.

'-k'
'--kibibytes'

        Set the default block size to its normal value of 1024 bytes, overriding any contrary specification in environment variables (see Section 2.3 [Block size], page 3). This option is in turn overridden by the --block-size, -h or --human-readable, and --si options.

        The -k or --kibibytes option affects the per-directory block count written by the -l and similar options, and the size written by the -s or --size option. It does not affect the file size written by -l.

'-m'
'--format=commas'

        List files horizontally, with as many as will fit on each line, separated by ', ' (a comma and a space).

'-p'
'--indicator-style=slash'

        Append a '/' to directory names.

'-x'
'--format=across'
'--format=horizontal'

        List the files in columns, sorted horizontally.

'-T *cols*'
'--tabsize=*cols*'

        Assume that each tab stop is *cols* columns wide. The default is 8. ls uses tabs where possible in the output, for efficiency. If *cols* is zero, do not use tabs at all.

        Some terminal emulators might not properly align columns to the right of a TAB following a non-ASCII byte. You can avoid that issue by using the -T0 option or put `TABSIZE=0` in your environment, to tell `ls` to align using spaces, not tabs.

'`-w`'
'`--width=cols`'

> Assume the screen is *cols* columns wide. The default is taken from the terminal settings if possible; otherwise the environment variable `COLUMNS` is used if it is set; otherwise the default is 80.

10.1.6 Formatting file timestamps

By default, file timestamps are listed in abbreviated form, using a date like '`Mar 30  2002`' for non-recent timestamps, and a date-without-year and time like '`Mar 30 23:45`' for recent timestamps. This format can change depending on the current locale as detailed below.

A timestamp is considered to be *recent* if it is less than six months old, and is not dated in the future. If a timestamp dated today is not listed in recent form, the timestamp is in the future, which means you probably have clock skew problems which may break programs like `make` that rely on file timestamps.

Time stamps are listed according to the time zone rules specified by the `TZ` environment variable, or by the system default rules if `TZ` is not set. See Section "Specifying the Time Zone with TZ" in *The GNU C Library Reference Manual*.

The following option changes how file timestamps are printed.

'`--time-style=style`'

> List timestamps in style *style*. The *style* should be one of the following:

> '`+format`' List timestamps using *format*, where *format* is interpreted like the format argument of `date` (see Section 21.1 [date invocation], page 175). For example, `--time-style="+%Y-%m-%d %H:%M:%S"` causes `ls` to list timestamps like '`2002-03-30 23:45:56`'. As with `date`, *format*'s interpretation is affected by the `LC_TIME` locale category.

> > If *format* contains two format strings separated by a newline, the former is used for non-recent files and the latter for recent files; if you want output columns to line up, you may need to insert spaces in one of the two formats.

> '`full-iso`'

> > List timestamps in full using ISO 8601 date, time, and time zone format with nanosecond precision, e.g., '`2002-03-30 23:45:56.477817180 -0700`'. This style is equivalent to '`+%Y-%m-%d %H:%M:%S.%N %z`'.

> > This is useful because the time output includes all the information that is available from the operating system. For example, this can help explain `make`'s behavior, since GNU `make` uses the full timestamp to determine whether a file is out of date.

> '`long-iso`'

> > List ISO 8601 date and time in minutes, e.g., '`2002-03-30 23:45`'. These timestamps are shorter than '`full-iso`' timestamps, and are

usually good enough for everyday work. This style is equivalent to '+%Y-%m-%d %H:%M'.

'iso'   List ISO 8601 dates for non-recent timestamps (e.g., '2002-03-30 '), and ISO 8601 month, day, hour, and minute for recent time-stamps (e.g., '03-30 23:45'). These timestamps are uglier than 'long-iso' timestamps, but they carry nearly the same information in a smaller space and their brevity helps ls output fit within traditional 80-column output lines. The following two ls invocations are equivalent:

```
newline='
'
ls -l --time-style="+%Y-%m-%d $newline%m-%d %H:%M"
ls -l --time-style="iso"
```

'locale'   List timestamps in a locale-dependent form. For example, a Finnish locale might list non-recent timestamps like 'maalis 30 2002' and recent timestamps like 'maalis 30 23:45'. Locale-dependent time-stamps typically consume more space than 'iso' timestamps and are harder for programs to parse because locale conventions vary so widely, but they are easier for many people to read.

The LC_TIME locale category specifies the timestamp format. The default POSIX locale uses timestamps like 'Mar 30 2002' and 'Mar 30 23:45'; in this locale, the following two ls invocations are equiv-alent:

```
newline='
'
ls -l --time-style="+%b %e  %Y$newline%b %e %H:%M"
ls -l --time-style="locale"
```

Other locales behave differently. For example, in a German locale, --time-style="locale" might be equivalent to --time-style="+%e. %b %Y $newline%e. %b %H:%M" and might generate timestamps like '30. Mär 2002 ' and '30. Mär 23:45'.

'posix-*style*'
             List POSIX-locale timestamps if the LC_TIME locale category is POSIX, *style* timestamps otherwise. For example, the 'posix-long-iso' style lists timestamps like 'Mar 30 2002' and 'Mar 30 23:45' when in the POSIX locale, and like '2002-03-30 23:45' otherwise.

You can specify the default value of the --time-style option with the environment variable TIME_STYLE; if TIME_STYLE is not set the default style is 'locale'. GNU Emacs 21.3 and later use the --dired option and therefore can parse any date format, but if you are using Emacs 21.1 or 21.2 and specify a non-POSIX locale you may need to set 'TIME_STYLE="posix-long-iso"'.

To avoid certain denial-of-service attacks, timestamps that would be longer than 1000 bytes may be treated as errors.

10.1.7 Formatting the file names

These options change how file names themselves are printed.

'-b'
'--escape'
'--quoting-style=escape'

> Quote nongraphic characters in file names using alphabetic and octal backslash sequences like those used in C.

'-N'
'--literal'
'--quoting-style=literal'

> Do not quote file names. However, with `ls` nongraphic characters are still printed as question marks if the output is a terminal and you do not specify the `--show-control-chars` option.

'-q'
'--hide-control-chars'

> Print question marks instead of nongraphic characters in file names. This is the default if the output is a terminal and the program is `ls`.

'-Q'
'--quote-name'
'--quoting-style=c'

> Enclose file names in double quotes and quote nongraphic characters as in C.

'--quoting-style=*word*'

> Use style *word* to quote file names and other strings that may contain arbitrary characters. The *word* should be one of the following:

> 'literal'   Output strings as-is; this is the same as the `-N` or `--literal` option.

> 'shell'   Quote strings for the shell if they contain shell metacharacters or would cause ambiguous output. The quoting is suitable for POSIX-compatible shells like `bash`, but it does not always work for incompatible shells like `csh`.

> 'shell-always'
> Quote strings for the shell, even if they would normally not require quoting.

> 'c'   Quote strings as for C character string literals, including the surrounding double-quote characters; this is the same as the `-Q` or `--quote-name` option.

> 'escape'   Quote strings as for C character string literals, except omit the surrounding double-quote characters; this is the same as the `-b` or `--escape` option.

> 'clocale'   Quote strings as for C character string literals, except use surrounding quotation marks appropriate for the locale.

> 'locale'   Quote strings as for C character string literals, except use surrounding quotation marks appropriate for the locale, and quote 'like

this' instead of "like this" in the default C locale. This looks nicer on many displays.

You can specify the default value of the --quoting-style option with the environment variable QUOTING_STYLE. If that environment variable is not set, the default value is 'literal', but this default may change to 'shell' in a future version of this package.

'--show-control-chars'

Print nongraphic characters as-is in file names. This is the default unless the output is a terminal and the program is ls.

10.2 dir: Briefly list directory contents

dir is equivalent to ls -C -b; that is, by default files are listed in columns, sorted vertically, and special characters are represented by backslash escape sequences.

See Section 10.1 [ls invocation], page 77.

10.3 vdir: Verbosely list directory contents

vdir is equivalent to ls -l -b; that is, by default files are listed in long format and special characters are represented by backslash escape sequences.

See Section 10.1 [ls invocation], page 77.

10.4 dircolors: Color setup for ls

dircolors outputs a sequence of shell commands to set up the terminal for color output from ls (and dir, etc.). Typical usage:

```
eval "$(dircolors [option]... [file])"
```

If file is specified, dircolors reads it to determine which colors to use for which file types and extensions. Otherwise, a precompiled database is used. For details on the format of these files, run 'dircolors --print-database'.

To make dircolors read a ~/.dircolors file if it exists, you can put the following lines in your ~/.bashrc (or adapt them to your favorite shell):

```
d=.dircolors
test -r $d && eval "$(dircolors $d)"
```

The output is a shell command to set the LS_COLORS environment variable. You can specify the shell syntax to use on the command line, or dircolors will guess it from the value of the SHELL environment variable.

The program accepts the following options. Also see Chapter 2 [Common options], page 2.

'-b'
'--sh'
'--bourne-shell'

Output Bourne shell commands. This is the default if the SHELL environment variable is set and does not end with 'csh' or 'tcsh'.

'`-c`'
'`--csh`'
'`--c-shell`'

> Output C shell commands. This is the default if `SHELL` ends with `csh` or `tcsh`.

'`-p`'
'`--print-database`'

> Print the (compiled-in) default color configuration database. This output is itself a valid configuration file, and is fairly descriptive of the possibilities.

An exit status of zero indicates success, and a nonzero value indicates failure.

11 Basic operations

This chapter describes the commands for basic file manipulation: copying, moving (renaming), and deleting (removing).

11.1 cp: Copy files and directories

cp copies files (or, optionally, directories). The copy is completely independent of the original. You can either copy one file to another, or copy arbitrarily many files to a destination directory. Synopses:

```
cp [option]... [-T] source dest
cp [option]... source... directory
cp [option]... -t directory source...
```

- If two file names are given, cp copies the first file to the second.

- If the --target-directory (-t) option is given, or failing that if the last file is a directory and the --no-target-directory (-T) option is not given, cp copies each *source* file to the specified directory, using the *sources*' names.

Generally, files are written just as they are read. For exceptions, see the --sparse option below.

By default, cp does not copy directories. However, the -R, -a, and -r options cause cp to copy recursively by descending into source directories and copying files to corresponding destination directories.

When copying from a symbolic link, cp normally follows the link only when not copying recursively or when --link (-l) is used. This default can be overridden with the --archive (-a), -d, --dereference (-L), --no-dereference (-P), and -H options. If more than one of these options is specified, the last one silently overrides the others.

When copying to a symbolic link, cp follows the link only when it refers to an existing regular file. However, when copying to a dangling symbolic link, cp refuses by default, and fails with a diagnostic, since the operation is inherently dangerous. This behavior is contrary to historical practice and to POSIX. Set POSIXLY_CORRECT to make cp attempt to create the target of a dangling destination symlink, in spite of the possible risk. Also, when an option like --backup or --link acts to rename or remove the destination before copying, cp renames or removes the symbolic link rather than the file it points to.

By default, cp copies the contents of special files only when not copying recursively. This default can be overridden with the --copy-contents option.

cp generally refuses to copy a file onto itself, with the following exception: if --force --backup is specified with *source* and *dest* identical, and referring to a regular file, cp will make a backup file, either regular or numbered, as specified in the usual ways (see Section 2.2 [Backup options], page 3). This is useful when you simply want to make a backup of an existing file before changing it.

The program accepts the following options. Also see Chapter 2 [Common options], page 2.

'-a'
'--archive'

Preserve as much as possible of the structure and attributes of the original files in the copy (but do not attempt to preserve internal directory structure; i.e., 'ls -U' may list the entries in a copied directory in a different order). Try to preserve SELinux security context and extended attributes (xattr), but ignore any failure to do that and print no corresponding diagnostic. Equivalent to -dR --preserve=all with the reduced diagnostics.

'--attributes-only'

Copy only the specified attributes of the source file to the destination. If the destination already exists, do not alter its contents. See the --preserve option for controlling which attributes to copy.

'-b'
'--backup[=method]'

See Section 2.2 [Backup options], page 3. Make a backup of each file that would otherwise be overwritten or removed. As a special case, cp makes a backup of source when the force and backup options are given and source and dest are the same name for an existing, regular file. One useful application of this combination of options is this tiny Bourne shell script:

```
#!/bin/sh
# Usage: backup FILE...
# Create a GNU-style backup of each listed FILE.
fail=0
for i; do
  cp --backup --force --preserve=all -- "$i" "$i" || fail=1
done
exit $fail
```

'--copy-contents'

If copying recursively, copy the contents of any special files (e.g., FIFOs and device files) as if they were regular files. This means trying to read the data in each source file and writing it to the destination. It is usually a mistake to use this option, as it normally has undesirable effects on special files like FIFOs and the ones typically found in the /dev directory. In most cases, cp -R --copy-contents will hang indefinitely trying to read from FIFOs and special files like /dev/console, and it will fill up your destination disk if you use it to copy /dev/zero. This option has no effect unless copying recursively, and it does not affect the copying of symbolic links.

'-d'
Copy symbolic links as symbolic links rather than copying the files that they point to, and preserve hard links between source files in the copies. Equivalent to --no-dereference --preserve=links.

'-f'
'--force'
When copying without this option and an existing destination file cannot be opened for writing, the copy fails. However, with --force, when a destination file cannot be opened, cp then removes it and tries to open it again. Contrast this behavior with that enabled by --link and --symbolic-link, whereby the

destination file is never opened but rather is removed unconditionally. Also see the description of --remove-destination.

This option is independent of the --interactive or -i option: neither cancels the effect of the other.

This option is ignored when the --no-clobber or -n option is also used.

'-H'   If a command line argument specifies a symbolic link, then copy the file it points to rather than the symbolic link itself. However, copy (preserving its nature) any symbolic link that is encountered via recursive traversal.

'-i'
'--interactive'
      When copying a file other than a directory, prompt whether to overwrite an existing destination file. The -i option overrides a previous -n option.

'-l'
'--link'   Make hard links instead of copies of non-directories.

'-L'
'--dereference'
      Follow symbolic links when copying from them. With this option, cp cannot create a symbolic link. For example, a symlink (to regular file) in the source tree will be copied to a regular file in the destination tree.

'-n'
'--no-clobber'
      Do not overwrite an existing file. The -n option overrides a previous -i option. This option is mutually exclusive with -b or --backup option.

'-P'
'--no-dereference'
      Copy symbolic links as symbolic links rather than copying the files that they point to. This option affects only symbolic links in the source; symbolic links in the destination are always followed if possible.

'-p'
'--preserve[=attribute_list]'
      Preserve the specified attributes of the original files. If specified, the *attribute_list* must be a comma-separated list of one or more of the following strings:

      'mode'   Preserve the file mode bits and access control lists.

      'ownership'
            Preserve the owner and group. On most modern systems, only users with appropriate privileges may change the owner of a file, and ordinary users may preserve the group ownership of a file only if they happen to be a member of the desired group.

      'timestamps'
            Preserve the times of last access and last modification, when possible. On older systems, it is not possible to preserve these attributes

when the affected file is a symbolic link. However, many systems now provide the `utimensat` function, which makes it possible even for symbolic links.

'links' Preserve in the destination files any links between corresponding source files. Note that with -L or -H, this option can convert symbolic links to hard links. For example,

```
$ mkdir c; : > a; ln -s a b; cp -aH a b c; ls -i1 c
74161745 a
74161745 b
```

Note the inputs: b is a symlink to regular file a, yet the files in destination directory, c/, are hard-linked. Since -a implies --no-dereference it would copy the symlink, but the later -H tells cp to dereference the command line arguments where it then sees two files with the same inode number. Then the --preserve=links option also implied by -a will preserve the perceived hard link.

Here is a similar example that exercises cp's -L option:

```
$ mkdir b c; (cd b; : > a; ln -s a b); cp -aL b c; ls -i1 c/b
74163295 a
74163295 b
```

'context' Preserve SELinux security context of the file, or fail with full diagnostics.

'xattr' Preserve extended attributes of the file, or fail with full diagnostics. If cp is built without xattr support, ignore this option. If SELinux context, ACLs or Capabilities are implemented using xattrs, they are preserved implicitly by this option as well, i.e., even without specifying --preserve=mode or --preserve=context.

'all' Preserve all file attributes. Equivalent to specifying all of the above, but with the difference that failure to preserve SELinux security context or extended attributes does not change cp's exit status. In contrast to -a, all but 'Operation not supported' warnings are output.

Using --preserve with no *attribute_list* is equivalent to --preserve=mode,ownership,time

In the absence of this option, the permissions of existing destination files are unchanged. Each new file is created with the mode of the corresponding source file minus the set-user-ID, set-group-ID, and sticky bits as the create mode; the operating system then applies either the umask or a default ACL, possibly resulting in a more restrictive file mode. See Chapter 27 [File permissions], page 206.

'--no-preserve=*attribute_list*'
Do not preserve the specified attributes. The *attribute_list* has the same form as for --preserve.

'`--parents`'

> Form the name of each destination file by appending to the target directory a slash and the specified name of the source file. The last argument given to `cp` must be the name of an existing directory. For example, the command:

>> `cp --parents a/b/c existing_dir`

> copies the file `a/b/c` to `existing_dir/a/b/c`, creating any missing intermediate directories.

'`-R`'
'`-r`'
'`--recursive`'

> Copy directories recursively. By default, do not follow symbolic links in the source unless used together with the `--link` (`-l`) option; see the `--archive` (`-a`), `-d`, `--dereference` (`-L`), `--no-dereference` (`-P`), and `-H` options. Special files are copied by creating a destination file of the same type as the source; see the `--copy-contents` option. It is not portable to use `-r` to copy symbolic links or special files. On some non-GNU systems, `-r` implies the equivalent of `-L` and `--copy-contents` for historical reasons. Also, it is not portable to use `-R` to copy symbolic links unless you also specify `-P`, as POSIX allows implementations that dereference symbolic links by default.

'`--reflink[=when]`'

> Perform a lightweight, copy-on-write (COW) copy, if supported by the file system. Once it has succeeded, beware that the source and destination files share the same disk data blocks as long as they remain unmodified. Thus, if a disk I/O error affects data blocks of one of the files, the other suffers the same fate.

> The *when* value can be one of the following:

> '`always`'   The default behavior: if the copy-on-write operation is not supported then report the failure for each file and exit with a failure status.

> '`auto`'   If the copy-on-write operation is not supported then fall back to the standard copy behavior.

> This option is overridden by the `--link`, `--symbolic-link` and `--attributes-only` options, thus allowing it to be used to configure the default data copying behavior for `cp`. For example, with the following alias, `cp` will use the minimum amount of space supported by the file system.

>> `alias cp='cp --reflink=auto --sparse=always'`

'`--remove-destination`'

> Remove each existing destination file before attempting to open it (contrast with `-f` above).

'`--sparse=when`'

> A *sparse file* contains *holes*—a sequence of zero bytes that does not occupy any physical disk blocks; the '`read`' system call reads these as zeros. This can both save considerable disk space and increase speed, since many binary files contain lots of consecutive zero bytes. By default, `cp` detects holes in input source files

via a crude heuristic and makes the corresponding output file sparse as well. Only regular files may be sparse.

The *when* value can be one of the following:

'`auto`'   The default behavior: if the input file is sparse, attempt to make the output file sparse, too. However, if an output file exists but refers to a non-regular file, then do not attempt to make it sparse.

'`always`'   For each sufficiently long sequence of zero bytes in the input file, attempt to create a corresponding hole in the output file, even if the input file does not appear to be sparse. This is useful when the input file resides on a file system that does not support sparse files (for example, '`efs`' file systems in SGI IRIX 5.3 and earlier), but the output file is on a type of file system that does support them. Holes may be created only in regular files, so if the destination file is of some other type, `cp` does not even try to make it sparse.

'`never`'   Never make the output file sparse. This is useful in creating a file for use with the `mkswap` command, since such a file must not have any holes.

'`--strip-trailing-slashes`'

Remove any trailing slashes from each *source* argument. See Section 2.9 [Trailing slashes], page 9.

'`-s`'
'`--symbolic-link`'

Make symbolic links instead of copies of non-directories. All source file names must be absolute (starting with '/') unless the destination files are in the current directory. This option merely results in an error message on systems that do not support symbolic links.

'`-S suffix`'
'`--suffix=suffix`'

Append *suffix* to each backup file made with `-b`. See Section 2.2 [Backup options], page 3.

'`-t directory`'
'`--target-directory=directory`'

Specify the destination *directory*. See Section 2.8 [Target directory], page 8.

'`-T`'
'`--no-target-directory`'

Do not treat the last operand specially when it is a directory or a symbolic link to a directory. See Section 2.8 [Target directory], page 8.

'`-u`'
'`--update`'

Do not copy a non-directory that has an existing destination with the same or newer modification time. If time stamps are being preserved, the comparison is to the source time stamp truncated to the resolutions of the destination file system and of the system calls used to update time stamps; this avoids duplicate work if several 'cp -pu' commands are executed with the same source and destination. If --preserve=links is also specified (like with 'cp -au' for example), that will take precedence. Consequently, depending on the order that files are processed from the source, newer files in the destination may be replaced, to mirror hard links in the source.

'-v'
'--verbose'

> Print the name of each file before copying it.

'-x'
'--one-file-system'

> Skip subdirectories that are on different file systems from the one that the copy started on. However, mount point directories *are* copied.

'-Z'
'--context[=*context*]'

> Without a specified *context*, adjust the SELinux security context according to the system default type for destination files, similarly to the **restorecon** command. The long form of this option with a specific context specified, will set the context for newly created files only. With a specified context, if both SELinux and SMACK are disabled, a warning is issued.This option is mutually exclusive with the --preserve=context option, and overrides the --preserve=all and -a options.

An exit status of zero indicates success, and a nonzero value indicates failure.

11.2 dd: Convert and copy a file

dd copies a file (from standard input to standard output, by default) with a changeable I/O block size, while optionally performing conversions on it. Synopses:

> dd [*operand*]...
> dd *option*

The only options are --help and --version. See Chapter 2 [Common options], page 2. dd accepts the following operands, whose syntax was inspired by the DD (data definition) statement of OS/360 JCL.

'if=*file*'   Read from *file* instead of standard input.

'of=*file*'   Write to *file* instead of standard output. Unless 'conv=notrunc' is given, dd truncates *file* to zero bytes (or the size specified with 'seek=').

'ibs=*bytes*'

> Set the input block size to *bytes*. This makes dd read *bytes* per block. The default is 512 bytes.

'obs=*bytes*'

> Set the output block size to *bytes*. This makes dd write *bytes* per block. The default is 512 bytes.

'bs=*bytes*'

> Set both input and output block sizes to *bytes*. This makes dd read and write *bytes* per block, overriding any 'ibs' and 'obs' settings. In addition, if no data-

transforming `conv` option is specified, input is copied to the output as soon as it's read, even if it is smaller than the block size.

'cbs=*bytes*'

Set the conversion block size to *bytes*. When converting variable-length records to fixed-length ones (`conv=block`) or the reverse (`conv=unblock`), use *bytes* as the fixed record length.

'skip=*n*'   Skip *n* 'ibs'-byte blocks in the input file before copying. If 'iflag=skip_bytes' is specified, *n* is interpreted as a byte count rather than a block count.

'seek=*n*'   Skip *n* 'obs'-byte blocks in the output file before copying. if 'oflag=seek_bytes' is specified, *n* is interpreted as a byte count rather than a block count.

'count=*n*'   Copy *n* 'ibs'-byte blocks from the input file, instead of everything until the end of the file. if 'iflag=count_bytes' is specified, *n* is interpreted as a byte count rather than a block count. Note if the input may return short reads as could be the case when reading from a pipe for example, 'iflag=fullblock' will ensure that 'count=' corresponds to complete input blocks rather than the traditional POSIX specified behavior of counting input read operations.

'status=*level*'

Transfer information is normally output to stderr upon receipt of the 'INFO' signal or when `dd` exits. Specifying *level* will adjust the amount of information printed, with the last *level* specified taking precedence.

'none'   Do not print any informational or warning messages to stderr. Error messages are output as normal.

'noxfer'   Do not print the final transfer rate and volume statistics that normally make up the last status line.

'progress'

Print the transfer rate and volume statistics on stderr, when processing each input block. Statistics are output on a single line at most once every second, but updates can be delayed when waiting on I/O.

'conv=*conversion*[,*conversion*]...'

Convert the file as specified by the *conversion* argument(s). (No spaces around any comma(s).)

Conversions:

'ascii'   Convert EBCDIC to ASCII, using the conversion table specified by POSIX. This provides a 1:1 translation for all 256 bytes. This option implies 'conv=unblock'; input is converted to ASCII before trailing spaces are deleted.

'ebcdic'   Convert ASCII to EBCDIC. This is the inverse of the 'ascii' conversion. This option implies 'conv=block'; trailing spaces are added before being converted to EBCDIC.

'ibm'   This acts like 'conv=ebcdic', except it uses the alternate conversion table specified by POSIX. This is not a 1:1 translation, but reflects common historical practice for '~', '[', and ']'.

The 'ascii', 'ebcdic', and 'ibm' conversions are mutually exclusive. If you use any of these options, you should also use the 'cbs=' option.

'block'   For each line in the input, output 'cbs' bytes, replacing the input newline with a space and padding with spaces as necessary.

'unblock'   Remove any trailing spaces in each 'cbs'-sized input block, and append a newline.

The 'block' and 'unblock' conversions are mutually exclusive.

'lcase'   Change uppercase letters to lowercase.

'ucase'   Change lowercase letters to uppercase.

The 'lcase' and 'ucase' conversions are mutually exclusive.

'sparse'   Try to seek rather than write NUL output blocks. On a file system that supports sparse files, this will create sparse output when extending the output file. Be careful when using this option in conjunction with 'conv=notrunc' or 'oflag=append'. With 'conv=notrunc', existing data in the output file corresponding to NUL blocks from the input, will be untouched. With 'oflag=append' the seeks performed will be ineffective. Similarly, when the output is a device rather than a file, NUL input blocks are not copied, and therefore this option is most useful with virtual or pre zeroed devices.

'swab'   Swap every pair of input bytes. GNU dd, unlike others, works when an odd number of bytes are read—the last byte is simply copied (since there is nothing to swap it with).

'sync'   Pad every input block to size of 'ibs' with trailing zero bytes. When used with 'block' or 'unblock', pad with spaces instead of zero bytes.

The following "conversions" are really file flags and don't affect internal processing:

'excl'   Fail if the output file already exists; dd must create the output file itself.

'nocreat'   Do not create the output file; the output file must already exist.

The 'excl' and 'nocreat' conversions are mutually exclusive.

'notrunc'   Do not truncate the output file.

'noerror'   Continue after read errors.

'fdatasync'
               Synchronize output data just before finishing. This forces a physical write of output data.

'fsync'   Synchronize output data and metadata just before finishing. This
            forces a physical write of output data and metadata.

'iflag=*flag*[,*flag*]...'
            Access the input file using the flags specified by the *flag* argument(s). (No
            spaces around any comma(s).)

'oflag=*flag*[,*flag*]...'
            Access the output file using the flags specified by the *flag* argument(s). (No
            spaces around any comma(s).)

            Here are the flags. Not every flag is supported on every operating system.

            'append'   Write in append mode, so that even if some other process is writ-
                        ing to this file, every dd write will append to the current contents
                        of the file. This flag makes sense only for output. If you com-
                        bine this flag with the 'of=*file*' operand, you should also specify
                        'conv=notrunc' unless you want the output file to be truncated
                        before being appended to.

            'cio'   Use concurrent I/O mode for data. This mode performs direct I/O
                        and drops the POSIX requirement to serialize all I/O to the same
                        file. A file cannot be opened in CIO mode and with a standard
                        open at the same time.

            'direct'   Use direct I/O for data, avoiding the buffer cache. Note that the
                        kernel may impose restrictions on read or write buffer sizes. For
                        example, with an ext4 destination file system and a Linux-based
                        kernel, using 'oflag=direct' will cause writes to fail with EINVAL
                        if the output buffer size is not a multiple of 512.

            'directory'
                        Fail unless the file is a directory. Most operating systems do not
                        allow I/O to a directory, so this flag has limited utility.

            'dsync'   Use synchronized I/O for data. For the output file, this forces a
                        physical write of output data on each write. For the input file,
                        this flag can matter when reading from a remote file that has been
                        written to synchronously by some other process. Metadata (e.g.,
                        last-access and last-modified time) is not necessarily synchronized.

            'sync'   Use synchronized I/O for both data and metadata.

            'nocache'   Discard the data cache for a file. When count=0 all cache is dis-
                        carded, otherwise the cache is dropped for the processed portion of
                        the file. Also when count=0 failure to discard the cache is diagnosed
                        and reflected in the exit status. Here as some usage examples:

                        ```
                        # Advise to drop cache for whole file
                        dd if=ifile iflag=nocache count=0

                        # Ensure drop cache for the whole file
                        dd of=ofile oflag=nocache conv=notrunc,fdatasync count=0
                        ```

```
# Drop cache for part of file
dd if=ifile iflag=nocache skip=10 count=10 of=/dev/null

# Stream data using just the read-ahead cache
dd if=ifile of=ofile iflag=nocache oflag=nocache
```

'nonblock'

Use non-blocking I/O.

'noatime'   Do not update the file's access time. Some older file systems silently ignore this flag, so it is a good idea to test it on your files before relying on it.

'noctty'   Do not assign the file to be a controlling terminal for **dd**. This has no effect when the file is not a terminal. On many hosts (e.g., GNU/Linux hosts), this option has no effect at all.

'nofollow'

Do not follow symbolic links.

'nolinks'   Fail if the file has multiple hard links.

'binary'   Use binary I/O. This option has an effect only on nonstandard platforms that distinguish binary from text I/O.

'text'   Use text I/O. Like 'binary', this option has no effect on standard platforms.

'fullblock'

Accumulate full blocks from input. The **read** system call may return early if a full block is not available. When that happens, continue calling **read** to fill the remainder of the block. This flag can be used only with **iflag**. This flag is useful with pipes for example as they may return short reads. In that case, this flag is needed to ensure that a 'count=' argument is interpreted as a block count rather than a count of read operations.

'count_bytes'

Interpret the 'count=' operand as a byte count, rather than a block count, which allows specifying a length that is not a multiple of the I/O block size. This flag can be used only with **iflag**.

'skip_bytes'

Interpret the 'skip=' operand as a byte count, rather than a block count, which allows specifying an offset that is not a multiple of the I/O block size. This flag can be used only with **iflag**.

'seek_bytes'

Interpret the 'seek=' operand as a byte count, rather than a block count, which allows specifying an offset that is not a multiple of the I/O block size. This flag can be used only with **oflag**.

These flags are not supported on all systems, and 'dd' rejects attempts to use them when they are not supported. When reading from standard input or writing to standard output, the 'nofollow' and 'noctty' flags should not be specified, and the other flags (e.g., 'nonblock') can affect how other processes behave with the affected file descriptors, even after dd exits.

The numeric-valued strings above (n and bytes) can be followed by a multiplier: 'b'=512, 'c'=1, 'w'=2, 'xm'=m, or any of the standard block size suffixes like 'k'=1024 (see Section 2.3 [Block size], page 3).

Any block size you specify via 'bs=', 'ibs=', 'obs=', 'cbs=' should not be too large— values larger than a few megabytes are generally wasteful or (as in the gigabyte..exabyte case) downright counterproductive or error-inducing.

To process data that is at an offset or size that is not a multiple of the I/O block size, you can use the 'skip_bytes', 'seek_bytes' and 'count_bytes' flags. Alternatively the traditional method of separate dd invocations can be used. For example, the following shell commands copy data in 512 KiB blocks between a disk and a tape, but do not save or restore a 4 KiB label at the start of the disk:

```
disk=/dev/rdsk/c0t1d0s2
tape=/dev/rmt/0


# Copy all but the label from disk to tape.
(dd bs=4k skip=1 count=0 && dd bs=512k) <$disk >$tape


# Copy from tape back to disk, but leave the disk label alone.
(dd bs=4k seek=1 count=0 && dd bs=512k) <$tape >$disk
```

For failing disks, other tools come with a great variety of extra functionality to ease the saving of as much data as possible before the disk finally dies, e.g. GNU ddrescue. However, in some cases such a tool is not available or the administrator feels more comfortable with the handling of dd. As a simple rescue method, call dd as shown in the following example: the options 'conv=noerror,sync' are used to continue after read errors and to pad out bad reads with NULs, while 'iflag=fullblock' caters for short reads (which traditionally never occur on disk based devices):

```
# Rescue data from an (unmounted!) partition of a failing disk.
dd conv=noerror,sync iflag=fullblock </dev/sda1 > /mnt/rescue.img
```

Sending an 'INFO' signal (or 'USR1' signal where that is unavailable) to a running dd process makes it print I/O statistics to standard error and then resume copying. In the example below, dd is run in the background to copy 5GB of data. The kill command makes it output intermediate I/O statistics, and when dd completes normally or is killed by the SIGINT signal, it outputs the final statistics.

```
# Ignore the signal so we never inadvertently terminate the dd child.
# Note this is not needed when SIGINFO is available.
trap '' USR1


# Run dd with the fullblock iflag to avoid short reads
# which can be triggered by reception of signals.
dd iflag=fullblock if=/dev/zero of=/dev/null count=5000000 bs=1000 & pid=$!
```

```
# Output stats every half second
until ! kill -s USR1 $pid 2>/dev/null; do sleep .5; done
```

The above script will output in the following format

```
859+0 records in
859+0 records out
4295000000 bytes (4.3 GB) copied, 0.539934 s, 8.0 GB/s
1000+0 records in
1000+0 records out
5000000000 bytes (5.0 GB) copied, 0.630785 s, 7.9 GB/s
```

Note also the 'status=progress' option which periodically updates the last line of the transfer statistics above.

On systems lacking the 'INFO' signal dd responds to the 'USR1' signal instead, unless the POSIXLY_CORRECT environment variable is set.

An exit status of zero indicates success, and a nonzero value indicates failure.

11.3 install: Copy files and set attributes

install copies files while setting their file mode bits and, if possible, their owner and group. Synopses:

```
install [option]... [-T] source dest
install [option]... source... directory
install [option]... -t directory source...
install [option]... -d directory...
```

- If two file names are given, install copies the first file to the second.

- If the --target-directory (-t) option is given, or failing that if the last file is a directory and the --no-target-directory (-T) option is not given, install copies each source file to the specified directory, using the sources' names.

- If the --directory (-d) option is given, install creates each directory and any missing parent directories. Parent directories are created with mode 'u=rwx,go=rx' (755), regardless of the -m option or the current umask. See Section 27.5 [Directory Setuid and Setgid], page 212, for how the set-user-ID and set-group-ID bits of parent directories are inherited.

install is similar to cp, but allows you to control the attributes of destination files. It is typically used in Makefiles to copy programs into their destination directories. It refuses to copy files onto themselves.

install never preserves extended attributes (xattr).

The program accepts the following options. Also see Chapter 2 [Common options], page 2.

'-b'
'--backup[=method]'
>   See Section 2.2 [Backup options], page 3. Make a backup of each file that would otherwise be overwritten or removed.

'-C'
'--compare'

> Compare each pair of source and destination files, and if the destination has
> identical content and any specified owner, group, permissions, and possibly
> SELinux context, then do not modify the destination at all. Note this option
> is best used in conjunction with `--user`, `--group` and `--mode` options, lest
> `install` incorrectly determines the default attributes that installed files would
> have (as it doesn't consider setgid directories and POSIX default ACLs for
> example). This could result in redundant copies or attributes that are not reset
> to the correct defaults.

'-c'   Ignored; for compatibility with old Unix versions of `install`.

'-D'   Create any missing parent directories of *dest*, then copy *source* to *dest*. Explicitly specifying the `--target-directory=dir` will similarly ensure the presence
of that hierarchy before copying *source* arguments.

'-d'
'--directory'

> Create any missing parent directories, giving them the default attributes. Then
> create each given directory, setting their owner, group and mode as given on
> the command line or to the defaults.

'-g *group*'
'--group=*group*'

> Set the group ownership of installed files or directories to *group*. The default
> is the process's current group. *group* may be either a group name or a numeric
> group ID.

'-m *mode*'
'--mode=*mode*'

> Set the file mode bits for the installed file or directory to *mode*, which can be
> either an octal number, or a symbolic mode as in `chmod`, with 'a=' (no access
> allowed to anyone) as the point of departure (see Chapter 27 [File permissions],
> page 206). The default mode is 'u=rwx,go=rx,a-s'—read, write, and execute
> for the owner, read and execute for group and other, and with set-user-ID and
> set-group-ID disabled. This default is not quite the same as '755', since it
> disables instead of preserving set-user-ID and set-group-ID on directories. See
> Section 27.5 [Directory Setuid and Setgid], page 212.

'-o *owner*'
'--owner=*owner*'

> If `install` has appropriate privileges (is run as root), set the ownership of
> installed files or directories to *owner*. The default is `root`. *owner* may be either
> a user name or a numeric user ID.

'--preserve-context'

> Preserve the SELinux security context of files and directories. Failure to pre-
> serve the context in all of the files or directories will result in an exit status of
> 1. If SELinux is disabled then print a warning and ignore the option.

'`-p`'
'`--preserve-timestamps`'
> Set the time of last access and the time of last modification of each installed file to match those of each corresponding original file. When a file is installed without this option, its last access and last modification times are both set to the time of installation. This option is useful if you want to use the last modification times of installed files to keep track of when they were last built as opposed to when they were last installed.

'`-s`'
'`--strip`'   Strip the symbol tables from installed binary executables.

'`--strip-program=program`'
> Program used to strip binaries.

'`-S suffix`'
'`--suffix=suffix`'
> Append *suffix* to each backup file made with `-b`. See Section 2.2 [Backup options], page 3.

'`-t directory`'
'`--target-directory=directory`'
> Specify the destination *directory*. See Section 2.8 [Target directory], page 8.

'`-T`'
'`--no-target-directory`'
> Do not treat the last operand specially when it is a directory or a symbolic link to a directory. See Section 2.8 [Target directory], page 8.

'`-v`'
'`--verbose`'
> Print the name of each file before copying it.

'`-Z`'
'`--context[=context]`'
> Without a specified *context*, adjust the SELinux security context according to the system default type for destination files, similarly to the `restorecon` command. The long form of this option with a specific context specified, will set the context for newly created files only. With a specified context, if both SELinux and SMACK are disabled, a warning is issued. This option is mutually exclusive with the `--preserve-context` option.

An exit status of zero indicates success, and a nonzero value indicates failure.

11.4 `mv`: Move (rename) files

`mv` moves or renames files (or directories). Synopses:

```
mv [option]... [-T] source dest
mv [option]... source... directory
mv [option]... -t directory source...
```

- If two file names are given, `mv` moves the first file to the second.

- If the `--target-directory` (`-t`) option is given, or failing that if the last file is a directory and the `--no-target-directory` (`-T`) option is not given, `mv` moves each *source* file to the specified directory, using the *sources'* names.

`mv` can move any type of file from one file system to another. Prior to version `4.0` of the fileutils, `mv` could move only regular files between file systems. For example, now `mv` can move an entire directory hierarchy including special device files from one partition to another. It first uses some of the same code that's used by `cp -a` to copy the requested directories and files, then (assuming the copy succeeded) it removes the originals. If the copy fails, then the part that was copied to the destination partition is removed. If you were to copy three directories from one partition to another and the copy of the first directory succeeded, but the second didn't, the first would be left on the destination partition and the second and third would be left on the original partition.

`mv` always tries to copy extended attributes (xattr), which may include SELinux context, ACLs or Capabilities. Upon failure all but '`Operation not supported`' warnings are output.

If a destination file exists but is normally unwritable, standard input is a terminal, and the `-f` or `--force` option is not given, `mv` prompts the user for whether to replace the file. (You might own the file, or have write permission on its directory.) If the response is not affirmative, the file is skipped.

Warning: Avoid specifying a source name with a trailing slash, when it might be a symlink to a directory. Otherwise, `mv` may do something very surprising, since its behavior depends on the underlying rename system call. On a system with a modern Linux-based kernel, it fails with `errno=ENOTDIR`. However, on other systems (at least FreeBSD 6.1 and Solaris 10) it silently renames not the symlink but rather the directory referenced by the symlink. See Section 2.9 [Trailing slashes], page 9.

The program accepts the following options. Also see Chapter 2 [Common options], page 2.

`'-b'`
`'--backup[=method]'`

> See Section 2.2 [Backup options], page 3. Make a backup of each file that would otherwise be overwritten or removed.

`'-f'`
`'--force'`   Do not prompt the user before removing a destination file. If you specify more than one of the `-i`, `-f`, `-n` options, only the final one takes effect.

`'-i'`
`'--interactive'`

> Prompt whether to overwrite each existing destination file, regardless of its permissions. If the response is not affirmative, the file is skipped. If you specify more than one of the `-i`, `-f`, `-n` options, only the final one takes effect.

`'-n'`
`'--no-clobber'`

> Do not overwrite an existing file. If you specify more than one of the `-i`, `-f`, `-n` options, only the final one takes effect.This option is mutually exclusive with `-b` or `--backup` option.

'`-u`'
'`--update`'

> Do not move a non-directory that has an existing destination with the same or newer modification time. If the move is across file system boundaries, the comparison is to the source time stamp truncated to the resolutions of the destination file system and of the system calls used to update time stamps; this avoids duplicate work if several '`mv -u`' commands are executed with the same source and destination.

'`-v`'
'`--verbose`'

> Print the name of each file before moving it.

'`--strip-trailing-slashes`'

> Remove any trailing slashes from each *source* argument. See Section 2.9 [Trailing slashes], page 9.

'`-S suffix`'
'`--suffix=suffix`'

> Append *suffix* to each backup file made with `-b`. See Section 2.2 [Backup options], page 3.

'`-t directory`'
'`--target-directory=directory`'

> Specify the destination *directory*. See Section 2.8 [Target directory], page 8.

'`-T`'
'`--no-target-directory`'

> Do not treat the last operand specially when it is a directory or a symbolic link to a directory. See Section 2.8 [Target directory], page 8.

'`-Z`'
'`--context`'

> This option functions similarly to the `restorecon` command, by adjusting the SELinux security context according to the system default type for destination files.

An exit status of zero indicates success, and a nonzero value indicates failure.

11.5 `rm`: Remove files or directories

`rm` removes each given *file*. By default, it does not remove directories. Synopsis:

    rm [option]... [file]...

If the `-I` or `--interactive=once` option is given, and there are more than three files or the `-r`, `-R`, or `--recursive` are given, then `rm` prompts the user for whether to proceed with the entire operation. If the response is not affirmative, the entire command is aborted.

Otherwise, if a file is unwritable, standard input is a terminal, and the `-f` or `--force` option is not given, or the `-i` or `--interactive=always` option *is* given, `rm` prompts the user for whether to remove the file. If the response is not affirmative, the file is skipped.

Any attempt to remove a file whose last file name component is . or .. is rejected without any prompting, as mandated by POSIX.

Warning: If you use `rm` to remove a file, it is usually possible to recover the contents of that file. If you want more assurance that the contents are truly unrecoverable, consider using `shred`.

The program accepts the following options. Also see Chapter 2 [Common options], page 2.

'`-d`'
'`--dir`'   Remove the listed directories if they are empty.

'`-f`'
'`--force`'   Ignore nonexistent files and missing operands, and never prompt the user. Ignore any previous `--interactive` (`-i`) option.

'`-i`'   Prompt whether to remove each file. If the response is not affirmative, the file is skipped. Ignore any previous `--force` (`-f`) option. Equivalent to `--interactive=always`.

'`-I`'   Prompt once whether to proceed with the command, if more than three files are named or if a recursive removal is requested. Ignore any previous `--force` (`-f`) option. Equivalent to `--interactive=once`.

'`--interactive [=when]`'
                Specify when to issue an interactive prompt. *when* may be omitted, or one of:

                - never - Do not prompt at all.

                - once - Prompt once if more than three files are named or if a recursive removal is requested. Equivalent to `-I`.

                - always - Prompt for every file being removed. Equivalent to `-i`.

                `--interactive` with no *when* is equivalent to `--interactive=always`.

'`--one-file-system`'
                When removing a hierarchy recursively, skip any directory that is on a file system different from that of the corresponding command line argument.

                This option is useful when removing a build "chroot" hierarchy, which normally contains no valuable data. However, it is not uncommon to bind-mount `/home` into such a hierarchy, to make it easier to use one's start-up file. The catch is that it's easy to forget to unmount `/home`. Then, when you use `rm -rf` to remove your normally throw-away chroot, that command will remove everything under `/home`, too. Use the `--one-file-system` option, and it will warn about and skip directories on other file systems. Of course, this will not save your `/home` if it and your chroot happen to be on the same file system.

'`--preserve-root`'
                Fail upon any attempt to remove the root directory, `/`, when used with the `--recursive` option. This is the default behavior. See Section 2.11 [Treating / specially], page 10.

'`--no-preserve-root`'
                Do not treat / specially when removing recursively. This option is not recommended unless you really want to remove all the files on your computer. See Section 2.11 [Treating / specially], page 10.

'`-r`'
'`-R`'
'`--recursive`'

> Remove the listed directories and their contents recursively.

'`-v`'
'`--verbose`'

> Print the name of each file before removing it.

One common question is how to remove files whose names begin with a '`-`'. GNU `rm`, like every program that uses the `getopt` function to parse its arguments, lets you use the '`--`' option to indicate that all following arguments are non-options. To remove a file called `-f` in the current directory, you could type either:

```
rm -- -f
```

or:

```
rm ./-f
```

The Unix `rm` program's use of a single '`-`' for this purpose predates the development of the `getopt` standard syntax.

An exit status of zero indicates success, and a nonzero value indicates failure.

11.6 `shred`: Remove files more securely

`shred` overwrites devices or files, to help prevent even very expensive hardware from recovering the data.

Ordinarily when you remove a file (see Section 11.5 [rm invocation], page 108), the data is not actually destroyed. Only the index listing where the file is stored is destroyed, and the storage is made available for reuse. There are undelete utilities that will attempt to reconstruct the index and can bring the file back if the parts were not reused.

On a busy system with a nearly-full drive, space can get reused in a few seconds. But there is no way to know for sure. If you have sensitive data, you may want to be sure that recovery is not possible by actually overwriting the file with non-sensitive data.

However, even after doing that, it is possible to take the disk back to a laboratory and use a lot of sensitive (and expensive) equipment to look for the faint "echoes" of the original data underneath the overwritten data. If the data has only been overwritten once, it's not even that hard.

The best way to remove something irretrievably is to destroy the media it's on with acid, melt it down, or the like. For cheap removable media like floppy disks, this is the preferred method. However, hard drives are expensive and hard to melt, so the `shred` utility tries to achieve a similar effect non-destructively.

This uses many overwrite passes, with the data patterns chosen to maximize the damage they do to the old data. While this will work on floppies, the patterns are designed for best effect on hard drives. For more details, see the source code and Peter Gutmann's paper *Secure Deletion of Data from Magnetic and Solid-State Memory*, from the proceedings of the Sixth USENIX Security Symposium (San Jose, California, July 22–25, 1996).

Please note that `shred` relies on a very important assumption: that the file system overwrites data in place. This is the traditional way to do things, but many modern file system designs do not satisfy this assumption. Exceptions include:

- Log-structured or journaled file systems, such as those supplied with AIX and Solaris, and JFS, ReiserFS, XFS, Ext3 (in `data=journal` mode), BFS, NTFS, etc., when they are configured to journal *data*.

- File systems that write redundant data and carry on even if some writes fail, such as RAID-based file systems.

- File systems that make snapshots, such as Network Appliance's NFS server.

- File systems that cache in temporary locations, such as NFS version 3 clients.

- Compressed file systems.

In the particular case of ext3 file systems, the above disclaimer applies (and `shred` is thus of limited effectiveness) only in `data=journal` mode, which journals file data in addition to just metadata. In both the `data=ordered` (default) and `data=writeback` modes, `shred` works as usual. Ext3 journaling modes can be changed by adding the `data=something` option to the mount options for a particular file system in the `/etc/fstab` file, as documented in the mount man page (man mount).

If you are not sure how your file system operates, then you should assume that it does not overwrite data in place, which means that shred cannot reliably operate on regular files in your file system.

Generally speaking, it is more reliable to shred a device than a file, since this bypasses the problem of file system design mentioned above. However, even shredding devices is not always completely reliable. For example, most disks map out bad sectors invisibly to the application; if the bad sectors contain sensitive data, `shred` won't be able to destroy it.

`shred` makes no attempt to detect or report this problem, just as it makes no attempt to do anything about backups. However, since it is more reliable to shred devices than files, `shred` by default does not truncate or remove the output file. This default is more suitable for devices, which typically cannot be truncated and should not be removed.

Finally, consider the risk of backups and mirrors. File system backups and remote mirrors may contain copies of the file that cannot be removed, and that will allow a shredded file to be recovered later. So if you keep any data you may later want to destroy using `shred`, be sure that it is not backed up or mirrored.

     `shred [option]... file[...]`

The program accepts the following options. Also see Chapter 2 [Common options], page 2.

`-f`
`--force`   Override file permissions if necessary to allow overwriting.

`-number`
`-n number`
`--iterations=number`

> By default, `shred` uses 3 passes of overwrite. You can reduce this to save time, or increase it if you think it's appropriate. After 25 passes all of the internal overwrite patterns will have been used at least once.

`--random-source=file`

> Use *file* as a source of random data used to overwrite and to choose pass ordering. See Section 2.7 [Random sources], page 7.

'-s *bytes*'

'--size=*bytes*'

> Shred the first *bytes* bytes of the file. The default is to shred the whole file. *bytes* can be followed by a size specification like 'K', 'M', or 'G' to specify a multiple. See Section 2.3 [Block size], page 3.

'-u'

'--remove[=*how*]'

> After shredding a file, truncate it (if possible) and then remove it. If a file has multiple links, only the named links will be removed. Often the file name is less sensitive than the file data, in which case the optional *how* parameter gives control of how to more efficiently remove each directory entry. The 'unlink' parameter will just use a standard unlink call, 'wipe' will also first obfuscate bytes in the name, and 'wipesync' will also sync each obfuscated byte in the name to disk. Note 'wipesync' is the default method, but can be expensive, requiring a sync for every character in every file. This can become significant with many files, or is redundant if your file system provides synchronous metadata updates.

'-v'

'--verbose'

> Display to standard error all status updates as sterilization proceeds.

'-x'

'--exact'   By default, **shred** rounds the size of a regular file up to the next multiple of the file system block size to fully erase the slack space in the last block of the file. This space may contain portions of the current system memory on some systems for example. Use **--exact** to suppress that behavior. Thus, by default if you shred a 10-byte regular file on a system with 512-byte blocks, the resulting file will be 512 bytes long. With this option, shred does not increase the apparent size of the file.

'-z'

'--zero'   Normally, the last pass that **shred** writes is made up of random data. If this would be conspicuous on your hard drive (for example, because it looks like encrypted data), or you just think it's tidier, the **--zero** option adds an additional overwrite pass with all zero bits. This is in addition to the number of passes specified by the **--iterations** option.

You might use the following command to erase all trace of the file system you'd created on the floppy disk in your first drive. That command takes about 20 minutes to erase a "1.44MB" (actually 1440 KiB) floppy.

```
shred --verbose /dev/fd0
```

Similarly, to erase all data on a selected partition of your hard disk, you could give a command like this:

```
shred --verbose /dev/sda5
```

On modern disks, a single pass should be adequate, and it will take one third the time of the default three-pass approach.

```
# 1 pass, write pseudo-random data; 3x faster than the default
shred --verbose -n1 /dev/sda5
```

To be on the safe side, use at least one pass that overwrites using pseudo-random data. I.e., don't be tempted to use '-n0 --zero', in case some disk controller optimizes the process of writing blocks of all zeros, and thereby does not clear all bytes in a block. Some SSDs may do just that.

A *file* of '-' denotes standard output. The intended use of this is to shred a removed temporary file. For example:

```
i=$(mktemp)
exec 3<>"$i"
rm -- "$i"
echo "Hello, world" >&3
shred - >&3
exec 3>-
```

However, the command 'shred - >file' does not shred the contents of *file*, since the shell truncates *file* before invoking shred. Use the command 'shred file' or (if using a Bourne-compatible shell) the command 'shred - 1<>file' instead.

An exit status of zero indicates success, and a nonzero value indicates failure.

12 Special file types

This chapter describes commands which create special types of files (and `rmdir`, which removes directories, one special file type).

Although Unix-like operating systems have markedly fewer special file types than others, not *everything* can be treated only as the undifferentiated byte stream of *normal files*. For example, when a file is created or removed, the system must record this information, which it does in a *directory*—a special type of file. Although you can read directories as normal files, if you're curious, in order for the system to do its job it must impose a structure, a certain order, on the bytes of the file. Thus it is a "special" type of file.

Besides directories, other special file types include named pipes (FIFOs), symbolic links, sockets, and so-called *special files*.

12.1 `link`: Make a hard link via the link syscall

`link` creates a single hard link at a time. It is a minimalist interface to the system-provided `link` function. See Section "Hard Links" in *The GNU C Library Reference Manual*. It avoids the bells and whistles of the more commonly-used `ln` command (see Section 12.2 [ln invocation], page 114). Synopsis:

```
link filename linkname
```

filename must specify an existing file, and *linkname* must specify a nonexistent entry in an existing directory. `link` simply calls `link (filename, linkname)` to create the link.

On a GNU system, this command acts like '`ln --directory --no-target-directory filename linkname`'. However, the `--directory` and `--no-target-directory` options are not specified by POSIX, and the `link` command is more portable in practice.

If *filename* is a symbolic link, it is unspecified whether *linkname* will be a hard link to the symbolic link or to the target of the symbolic link. Use `ln -P` or `ln -L` to specify which behavior is desired.

An exit status of zero indicates success, and a nonzero value indicates failure.

12.2 `ln`: Make links between files

`ln` makes links between files. By default, it makes hard links; with the `-s` option, it makes symbolic (or *soft*) links. Synopses:

```
ln [option]... [-T] target linkname
ln [option]... target
ln [option]... target... directory
ln [option]... -t directory target...
```

- If two file names are given, `ln` creates a link to the first file from the second.

- If one *target* is given, `ln` creates a link to that file in the current directory.

- If the `--target-directory` (`-t`) option is given, or failing that if the last file is a directory and the `--no-target-directory` (`-T`) option is not given, `ln` creates a link to each *target* file in the specified directory, using the *targets'* names.

Normally `ln` does not remove existing files. Use the `--force` (`-f`) option to remove them unconditionally, the `--interactive` (`-i`) option to remove them conditionally, and the `--backup` (`-b`) option to rename them.

A *hard link* is another name for an existing file; the link and the original are indistinguishable. Technically speaking, they share the same inode, and the inode contains all the information about a file—indeed, it is not incorrect to say that the inode *is* the file. Most systems prohibit making a hard link to a directory; on those where it is allowed, only the super-user can do so (and with caution, since creating a cycle will cause problems to many other utilities). Hard links cannot cross file system boundaries. (These restrictions are not mandated by POSIX, however.)

Symbolic links (*symlinks* for short), on the other hand, are a special file type (which not all kernels support: System V release 3 (and older) systems lack symlinks) in which the link file actually refers to a different file, by name. When most operations (opening, reading, writing, and so on) are passed the symbolic link file, the kernel automatically *dereferences* the link and operates on the target of the link. But some operations (e.g., removing) work on the link file itself, rather than on its target. The owner and group of a symlink are not significant to file access performed through the link, but do have implications on deleting a symbolic link from a directory with the restricted deletion bit set. On the GNU system, the mode of a symlink has no significance and cannot be changed, but on some BSD systems, the mode can be changed and will affect whether the symlink will be traversed in file name resolution. See Section "Symbolic Links" in *The GNU C Library Reference Manual*.

Symbolic links can contain arbitrary strings; a *dangling symlink* occurs when the string in the symlink does not resolve to a file. There are no restrictions against creating dangling symbolic links. There are trade-offs to using absolute or relative symlinks. An absolute symlink always points to the same file, even if the directory containing the link is moved. However, if the symlink is visible from more than one machine (such as on a networked file system), the file pointed to might not always be the same. A relative symbolic link is resolved in relation to the directory that contains the link, and is often useful in referring to files on the same device without regards to what name that device is mounted on when accessed via networked machines.

When creating a relative symlink in a different location than the current directory, the resolution of the symlink will be different than the resolution of the same string from the current directory. Therefore, many users prefer to first change directories to the location where the relative symlink will be created, so that tab-completion or other file resolution will find the same target as what will be placed in the symlink.

The program accepts the following options. Also see Chapter 2 [Common options], page 2.

'`-b`'
'`--backup[=method]`'

        See Section 2.2 [Backup options], page 3. Make a backup of each file that would otherwise be overwritten or removed.

'-d'
'-F'
'--directory'

> Allow users with appropriate privileges to attempt to make hard links to directories. However, note that this will probably fail due to system restrictions, even for the super-user.

'-f'
'--force'   Remove existing destination files.

'-i'
'--interactive'

> Prompt whether to remove existing destination files.

'-L'
'--logical'

> If -s is not in effect, and the source file is a symbolic link, create the hard link to the file referred to by the symbolic link, rather than the symbolic link itself.

'-n'
'--no-dereference'

> Do not treat the last operand specially when it is a symbolic link to a directory. Instead, treat it as if it were a normal file.
>
> When the destination is an actual directory (not a symlink to one), there is no ambiguity. The link is created in that directory. But when the specified destination is a symlink to a directory, there are two ways to treat the user's request. ln can treat the destination just as it would a normal directory and create the link in it. On the other hand, the destination can be viewed as a non-directory—as the symlink itself. In that case, ln must delete or backup that symlink before creating the new link. The default is to treat a destination that is a symlink to a directory just like a directory.
>
> This option is weaker than the --no-target-directory (-T) option, so it has no effect if both options are given.

'-P'
'--physical'

> If -s is not in effect, and the source file is a symbolic link, create the hard link to the symbolic link itself. On platforms where this is not supported by the kernel, this option creates a symbolic link with identical contents; since symbolic link contents cannot be edited, any file name resolution performed through either link will be the same as if a hard link had been created.

'-r'
'--relative'

> Make symbolic links relative to the link location.
>
> Example:
> ```
> ln -srv /a/file /tmp
> '/tmp/file' -> '../a/file'
> ```
> Relative symbolic links are generated based on their canonicalized containing directory, and canonicalized targets. I.e., all symbolic links in these file names

will be resolved. See Section 18.5 [realpath invocation], page 161, which gives greater control over relative file name generation, as demonstrated in the following example:

```
ln--relative() {
  test "$1" = --no-symlinks && { nosym=$1; shift; }
  target="$1";
  test -d "$2" && link="$2/." || link="$2"
  rtarget="$(realpath $nosym -m "$target" \
             --relative-to "$(dirname "$link")")"
  ln -s -v "$rtarget" "$link"
}
```

'-s'

'--symbolic'

> Make symbolic links instead of hard links. This option merely produces an error message on systems that do not support symbolic links.

'-S suffix'

'--suffix=suffix'

> Append suffix to each backup file made with -b. See Section 2.2 [Backup options], page 3.

'-t directory'

'--target-directory=directory'

> Specify the destination directory. See Section 2.8 [Target directory], page 8.

'-T'

'--no-target-directory'

> Do not treat the last operand specially when it is a directory or a symbolic link to a directory. See Section 2.8 [Target directory], page 8.

'-v'

'--verbose'

> Print the name of each file after linking it successfully.

If -L and -P are both given, the last one takes precedence. If -s is also given, -L and -P are silently ignored. If neither option is given, then this implementation defaults to -P if the system `link` supports hard links to symbolic links (such as the GNU system), and -L if `link` follows symbolic links (such as on BSD).

An exit status of zero indicates success, and a nonzero value indicates failure.

Examples:

```
Bad Example:

# Create link ../a pointing to a in that directory.
# Not really useful because it points to itself.
ln -s a ..

Better Example:

# Change to the target before creating symlinks to avoid being confused.
cd ..
```

```
ln -s adir/a .
```

```
Bad Example:
```

```
# Hard coded file names don't move well.
ln -s $(pwd)/a /some/dir/
```

```
Better Example:
```

```
# Relative file names survive directory moves and also
# work across networked file systems.
ln -s afile anotherfile
ln -s ../adir/afile yetanotherfile
```

12.3 mkdir: Make directories

mkdir creates directories with the specified names. Synopsis:

    mkdir [option]... name...

mkdir creates each directory *name* in the order given. It reports an error if *name* already exists, unless the -p option is given and *name* is a directory.

The program accepts the following options. Also see Chapter 2 [Common options], page 2.

'-m *mode*'
'--mode=*mode*'

> Set the file permission bits of created directories to *mode*, which uses the same syntax as in chmod and uses 'a=rwx' (read, write and execute allowed for everyone) for the point of the departure. See Chapter 27 [File permissions], page 206.
>
> Normally the directory has the desired file mode bits at the moment it is created. As a GNU extension, *mode* may also mention special mode bits, but in this case there may be a temporary window during which the directory exists but its special mode bits are incorrect. See Section 27.5 [Directory Setuid and Setgid], page 212, for how the set-user-ID and set-group-ID bits of directories are inherited unless overridden in this way.

'-p'
'--parents'

> Make any missing parent directories for each argument, setting their file permission bits to the umask modified by 'u+wx'. Ignore existing parent directories, and do not change their file permission bits.
>
> To set the file permission bits of any newly-created parent directories to a value that includes 'u+wx', you can set the umask before invoking mkdir. For example, if the shell command '(umask u=rwx,go=rx; mkdir -p P/Q)' creates the parent P it sets the parent's permission bits to 'u=rwx,go=rx'. To set a parent's special mode bits as well, you can invoke chmod after mkdir. See Section 27.5 [Directory Setuid and Setgid], page 212, for how the set-user-ID and set-group-ID bits of newly-created parent directories are inherited.

'-v'
'--verbose'

> Print a message for each created directory. This is most useful with **--parents**.

'`-Z`'
'`--context[=`*`context`*`]`'

> Without a specified *context*, adjust the SELinux security context according
> to the system default type for destination files, similarly to the `restorecon`
> command. The long form of this option with a specific context specified, will
> set the context for newly created files only. With a specified context, if both
> SELinux and SMACK are disabled, a warning is issued.

An exit status of zero indicates success, and a nonzero value indicates failure.

12.4 `mkfifo`: Make FIFOs (named pipes)

`mkfifo` creates FIFOs (also called *named pipes*) with the specified names. Synopsis:

    mkfifo [option] name...

A *FIFO* is a special file type that permits independent processes to communicate. One
process opens the FIFO file for writing, and another for reading, after which data can flow
as with the usual anonymous pipe in shells or elsewhere.

The program accepts the following options. Also see Chapter 2 [Common options],
page 2.

'`-m `*`mode`*'
'`--mode=`*`mode`*'

> Set the mode of created FIFOs to *mode*, which is symbolic as in `chmod` and
> uses '`a=rw`' (read and write allowed for everyone) for the point of departure.
> *mode* should specify only file permission bits. See Chapter 27 [File permissions],
> page 206.

'`-Z`'
'`--context[=`*`context`*`]`'

> Without a specified *context*, adjust the SELinux security context according
> to the system default type for destination files, similarly to the `restorecon`
> command. The long form of this option with a specific context specified, will
> set the context for newly created files only. With a specified context, if both
> SELinux and SMACK are disabled, a warning is issued.

An exit status of zero indicates success, and a nonzero value indicates failure.

12.5 `mknod`: Make block or character special files

`mknod` creates a FIFO, character special file, or block special file with the specified name.
Synopsis:

    mknod [option]... name type [major minor]

Unlike the phrase "special file type" above, the term *special file* has a technical meaning
on Unix: something that can generate or receive data. Usually this corresponds to a physical
piece of hardware, e.g., a printer or a disk. (These files are typically created at system-
configuration time.) The `mknod` command is what creates files of this type. Such devices
can be read either a character at a time or a "block" (many characters) at a time, hence
we say there are *block special* files and *character special* files.

Due to shell aliases and built-in `mknod` functions, using an unadorned `mknod` interactively or in a script may get you different functionality than that described here. Invoke it via env (i.e., `env mknod ...`) to avoid interference from the shell.

The arguments after *name* specify the type of file to make:

'p'   for a FIFO

'b'   for a block special file

'c'   for a character special file

When making a block or character special file, the major and minor device numbers must be given after the file type. If a major or minor device number begins with '0x' or '0X', it is interpreted as hexadecimal; otherwise, if it begins with '0', as octal; otherwise, as decimal.

The program accepts the following options. Also see Chapter 2 [Common options], page 2.

'-m *mode*'
'--mode=*mode*'

> Set the mode of created files to *mode*, which is symbolic as in `chmod` and uses 'a=rw' as the point of departure. *mode* should specify only file permission bits. See Chapter 27 [File permissions], page 206.

'-Z'
'--context[=*context*]'

> Without a specified *context*, adjust the SELinux security context according to the system default type for destination files, similarly to the `restorecon` command. The long form of this option with a specific context specified, will set the context for newly created files only. With a specified context, if both SELinux and SMACK are disabled, a warning is issued.

An exit status of zero indicates success, and a nonzero value indicates failure.

12.6 `readlink`: Print value of a symlink or canonical file name

`readlink` may work in one of two supported modes:

'Readlink mode'

> `readlink` outputs the value of the given symbolic links. If `readlink` is invoked with an argument other than the name of a symbolic link, it produces no output and exits with a nonzero exit code.

'Canonicalize mode'

> `readlink` outputs the absolute name of the given files which contain no ., .. components nor any repeated separators (/) or symbolic links.

  readlink [*option*]... *file*...

By default, `readlink` operates in readlink mode.

The program accepts the following options. Also see Chapter 2 [Common options], page 2.

'`-f`'
'`--canonicalize`'

> Activate canonicalize mode. If any component of the file name except the last one is missing or unavailable, `readlink` produces no output and exits with a nonzero exit code. A trailing slash is ignored.

'`-e`'
'`--canonicalize-existing`'

> Activate canonicalize mode. If any component is missing or unavailable, `readlink` produces no output and exits with a nonzero exit code. A trailing slash requires that the name resolve to a directory.

'`-m`'
'`--canonicalize-missing`'

> Activate canonicalize mode. If any component is missing or unavailable, `readlink` treats it as a directory.

'`-n`'
'`--no-newline`'

> Do not print the output delimiter, when a single *file* is specified. Print a warning if specified along with multiple *files*.

'`-s`'
'`-q`'
'`--silent`'
'`--quiet`' Suppress most error messages.

'`-v`'
'`--verbose`'

> Report error messages.

'`-z`'
'`--zero`' Output a zero byte (ASCII NUL) at the end of each line, rather than a newline. This option enables other programs to parse the output even when that output would contain data with embedded newlines.

The `readlink` utility first appeared in OpenBSD 2.1.

The `realpath` command without options, operates like `readlink` in canonicalize mode.

An exit status of zero indicates success, and a nonzero value indicates failure.

12.7 `rmdir`: Remove empty directories

`rmdir` removes empty directories. Synopsis:

        rmdir [*option*]... *directory*...

If any *directory* argument does not refer to an existing empty directory, it is an error.

The program accepts the following options. Also see Chapter 2 [Common options], page 2.

'`--ignore-fail-on-non-empty`'

> Ignore each failure to remove a directory that is solely because the directory is non-empty.

'`-p`'
'`--parents`'

> Remove *directory*, then try to remove each component of *directory*. So, for example, '`rmdir -p a/b/c`' is similar to '`rmdir a/b/c a/b a`'. As such, it fails if any of those directories turns out not to be empty. Use the `--ignore-fail-on-non-empty` option to make it so such a failure does not evoke a diagnostic and does not cause `rmdir` to exit unsuccessfully.

'`-v`'
'`--verbose`'

> Give a diagnostic for each successful removal. *directory* is removed.

See Section 11.5 [rm invocation], page 108, for how to remove non-empty directories (recursively).

An exit status of zero indicates success, and a nonzero value indicates failure.

12.8 `unlink`: Remove files via the unlink syscall

`unlink` deletes a single specified file name. It is a minimalist interface to the system-provided `unlink` function. See Section "Deleting Files" in *The GNU C Library Reference Manual*. Synopsis: It avoids the bells and whistles of the more commonly-used `rm` command (see Section 11.5 [rm invocation], page 108).

        unlink *filename*

On some systems `unlink` can be used to delete the name of a directory. On others, it can be used that way only by a privileged user. In the GNU system `unlink` can never delete the name of a directory.

The `unlink` command honors the `--help` and `--version` options. To remove a file whose name begins with '`-`', prefix the name with '`./`', e.g., '`unlink ./--help`'.

An exit status of zero indicates success, and a nonzero value indicates failure.

13 Changing file attributes

A file is not merely its contents, a name, and a file type (see Chapter 12 [Special file types], page 114). A file also has an owner (a user ID), a group (a group ID), permissions (what the owner can do with the file, what people in the group can do, and what everyone else can do), various timestamps, and other information. Collectively, we call these a file's *attributes*.

These commands change file attributes.

13.1 `chown`: Change file owner and group

`chown` changes the user and/or group ownership of each given *file* to *new-owner* or to the user and group of an existing reference file. Synopsis:

```
chown [option]... {new-owner | --reference=ref_file} file...
```

If used, *new-owner* specifies the new owner and/or group as follows (with no embedded white space):

```
[owner] [ : [group] ]
```

Specifically:

owner   If only an *owner* (a user name or numeric user ID) is given, that user is made the owner of each given file, and the files' group is not changed.

owner': '*group*

      If the *owner* is followed by a colon and a *group* (a group name or numeric group ID), with no spaces between them, the group ownership of the files is changed as well (to *group*).

owner': '   If a colon but no group name follows *owner*, that user is made the owner of the files and the group of the files is changed to *owner*'s login group.

': '*group*   If the colon and following *group* are given, but the owner is omitted, only the group of the files is changed; in this case, `chown` performs the same function as `chgrp`.

': '   If only a colon is given, or if *new-owner* is empty, neither the owner nor the group is changed.

If *owner* or *group* is intended to represent a numeric user or group ID, then you may specify it with a leading '+'. See Section 2.6 [Disambiguating names and IDs], page 7.

Some older scripts may still use '.' in place of the ':' separator. POSIX 1003.1-2001 (see Section 2.13 [Standards conformance], page 11) does not require support for that, but for backward compatibility GNU `chown` supports '.' so long as no ambiguity results. New scripts should avoid the use of '.' because it is not portable, and because it has undesirable results if the entire *owner*'.'*group* happens to identify a user whose name contains '.'.

It is system dependent whether a user can change the group to an arbitrary one, or the more portable behavior of being restricted to setting a group of which the user is a member.

The `chown` command sometimes clears the set-user-ID or set-group-ID permission bits. This behavior depends on the policy and functionality of the underlying `chown` system call, which may make system-dependent file mode modifications outside the control of the `chown` command. For example, the `chown` command might not affect those bits when invoked by a user with appropriate privileges, or when the bits signify some function other than executable permission (e.g., mandatory locking). When in doubt, check the underlying system behavior.

The program accepts the following options. Also see Chapter 2 [Common options], page 2.

'-c'
'--changes'

> Verbosely describe the action for each *file* whose ownership actually changes.

'-f'
'--silent'
'--quiet' Do not print error messages about files whose ownership cannot be changed.

'--from=*old-owner*'

> Change a *file*'s ownership only if it has current attributes specified by *old-owner*. *old-owner* has the same form as *new-owner* described above. This option is useful primarily from a security standpoint in that it narrows considerably the window of potential abuse. For example, to reflect a user ID numbering change for one user's files without an option like this, **root** might run

> > find / -owner OLDUSER -print0 | xargs -0 chown -h NEWUSER

> But that is dangerous because the interval between when the **find** tests the existing file's owner and when the **chown** is actually run may be quite large. One way to narrow the gap would be to invoke chown for each file as it is found:

> > find / -owner OLDUSER -exec chown -h NEWUSER {} \;

> But that is very slow if there are many affected files. With this option, it is safer (the gap is narrower still) though still not perfect:

> > chown -h -R --from=OLDUSER NEWUSER /

'--dereference'

> Do not act on symbolic links themselves but rather on what they point to. This is the default.

'-h'
'--no-dereference'

> Act on symbolic links themselves instead of what they point to. This mode relies on the **lchown** system call. On systems that do not provide the **lchown** system call, **chown** fails when a file specified on the command line is a symbolic link. By default, no diagnostic is issued for symbolic links encountered during a recursive traversal, but see **--verbose**.

'--preserve-root'

> Fail upon any attempt to recursively change the root directory, /. Without **--recursive**, this option has no effect. See Section 2.11 [Treating / specially], page 10.

'--no-preserve-root'

> Cancel the effect of any preceding **--preserve-root** option. See Section 2.11 [Treating / specially], page 10.

'`--reference=ref_file`'

>Change the user and group of each *file* to be the same as those of *ref_file*. If *ref_file* is a symbolic link, do not use the user and group of the symbolic link, but rather those of the file it refers to.

'`-v`'
'`--verbose`'

>Output a diagnostic for every file processed. If a symbolic link is encountered during a recursive traversal on a system without the lchown system call, and `--no-dereference` is in effect, then issue a diagnostic saying neither the symbolic link nor its referent is being changed.

'`-R`'
'`--recursive`'

>Recursively change ownership of directories and their contents.

'`-H`'   If `--recursive` (`-R`) is specified and a command line argument is a symbolic link to a directory, traverse it.See Section 2.10 [Traversing symlinks], page 9.

'`-L`'   In a recursive traversal, traverse every symbolic link to a directory that is encountered.See Section 2.10 [Traversing symlinks], page 9.

'`-P`'   Do not traverse any symbolic links. This is the default if none of `-H`, `-L`, or `-P` is specified.See Section 2.10 [Traversing symlinks], page 9.

An exit status of zero indicates success, and a nonzero value indicates failure.

Examples:

```
# Change the owner of /u to "root".
chown root /u

# Likewise, but also change its group to "staff".
chown root:staff /u

# Change the owner of /u and subfiles to "root".
chown -hR root /u
```

13.2 `chgrp`: Change group ownership

`chgrp` changes the group ownership of each given *file* to *group* (which can be either a group name or a numeric group ID) or to the group of an existing reference file. See Section 13.1 [chown invocation], page 123. Synopsis:

>`chgrp [option]... {group | --reference=ref_file} file...`

If *group* is intended to represent a numeric group ID, then you may specify it with a leading '+'. See Section 2.6 [Disambiguating names and IDs], page 7.

It is system dependent whether a user can change the group to an arbitrary one, or the more portable behavior of being restricted to setting a group of which the user is a member.

The program accepts the following options. Also see Chapter 2 [Common options], page 2.

'`-c`'
'`--changes`'

>Verbosely describe the action for each *file* whose group actually changes.

`'-f'`
`'--silent'`
`'--quiet'` Do not print error messages about files whose group cannot be changed.

`'--dereference'`

Do not act on symbolic links themselves but rather on what they point to. This is the default.

`'-h'`
`'--no-dereference'`

Act on symbolic links themselves instead of what they point to. This mode relies on the `lchown` system call. On systems that do not provide the `lchown` system call, `chgrp` fails when a file specified on the command line is a symbolic link. By default, no diagnostic is issued for symbolic links encountered during a recursive traversal, but see `--verbose`.

`'--preserve-root'`

Fail upon any attempt to recursively change the root directory, `/`. Without `--recursive`, this option has no effect. See Section 2.11 [Treating / specially], page 10.

`'--no-preserve-root'`

Cancel the effect of any preceding `--preserve-root` option. See Section 2.11 [Treating / specially], page 10.

`'--reference=ref_file'`

Change the group of each *file* to be the same as that of *ref_file*. If *ref_file* is a symbolic link, do not use the group of the symbolic link, but rather that of the file it refers to.

`'-v'`
`'--verbose'`

Output a diagnostic for every file processed. If a symbolic link is encountered during a recursive traversal on a system without the `lchown` system call, and `--no-dereference` is in effect, then issue a diagnostic saying neither the symbolic link nor its referent is being changed.

`'-R'`
`'--recursive'`

Recursively change the group ownership of directories and their contents.

`'-H'` If `--recursive` (`-R`) is specified and a command line argument is a symbolic link to a directory, traverse it.See Section 2.10 [Traversing symlinks], page 9.

`'-L'` In a recursive traversal, traverse every symbolic link to a directory that is encountered.See Section 2.10 [Traversing symlinks], page 9.

`'-P'` Do not traverse any symbolic links. This is the default if none of `-H`, `-L`, or `-P` is specified.See Section 2.10 [Traversing symlinks], page 9.

An exit status of zero indicates success, and a nonzero value indicates failure.

Examples:

```
# Change the group of /u to "staff".
chgrp staff /u

# Change the group of /u and subfiles to "staff".
chgrp -hR staff /u
```

13.3 chmod: Change access permissions

chmod changes the access permissions of the named files. Synopsis:

> chmod [option]... {mode | --reference=ref_file} file...

chmod never changes the permissions of symbolic links, since the chmod system call cannot change their permissions. This is not a problem since the permissions of symbolic links are never used. However, for each symbolic link listed on the command line, chmod changes the permissions of the pointed-to file. In contrast, chmod ignores symbolic links encountered during recursive directory traversals.

A successful use of chmod clears the set-group-ID bit of a regular file if the file's group ID does not match the user's effective group ID or one of the user's supplementary group IDs, unless the user has appropriate privileges. Additional restrictions may cause the set-user-ID and set-group-ID bits of *mode* or *ref_file* to be ignored. This behavior depends on the policy and functionality of the underlying chmod system call. When in doubt, check the underlying system behavior.

If used, *mode* specifies the new file mode bits. For details, see the section on Chapter 27 [File permissions], page 206. If you really want *mode* to have a leading '-', you should use -- first, e.g., 'chmod -- -w file'. Typically, though, 'chmod a-w file' is preferable, and chmod -w file (without the --) complains if it behaves differently from what 'chmod a-w file' would do.

The program accepts the following options. Also see Chapter 2 [Common options], page 2.

'-c'
'--changes'
> Verbosely describe the action for each *file* whose permissions actually changes.

'-f'
'--silent'
'--quiet' Do not print error messages about files whose permissions cannot be changed.

'--preserve-root'
> Fail upon any attempt to recursively change the root directory, /. Without --recursive, this option has no effect. See Section 2.11 [Treating / specially], page 10.

'--no-preserve-root'
> Cancel the effect of any preceding --preserve-root option. See Section 2.11 [Treating / specially], page 10.

'-v'
'--verbose'
> Verbosely describe the action or non-action taken for every *file*.

'`--reference=ref_file`'

> Change the mode of each *file* to be the same as that of *ref_file*. See Chapter 27 [File permissions], page 206. If *ref_file* is a symbolic link, do not use the mode of the symbolic link, but rather that of the file it refers to.

'`-R`'

'`--recursive`'

> Recursively change permissions of directories and their contents.

An exit status of zero indicates success, and a nonzero value indicates failure.

13.4 `touch`: Change file timestamps

`touch` changes the access and/or modification times of the specified files. Synopsis:

        touch [option]... file...

Any *file* argument that does not exist is created empty, unless option `--no-create` (`-c`) or `--no-dereference` (`-h`) was in effect.

A *file* argument string of '`-`' is handled specially and causes `touch` to change the times of the file associated with standard output.

By default, `touch` sets file timestamps to the current time. Because `touch` acts on its operands left to right, the resulting timestamps of earlier and later operands may disagree. Also, the determination of what time is "current" depends on the platform. Platforms with network file systems often use different clocks for the operating system and for file systems; because `touch` typically uses file systems' clocks by default, clock skew can cause the resulting file timestamps to appear to be in a program's "future" or "past".

The `touch` command sets the file's timestamp to the greatest representable value that is not greater than the requested time. This can differ from the requested time for several reasons. First, the requested time may have a higher resolution than supported. Second, a file system may use different resolutions for different types of times. Third, file timestamps may use a different resolution than operating system timestamps. Fourth, the operating system primitives used to update timestamps may employ yet a different resolution. For example, in theory a file system might use 10-microsecond resolution for access time and 100-nanosecond resolution for modification time, and the operating system might use nanosecond resolution for the current time and microsecond resolution for the primitive that `touch` uses to set a file's timestamp to an arbitrary value.

When setting file timestamps to the current time, `touch` can change the timestamps for files that the user does not own but has write permission for. Otherwise, the user must own the files. Some older systems have a further restriction: the user must own the files unless both the access and modification times are being set to the current time.

Although `touch` provides options for changing two of the times—the times of last access and modification—of a file, there is actually a standard third one as well: the inode change time. This is often referred to as a file's `ctime`. The inode change time represents the time when the file's meta-information last changed. One common example of this is when the permissions of a file change. Changing the permissions doesn't access the file, so the atime doesn't change, nor does it modify the file, so the mtime doesn't change. Yet, something about the file itself has changed, and this must be noted somewhere. This is the job of the ctime field. This is necessary, so that, for example, a backup program can make a fresh copy of the file, including the new permissions value. Another operation that modifies a file's ctime without affecting the others is renaming. In any case, it is not possible, in normal operations, for a user to change the ctime field to a user-specified value. Some operating systems and file systems support a fourth time: the birth time, when the file was first created; by definition, this timestamp never changes.

Time stamps assume the time zone rules specified by the TZ environment variable, or by the system default rules if TZ is not set. See Section "Specifying the Time Zone with TZ" in *The GNU C Library Reference Manual*. You can avoid ambiguities during daylight saving transitions by using UTC time stamps.

The program accepts the following options. Also see Chapter 2 [Common options], page 2.

'-a'
'--time=atime'
'--time=access'
'--time=use'

>   Change the access time only.

'-c'
'--no-create'

>   Do not warn about or create files that do not exist.

'-d'
'--date=*time*'

>   Use *time* instead of the current time. It can contain month names, time zones, 'am' and 'pm', 'yesterday', etc. For example, --date="2004-02-27 14:19:13.489392193 +0530" specifies the instant of time that is 489,392,193 nanoseconds after February 27, 2004 at 2:19:13 PM in a time zone that is 5 hours and 30 minutes east of UTC. See Chapter 28 [Date input formats], page 214. File systems that do not support high-resolution time stamps silently ignore any excess precision here.

'-f'   Ignored; for compatibility with BSD versions of touch.

'-h'
'--no-dereference'

>   Attempt to change the timestamps of a symbolic link, rather than what the link refers to. When using this option, empty files are not created, but option -c must also be used to avoid warning about files that do not exist. Not all systems support changing the timestamps of symlinks, since underlying system support for this action was not required until POSIX 2008. Also, on some systems, the mere act of examining a symbolic link changes the access time, such that only changes to the modification time will persist long enough to be observable. When coupled with option -r, a reference timestamp is taken from a symbolic link rather than the file it refers to.

'-m'
'--time=mtime'
'--time=modify'

>   Change the modification time only.

'-r *file*'
'--reference=*file*'

> Use the times of the reference *file* instead of the current time. If this option is combined with the --date=*time* (-d *time*) option, the reference *file*'s time is the origin for any relative *time*s given, but is otherwise ignored. For example, '-r foo -d '-5 seconds'' specifies a time stamp equal to five seconds before the corresponding time stamp for foo. If *file* is a symbolic link, the reference timestamp is taken from the target of the symlink, unless -h was also in effect.

'-t [[*cc*]*yy*]*mmddhhmm*[.*ss*]'

> Use the argument (optional four-digit or two-digit years, months, days, hours, minutes, optional seconds) instead of the current time. If the year is specified with only two digits, then *cc* is 20 for years in the range 0 ... 68, and 19 for years in 69 ... 99. If no digits of the year are specified, the argument is interpreted as a date in the current year. On the atypical systems that support leap seconds, *ss* may be '60'.

On older systems, touch supports an obsolete syntax, as follows. If no timestamp is given with any of the -d, -r, or -t options, and if there are two or more *files* and the first *file* is of the form '*mmddhhmm*[*yy*]' and this would be a valid argument to the -t option (if the *yy*, if any, were moved to the front), and if the represented year is in the range 1969–1999, that argument is interpreted as the time for the other files instead of as a file name. This obsolete behavior can be enabled or disabled with the _POSIX2_VERSION environment variable (see Section 2.13 [Standards conformance], page 11), but portable scripts should avoid commands whose behavior depends on this variable. For example, use 'touch ./12312359 main.c' or 'touch -t 12312359 main.c' rather than the ambiguous 'touch 12312359 main.c'.

An exit status of zero indicates success, and a nonzero value indicates failure.

14 Disk usage

No disk can hold an infinite amount of data. These commands report how much disk storage is in use or available, report other file and file status information, and write buffers to disk.

14.1 `df`: Report file system disk space usage

`df` reports the amount of disk space used and available on file systems. Synopsis:

       `df [option]... [file]...`

With no arguments, `df` reports the space used and available on all currently mounted file systems (of all types). Otherwise, `df` reports on the file system containing each argument *file*.

Normally the disk space is printed in units of 1024 bytes, but this can be overridden (see Section 2.3 [Block size], page 3). Non-integer quantities are rounded up to the next higher unit.

For bind mounts and without arguments, `df` only outputs the statistics for that device with the shortest mount point name in the list of file systems (*mtab*), i.e., it hides duplicate entries, unless the `-a` option is specified.

With the same logic, `df` elides a mount entry of a dummy pseudo device if there is another mount entry of a real block device for that mount point with the same device number, e.g. the early-boot pseudo file system '`rootfs`' is not shown per default when already the real root device has been mounted.

If an argument *file* resolves to a special file containing a mounted file system, `df` shows the space available on that file system rather than on the file system containing the device node. GNU `df` does not attempt to determine the disk usage on unmounted file systems, because on most kinds of systems doing so requires extremely nonportable intimate knowledge of file system structures.

The program accepts the following options. Also see Chapter 2 [Common options], page 2.

'`-a`'
'`--all`'   Include in the listing dummy, duplicate, or inaccessible file systems, which are omitted by default. Dummy file systems are typically special purpose pseudo file systems such as '`/proc`', with no associated storage. Duplicate file systems are local or remote file systems that are mounted at separate locations in the local file hierarchy, or bind mounted locations. Inaccessible file systems are those which are mounted but subsequently over-mounted by another file system at that point, or otherwise inaccessible due to permissions of the mount point etc.

'`-B size`'
'`--block-size=size`'
                   Scale sizes by *size* before printing them (see Section 2.3 [Block size], page 3). For example, `-BG` prints sizes in units of 1,073,741,824 bytes.

'`-h`'
'`--human-readable`'
                   Append a size letter to each size, such as '`M`' for mebibytes. Powers of 1024 are used, not 1000; '`M`' stands for 1,048,576 bytes. This option is equivalent to

--block-size=human-readable. Use the --si option if you prefer powers of
1000.

'-H'   Equivalent to --si.

'-i'
'--inodes'
            List inode usage information instead of block usage. An inode (short for index
            node) contains information about a file such as its owner, permissions, time-
            stamps, and location on the disk.

'-k'   Print sizes in 1024-byte blocks, overriding the default block size (see Section 2.3
            [Block size], page 3). This option is equivalent to --block-size=1K.

'-l'
'--local'   Limit the listing to local file systems. By default, remote file systems are also
            listed.

'--no-sync'
            Do not invoke the sync system call before getting any usage data. This may
            make df run significantly faster on systems with many disks, but on some
            systems (notably SunOS) the results may be slightly out of date. This is the
            default.

'--output'
'--output[=field_list]'
            Use the output format defined by field_list, or print all fields if field_list is
            omitted. In the latter case, the order of the columns conforms to the order of
            the field descriptions below.

            The use of the --output together with each of the options -i, -P, and -T is
            mutually exclusive.

            FIELD_LIST is a comma-separated list of columns to be included in df's output
            and therefore effectively controls the order of output columns. Each field can
            thus be used at the place of choice, but yet must only be used once.

            Valid field names in the field_list are:

            'source'   The source of the mount point, usually a device.

            'fstype'   File system type.

            'itotal'   Total number of inodes.

            'iused'   Number of used inodes.

            'iavail'   Number of available inodes.

            'ipcent'   Percentage of iused divided by itotal.

            'size'   Total number of blocks.

            'used'   Number of used blocks.

            'avail'   Number of available blocks.

            'pcent'   Percentage of used divided by size.

'`file`'   The file name if specified on the command line.

'`target`'   The mount point.

The fields for block and inodes statistics are affected by the scaling options like
-h as usual.

The definition of the *field_list* can even be split among several --output uses.

```
#!/bin/sh
# Print the TARGET (i.e., the mount point) along with their percentage
# statistic regarding the blocks and the inodes.
df --out=target --output=pcent,ipcent

# Print all available fields.
df --o
```

'`-p`'

'`--portability`'

Use the POSIX output format. This is like the default format except for the
following:

1. The information about each file system is always printed on exactly one
   line; a mount device is never put on a line by itself. This means that if the
   mount device name is more than 20 characters long (e.g., for some network
   mounts), the columns are misaligned.

2. The labels in the header output line are changed to conform to POSIX.

3. The default block size and output format are unaffected by the
   DF_BLOCK_SIZE, **BLOCK_SIZE** and **BLOCKSIZE** environment variables.
   However, the default block size is still affected by **POSIXLY_CORRECT**: it
   is 512 if **POSIXLY_CORRECT** is set, 1024 otherwise. See Section 2.3 [Block
   size], page 3.

'`--si`'   Append an SI-style abbreviation to each size, such as 'M' for megabytes. Pow-
              ers of 1000 are used, not 1024; 'M' stands for 1,000,000 bytes. This option is
              equivalent to --block-size=si. Use the -h or --human-readable option if
              you prefer powers of 1024.

'`--sync`'   Invoke the **sync** system call before getting any usage data. On some systems
              (notably SunOS), doing this yields more up to date results, but in general this
              option makes **df** much slower, especially when there are many or very busy file
              systems.

'`--total`'   Print a grand total of all arguments after all arguments have been processed.
              This can be used to find out the total disk size, usage and available space
              of all listed devices. If no arguments are specified df will try harder to elide
              file systems insignificant to the total available space, by suppressing duplicate
              remote file systems.

              For the grand total line, df prints '"total"' into the *source* column, and '"-"'
              into the *target* column. If there is no *source* column (see --output), then df
              prints '"total"' into the *target* column, if present.

'-t *fstype*'
'--type=*fstype*'
> Limit the listing to file systems of type *fstype*. Multiple file system types can be specified by giving multiple -t options. By default, nothing is omitted.

'-T'
'--print-type'
> Print each file system's type. The types printed here are the same ones you can include or exclude with -t and -x. The particular types printed are whatever is supported by the system. Here are some of the common names (this list is certainly not exhaustive):
>
> 'nfs'   An NFS file system, i.e., one mounted over a network from another machine. This is the one type name which seems to be used uniformly by all systems.
>
> 'ext2, ext3, ext4, xfs, btrfs...'
> > A file system on a locally-mounted hard disk. (The system might even support more than one type here; Linux does.)
>
> 'iso9660, cdfs'
> > A file system on a CD or DVD drive. HP-UX uses 'cdfs', most other systems use 'iso9660'.
>
> 'ntfs,fat' File systems used by MS-Windows / MS-DOS.

'-x *fstype*'
'--exclude-type=*fstype*'
> Limit the listing to file systems not of type *fstype*. Multiple file system types can be eliminated by giving multiple -x options. By default, no file system types are omitted.

'-v'   Ignored; for compatibility with System V versions of df.

df is installed only on systems that have usable mount tables, so portable scripts should not rely on its existence.

An exit status of zero indicates success, and a nonzero value indicates failure.Failure includes the case where no output is generated, so you can inspect the exit status of a command like 'df -t ext3 -t reiserfs *dir*' to test whether *dir* is on a file system of type 'ext3' or 'reiserfs'.

Since the list of file systems (*mtab*) is needed to determine the file system type, failure includes the cases when that list cannot be read and one or more of the options -a, -l, -t or -x is used together with a file name argument.

14.2 du: Estimate file space usage

du reports the amount of disk space used by the set of specified files and for each subdirectory (of directory arguments). Synopsis:

> du [*option*]... [*file*]...

With no arguments, du reports the disk space for the current directory. Normally the disk space is printed in units of 1024 bytes, but this can be overridden (see Section 2.3 [Block size], page 3). Non-integer quantities are rounded up to the next higher unit.

If two or more hard links point to the same file, only one of the hard links is counted. The *file* argument order affects which links are counted, and changing the argument order may change the numbers and entries that du outputs.

The program accepts the following options. Also see Chapter 2 [Common options], page 2.

'-0'

'--null'   Output a zero byte (ASCII NUL) at the end of each line, rather than a newline. This option enables other programs to parse the output even when that output would contain data with embedded newlines.

'-a'

'--all'   Show counts for all files, not just directories.

'--apparent-size'

Print apparent sizes, rather than disk usage. The apparent size of a file is the number of bytes reported by wc -c on regular files, or more generally, ls -l --block-size=1 or stat --format=%s. For example, a file containing the word 'zoo' with no newline would, of course, have an apparent size of 3. Such a small file may require anywhere from 0 to 16 KiB or more of disk space, depending on the type and configuration of the file system on which the file resides. However, a sparse file created with this command:

        dd bs=1 seek=2GiB if=/dev/null of=big

has an apparent size of 2 GiB, yet on most modern systems, it actually uses almost no disk space.

'-B size'

'--block-size=size'

Scale sizes by *size* before printing them (see Section 2.3 [Block size], page 3). For example, -BG prints sizes in units of 1,073,741,824 bytes.

'-b'

'--bytes'   Equivalent to --apparent-size --block-size=1.

'-c'

'--total'   Print a grand total of all arguments after all arguments have been processed. This can be used to find out the total disk usage of a given set of files or directories.

'-D'

'--dereference-args'

Dereference symbolic links that are command line arguments. Does not affect other symbolic links. This is helpful for finding out the disk usage of directories, such as /usr/tmp, which are often symbolic links.

'-d depth'

'--max-depth=depth'

Show the total for each directory (and file if –all) that is at most MAX_DEPTH levels down from the root of the hierarchy. The root is at level 0, so du --max-depth=0 is equivalent to du -s.

'`--files0-from=`*`file`*'

Disallow processing files named on the command line, and instead process those named in file *file*; each name being terminated by a zero byte (ASCII NUL). This is useful when the list of file names is so long that it may exceed a command line length limitation. In such cases, running `du` via `xargs` is undesirable because it splits the list into pieces and makes `du` print with the `--total` (`-c`) option for each sublist rather than for the entire list. One way to produce a list of ASCII NUL terminated file names is with GNU `find`, using its `-print0` predicate. If *file* is '`-`' then the ASCII NUL terminated file names are read from standard input.

'`-H`'   Equivalent to `--dereference-args` (`-D`).

'`-h`'
'`--human-readable`'

Append a size letter to each size, such as 'M' for mebibytes. Powers of 1024 are used, not 1000; 'M' stands for 1,048,576 bytes. This option is equivalent to `--block-size=human-readable`. Use the `--si` option if you prefer powers of 1000.

'`--inodes`'

List inode usage information instead of block usage. This option is useful for finding directories which contain many files, and therefore eat up most of the inodes space of a file system (see `df`, option `--inodes`). It can well be combined with the options `-a`, `-c`, `-h`, `-l`, `-s`, `-S`, `-t` and `-x`; however, passing other options regarding the block size, for example `-b`, `-m` and `--apparent-size`, is ignored.

'`-k`'   Print sizes in 1024-byte blocks, overriding the default block size (see Section 2.3 [Block size], page 3). This option is equivalent to `--block-size=1K`.

'`-L`'
'`--dereference`'

Dereference symbolic links (show the disk space used by the file or directory that the link points to instead of the space used by the link).

'`-l`'
'`--count-links`'

Count the size of all files, even if they have appeared already (as a hard link).

'`-m`'   Print sizes in 1,048,576-byte blocks, overriding the default block size (see Section 2.3 [Block size], page 3). This option is equivalent to `--block-size=1M`.

'`-P`'
'`--no-dereference`'

For each symbolic links encountered by `du`, consider the disk space used by the symbolic link.

'`-S`'
'`--separate-dirs`'

Normally, in the output of `du` (when not using `--summarize`), the size listed next to a directory name, *d*, represents the sum of sizes of all entries beneath d as well as the size of d itself. With --separate-dirs, the size reported for a directory name, d, will exclude the size of any subdirectories.

'--si'   Append an SI-style abbreviation to each size, such as 'M' for megabytes. Powers of 1000 are used, not 1024; 'M' stands for 1,000,000 bytes. This option is equivalent to --block-size=si. Use the -h or --human-readable option if you prefer powers of 1024.

'-s'
'--summarize'
            Display only a total for each argument.

'-t size'
'--threshold=size'
            Exclude entries based on a given size. The size refers to used blocks in normal mode (see Section 2.3 [Block size], page 3), or inodes count in conjunction with the --inodes option.

            If size is positive, then du will only print entries with a size greater than or equal to that.

            If size is negative, then du will only print entries with a size smaller than or equal to that.

            Although GNU find can be used to find files of a certain size, du's --threshold option can be used to also filter directories based on a given size.

            Please note that the --threshold option can be combined with the --apparent-size option, and in this case would elide entries based on its apparent size.

            Please note that the --threshold option can be combined with the --inodes option, and in this case would elide entries based on its inodes count.

            Here's how you would use --threshold to find directories with a size greater than or equal to 200 megabytes:

                 du --threshold=200MB

            Here's how you would use --threshold to find directories and files - note the -a - with an apparent size smaller than or equal to 500 bytes:

                 du -a -t -500 --apparent-size

            Here's how you would use --threshold to find directories on the root file system with more than 20000 inodes used in the directory tree below:

                 du --inodes -x --threshold=20000 /

'--time'   Show time of the most recent modification of any file in the directory, or any of its subdirectories.

'--time=ctime'
'--time=status'
'--time=use'
            Show the most recent status change time (the 'ctime' in the inode) of any file in the directory, instead of the modification time.

'`--time=atime`'

'`--time=access`'

> Show the most recent access time (the '`atime`' in the inode) of any file in the
> directory, instead of the modification time.

'`--time-style=style`'

> List timestamps in style *style*. This option has an effect only if the `--time`
> option is also specified. The *style* should be one of the following:

> '`+format`' List timestamps using *format*, where *format* is interpreted like
> the format argument of `date` (see Section 21.1 [date invocation],
> page 175). For example, `--time-style="+%Y-%m-%d %H:%M:%S"`
> causes `du` to list timestamps like '`2002-03-30 23:45:56`'. As with
> `date`, *format*'s interpretation is affected by the `LC_TIME` locale cat-
> egory.

> '`full-iso`'
>
> List timestamps in full using ISO 8601 date, time, and time
> zone format with nanosecond precision, e.g., '`2002-03-30`
> `23:45:56.477817180 -0700`'. This style is equivalent to
> '`+%Y-%m-%d %H:%M:%S.%N %z`'.

> '`long-iso`'
>
> List ISO 8601 date and time in minutes, e.g., '`2002-03-30 23:45`'.
> These timestamps are shorter than '`full-iso`' timestamps, and are
> usually good enough for everyday work. This style is equivalent to
> '`+%Y-%m-%d %H:%M`'.

> '`iso`' List ISO 8601 dates for timestamps, e.g., '`2002-03-30`'. This style
> is equivalent to '`+%Y-%m-%d`'.

> You can specify the default value of the `--time-style` option with the en-
> vironment variable `TIME_STYLE`; if `TIME_STYLE` is not set the default style is
> '`long-iso`'. For compatibility with `ls`, if `TIME_STYLE` begins with '`+`' and con-
> tains a newline, the newline and any later characters are ignored; if `TIME_STYLE`
> begins with '`posix-`' the '`posix-`' is ignored; and if `TIME_STYLE` is '`locale`' it
> is ignored.

'`-X file`'

'`--exclude-from=file`'

> Like `--exclude`, except take the patterns to exclude from *file*, one per line. If
> *file* is '`-`', take the patterns from standard input.

'`--exclude=pattern`'

> When recursing, skip subdirectories or files matching *pattern*. For example, `du`
> `--exclude='*.o'` excludes files whose names end in '`.o`'.

'`-x`'

'`--one-file-system`'

> Skip directories that are on different file systems from the one that the argument
> being processed is on.

On BSD systems, du reports sizes that are half the correct values for files that are NFS-mounted from HP-UX systems. On HP-UX systems, it reports sizes that are twice the correct values for files that are NFS-mounted from BSD systems. This is due to a flaw in HP-UX; it also affects the HP-UX du program.

An exit status of zero indicates success, and a nonzero value indicates failure.

14.3 stat: Report file or file system status

stat displays information about the specified file(s). Synopsis:

    stat [option]... [file]...

With no option, stat reports all information about the given files. But it also can be used to report the information of the file systems the given files are located on. If the files are links, stat can also give information about the files the links point to.

Due to shell aliases and built-in stat functions, using an unadorned stat interactively or in a script may get you different functionality than that described here. Invoke it via env (i.e., env stat ...) to avoid interference from the shell.

'-L'
'--dereference'

> Change how stat treats symbolic links. With this option, stat acts on the file referenced by each symbolic link argument. Without it, stat acts on any symbolic link argument directly.

'-f'
'--file-system'

> Report information about the file systems where the given files are located instead of information about the files themselves. This option implies the -L option.

'-c'
'--format=format'

> Use format rather than the default format. format is automatically newline-terminated, so running a command like the following with two or more file operands produces a line of output for each operand:

        $ stat --format=%d:%i / /usr
        2050:2
        2057:2

'--printf=format'

> Use format rather than the default format. Like --format, but interpret backslash escapes, and do not output a mandatory trailing newline. If you want a newline, include '\n' in the format. Here's how you would use --printf to print the device and inode numbers of / and /usr:

        $ stat --printf='%d:%i\n' / /usr
        2050:2
        2057:2

'-t'
'--terse' Print the information in terse form, suitable for parsing by other programs.

The output of the following commands are identical and the `--format` also identifies the items printed (in fuller form) in the default format. Note the format string would include another '%C' at the end with an active SELinux security context.

```
$ stat --format="%n %s %b %f %u %g %D %i %h %t %T %X %Y %Z %W %o" ...
$ stat --terse ...
```

The same illustrating terse output in `--file-system` mode:

```
$ stat -f --format="%n %i %l %t %s %S %b %f %a %c %d" ...
$ stat -f --terse ...
```

The valid *format* directives for files with `--format` and `--printf` are:

- %a - Access rights in octal
- %A - Access rights in human readable form
- %b - Number of blocks allocated (see '%B')
- %B - The size in bytes of each block reported by '%b'
- %C - The SELinux security context of a file, if available
- %d - Device number in decimal
- %D - Device number in hex
- %f - Raw mode in hex
- %F - File type
- %g - Group ID of owner
- %G - Group name of owner
- %h - Number of hard links
- %i - Inode number
- %m - Mount point (See note below)
- %n - File name
- %N - Quoted file name with dereference if symbolic link
- %o - Optimal I/O transfer size hint
- %s - Total size, in bytes
- %t - Major device type in hex (see below)
- %T - Minor device type in hex (see below)
- %u - User ID of owner
- %U - User name of owner
- %w - Time of file birth, or '-' if unknown
- %W - Time of file birth as seconds since Epoch, or '0'
- %x - Time of last access
- %X - Time of last access as seconds since Epoch
- %y - Time of last data modification
- %Y - Time of last data modification as seconds since Epoch
- %z - Time of last status change

- %Z - Time of last status change as seconds since Epoch

The '%t' and '%T' formats operate on the st_rdev member of the stat(2) structure, and are only defined for character and block special files. On some systems or file types, st_rdev may be used to represent other quantities.

The '%W', '%X', '%Y', and '%Z' formats accept a precision preceded by a period to specify the number of digits to print after the decimal point. For example, '%.3X' outputs the last access time to millisecond precision. If a period is given but no precision, stat uses 9 digits, so '%.X' is equivalent to '%.9X'. When discarding excess precision, time stamps are truncated toward minus infinity.

```
zero pad:
  $ stat -c '[%015Y]' /usr
  [000001288929712]
space align:
  $ stat -c '[%15Y]' /usr
  [     1288929712]
  $ stat -c '[%-15Y]' /usr
  [1288929712     ]
precision:
  $ stat -c '[%.3Y]' /usr
  [1288929712.114]
  $ stat -c '[%.Y]' /usr
  [1288929712.114951834]
```

The mount point printed by '%m' is similar to that output by df, except that:

- stat does not dereference symlinks by default (unless -L is specified)

- stat does not search for specified device nodes in the file system list, instead operating on them directly

- stat outputs the alias for a bind mounted file, rather than the initial mount point of its backing device. One can recursively call stat until there is no change in output, to get the current base mount point

When listing file system information (--file-system (-f)), you must use a different set of *format* directives:

- %a - Free blocks available to non-super-user

- %b - Total data blocks in file system

- %c - Total file nodes in file system

- %d - Free file nodes in file system

- %f - Free blocks in file system

- %i - File System ID in hex

- %l - Maximum length of file names

- %n - File name

- %s - Block size (for faster transfers)

- %S - Fundamental block size (for block counts)

- %t - Type in hex

- %T - Type in human readable form

Time stamps are listed according to the time zone rules specified by the `TZ` environment variable, or by the system default rules if `TZ` is not set. See Section "Specifying the Time Zone with TZ" in *The GNU C Library Reference Manual*.

An exit status of zero indicates success, and a nonzero value indicates failure.

14.4 `sync`: Synchronize cached writes to persistent storage

`sync` synchronizes in memory files or file systems to persistent storage. Synopsis:

    sync [option] [file]...

`sync` writes any data buffered in memory out to disk. This can include (but is not limited to) modified superblocks, modified inodes, and delayed reads and writes. This must be implemented by the kernel; The `sync` program does nothing but exercise the `sync`, `syncfs`, `fsync`, and `fdatasync` system calls.

The kernel keeps data in memory to avoid doing (relatively slow) disk reads and writes. This improves performance, but if the computer crashes, data may be lost or the file system corrupted as a result. The `sync` command instructs the kernel to write data in memory to persistent storage.

If any argument is specified then only those files will be synchronized using the fsync(2) syscall by default.

If at least one file is specified, it is possible to change the synchronization method with the following options. Also see Chapter 2 [Common options], page 2.

'`-d`'
'`--data`'   Use fdatasync(2) to sync only the data for the file, and any metadata required to maintain file system consistency.

'`-f`'
'`--file-system`'
              Synchronize all the I/O waiting for the file systems that contain the file, using the syscall syncfs(2). Note you would usually *not* specify this option if passing a device node like '`/dev/sda`' for example, as that would sync the containing file system rather than the referenced one. Note also that depending on the system, passing individual device nodes or files may have different sync characteristics than using no arguments. I.e., arguments passed to fsync(2) may provide greater guarantees through write barriers, than a global sync(2) used when no arguments are provided.

An exit status of zero indicates success, and a nonzero value indicates failure.

14.5 `truncate`: Shrink or extend the size of a file

`truncate` shrinks or extends the size of each *file* to the specified size. Synopsis:

    truncate option... file...

Any *file* that does not exist is created.

If a *file* is larger than the specified size, the extra data is lost. If a *file* is shorter, it is extended and the extended part (or hole) reads as zero bytes.

The program accepts the following options. Also see Chapter 2 [Common options], page 2.

'-c'
'--no-create'

>Do not create files that do not exist.

'-o'
'--io-blocks'

>Treat *size* as number of I/O blocks of the *file* rather than bytes.

'-r *rfile*'
'--reference=*rfile*'

>Base the size of each *file* on the size of *rfile*.

'-s *size*'
'--size=*size*'

>Set or adjust the size of each *file* according to *size*. *size* is in bytes unless --io-blocks is specified. *size* may be, or may be an integer optionally followed by, one of the following multiplicative suffixes:

>>'KB' => 1000 (KiloBytes)
>>'K' => 1024 (KibiBytes)
>>'MB' => 1000*1000 (MegaBytes)
>>'M' => 1024*1024 (MebiBytes)
>>'GB' => 1000*1000*1000 (GigaBytes)
>>'G' => 1024*1024*1024 (GibiBytes)

>and so on for 'T', 'P', 'E', 'Z', and 'Y'.

>*size* may also be prefixed by one of the following to adjust the size of each *file* based on its current size:

>>'+' => extend by
>>'-' => reduce by
>>'<' => at most
>>'>' => at least
>>'/' => round down to multiple of
>>'%' => round up to multiple of

An exit status of zero indicates success, and a nonzero value indicates failure.

15 Printing text

This section describes commands that display text strings.

15.1 `echo`: Print a line of text

`echo` writes each given *string* to standard output, with a space between each and a newline after the last one. Synopsis:

    echo [option]... [string]...

Due to shell aliases and built-in `echo` functions, using an unadorned `echo` interactively or in a script may get you different functionality than that described here. Invoke it via `env` (i.e., `env echo ...`) to avoid interference from the shell.

The program accepts the following options. Also see Chapter 2 [Common options], page 2. Options must precede operands, and the normally-special argument '--' has no special meaning and is treated like any other *string*.

'-n'   Do not output the trailing newline.

'-e'   Enable interpretation of the following backslash-escaped characters in each *string*:

        '\a'   alert (bell)

        '\b'   backspace

        '\c'   produce no further output

        '\e'   escape

        '\f'   form feed

        '\n'   newline

        '\r'   carriage return

        '\t'   horizontal tab

        '\v'   vertical tab

        '\\'   backslash

        '\0nnn'   the eight-bit value that is the octal number *nnn* (zero to three octal digits), if *nnn* is a nine-bit value, the ninth bit is ignored

        '\nnn'   the eight-bit value that is the octal number *nnn* (one to three octal digits), if *nnn* is a nine-bit value, the ninth bit is ignored

        '\xhh'   the eight-bit value that is the hexadecimal number *hh* (one or two hexadecimal digits)

'-E'   Disable interpretation of backslash escapes in each *string*. This is the default. If -e and -E are both specified, the last one given takes effect.

If the `POSIXLY_CORRECT` environment variable is set, then when `echo`'s first argument is not -n it outputs option-like arguments instead of treating them as options. For example, `echo -ne hello` outputs '-ne hello' instead of plain '`hello`'.

POSIX does not require support for any options, and says that the behavior of echo is implementation-defined if any *string* contains a backslash or if the first argument is -n. Portable programs can use the printf command if they need to omit trailing newlines or output control characters or backslashes. See Section 15.2 [printf invocation], page 145.

An exit status of zero indicates success, and a nonzero value indicates failure.

15.2 printf: Format and print data

printf does formatted printing of text. Synopsis:

```
printf format [argument]...
```

printf prints the *format* string, interpreting '%' directives and '\' escapes to format numeric and string arguments in a way that is mostly similar to the C 'printf' function. See Section "printf format directives" in *The GNU C Library Reference Manual*, for details. The differences are listed below.

Due to shell aliases and built-in printf functions, using an unadorned printf interactively or in a script may get you different functionality than that described here. Invoke it via env (i.e., env printf ...) to avoid interference from the shell.

- The *format* argument is reused as necessary to convert all the given *argument*s. For example, the command 'printf %s a b' outputs 'ab'.

- Missing *argument*s are treated as null strings or as zeros, depending on whether the context expects a string or a number. For example, the command 'printf %sx%d' prints 'x0'.

- An additional escape, '\c', causes printf to produce no further output. For example, the command 'printf 'A%sC\cD%sF' B E' prints 'ABC'.

- The hexadecimal escape sequence '\x*hh*' has at most two digits, as opposed to C where it can have an unlimited number of digits. For example, the command 'printf '\x07e'' prints two bytes, whereas the C statement 'printf ("\x07e")' prints just one.

- printf has an additional directive, '%b', which prints its argument string with '\' escapes interpreted in the same way as in the *format* string, except that octal escapes are of the form '\0*ooo*' where *ooo* is 0 to 3 octal digits. If '*ooo*' is nine-bit value, ignore the ninth bit. If a precision is also given, it limits the number of bytes printed from the converted string.

- Numeric arguments must be single C constants, possibly with leading '+' or '-'. For example, 'printf %.4d -3' outputs '-0003'.

- If the leading character of a numeric argument is '"' or ''' then its value is the numeric value of the immediately following character. Any remaining characters are silently ignored if the POSIXLY_CORRECT environment variable is set; otherwise, a warning is printed. For example, 'printf "%d" "'a"' outputs '97' on hosts that use the ASCII character set, since 'a' has the numeric value 97 in ASCII.

A floating-point argument must use a period before any fractional digits, but is printed according to the LC_NUMERIC category of the current locale. For example, in a locale whose radix character is a comma, the command 'printf %g 3.14' outputs '3,14' whereas the command 'printf %g 3,14' is an error. See Section 2.4 [Floating point], page 5.

printf interprets '*ooo*' in *format* as an octal number (if *ooo* is 1 to 3 octal digits) specifying a byte to print, and '\x*hh*' as a hexadecimal number (if *hh* is 1 to 2 hex digits) specifying a character to print. Note however that when '*ooo*' specifies a number larger than 255, printf ignores the ninth bit. For example, 'printf '\400'' is equivalent to 'printf '\0''.

printf interprets two character syntaxes introduced in ISO C 99: '\u' for 16-bit Unicode (ISO/IEC 10646) characters, specified as four hexadecimal digits *hhhh*, and '\U' for 32-bit Unicode characters, specified as eight hexadecimal digits *hhhhhhhh*. printf outputs the Unicode characters according to the LC_CTYPE locale. Unicode characters in the ranges U+0000...U+009F, U+D800...U+DFFF cannot be specified by this syntax, except for U+0024 ($), U+0040 (@), and U+0060 (`).

The processing of '\u' and '\U' requires a full-featured iconv facility. It is activated on systems with glibc 2.2 (or newer), or when libiconv is installed prior to this package. Otherwise '\u' and '\U' will print as-is.

The only options are a lone --help or --version. See Chapter 2 [Common options], page 2. Options must precede operands.

The Unicode character syntaxes are useful for writing strings in a locale independent way. For example, a string containing the Euro currency symbol

```
$ env printf '\u20AC 14.95'
```

will be output correctly in all locales supporting the Euro symbol (ISO-8859-15, UTF-8, and others). Similarly, a Chinese string

```
$ env printf '\u4e2d\u6587'
```

will be output correctly in all Chinese locales (GB2312, BIG5, UTF-8, etc).

Note that in these examples, the printf command has been invoked via env to ensure that we run the program found via your shell's search path, and not a shell alias or a built-in function.

For larger strings, you don't need to look up the hexadecimal code values of each character one by one. ASCII characters mixed with \u escape sequences is also known as the JAVA source file encoding. You can use GNU recode 3.5c (or newer) to convert strings to this encoding. Here is how to convert a piece of text into a shell script which will output this text in a locale-independent way:

```
$ LC_CTYPE=zh_CN.big5 /usr/local/bin/printf \
    '\u4e2d\u6587\n' > sample.txt
$ recode BIG5..JAVA < sample.txt \
    | sed -e "s|^|/usr/local/bin/printf '|" -e "s|$|\\\n'|" \
    > sample.sh
```

An exit status of zero indicates success, and a nonzero value indicates failure.

15.3 yes: Print a string until interrupted

yes prints the command line arguments, separated by spaces and followed by a newline, forever until it is killed. If no arguments are given, it prints 'y' followed by a newline forever until killed.

Upon a write error, yes exits with status '1'.

The only options are a lone --help or --version. To output an argument that begins with '-', precede it with --, e.g., 'yes -- --help'. See Chapter 2 [Common options], page 2.

16 Conditions

This section describes commands that are primarily useful for their exit status, rather than their output. Thus, they are often used as the condition of shell `if` statements, or as the last command in a pipeline.

16.1 `false`: Do nothing, unsuccessfully

`false` does nothing except return an exit status of 1, meaning *failure*. It can be used as a place holder in shell scripts where an unsuccessful command is needed. In most modern shells, `false` is a built-in command, so when you use '`false`' in a script, you're probably using the built-in command, not the one documented here.

`false` honors the `--help` and `--version` options.

This version of `false` is implemented as a C program, and is thus more secure and faster than a shell script implementation, and may safely be used as a dummy shell for the purpose of disabling accounts.

Note that `false` (unlike all other programs documented herein) exits unsuccessfully, even when invoked with `--help` or `--version`.

Portable programs should not assume that the exit status of `false` is 1, as it is greater than 1 on some non-GNU hosts.

16.2 `true`: Do nothing, successfully

`true` does nothing except return an exit status of 0, meaning *success*. It can be used as a place holder in shell scripts where a successful command is needed, although the shell built-in command : (colon) may do the same thing faster. In most modern shells, `true` is a built-in command, so when you use '`true`' in a script, you're probably using the built-in command, not the one documented here.

`true` honors the `--help` and `--version` options.

Note, however, that it is possible to cause `true` to exit with nonzero status: with the `--help` or `--version` option, and with standard output already closed or redirected to a file that evokes an I/O error. For example, using a Bourne-compatible shell:

```
$ ./true --version >&-
./true: write error: Bad file number
$ ./true --version > /dev/full
./true: write error: No space left on device
```

This version of `true` is implemented as a C program, and is thus more secure and faster than a shell script implementation, and may safely be used as a dummy shell for the purpose of disabling accounts.

16.3 `test`: Check file types and compare values

`test` returns a status of 0 (true) or 1 (false) depending on the evaluation of the conditional expression *expr*. Each part of the expression must be a separate argument.

`test` has file status checks, string operators, and numeric comparison operators.

`test` has an alternate form that uses opening and closing square brackets instead a leading '`test`'. For example, instead of '`test -d /`', you can write '`[ -d / ]`'. The square brackets must be separate arguments; for example, '`[-d /]`' does not have the desired effect. Since '`test` *expr*' and '`[` *expr* `]`' have the same meaning, only the former form is discussed below.

Synopses:

```
test expression
test
[ expression ]
[ ]
[ option
```

Due to shell aliases and built-in `test` functions, using an unadorned `test` interactively or in a script may get you different functionality than that described here. Invoke it via `env` (i.e., `env test ...`) to avoid interference from the shell.

If *expression* is omitted, `test` returns false. If *expression* is a single argument, `test` returns false if the argument is null and true otherwise. The argument can be any string, including strings like '`-d`', '`-1`', '`--`', '`--help`', and '`--version`' that most other programs would treat as options. To get help and version information, invoke the commands '`[ --help`' and '`[ --version`', without the usual closing brackets. See Chapter 2 [Common options], page 2.

Exit status:

> 0 if the expression is true,
> 1 if the expression is false,
> 2 if an error occurred.

16.3.1 File type tests

These options test for particular types of files. (Everything's a file, but not all files are the same!)

'`-b` *file*'   True if *file* exists and is a block special device.

'`-c` *file*'   True if *file* exists and is a character special device.

'`-d` *file*'   True if *file* exists and is a directory.

'`-f` *file*'   True if *file* exists and is a regular file.

'`-h` *file*'
'`-L` *file*'   True if *file* exists and is a symbolic link. Unlike all other file-related tests, this test does not dereference *file* if it is a symbolic link.

'`-p` *file*'   True if *file* exists and is a named pipe.

'`-S` *file*'   True if *file* exists and is a socket.

'`-t` *fd*'   True if *fd* is a file descriptor that is associated with a terminal.

16.3.2 Access permission tests

These options test for particular access permissions.

'-g *file*'   True if *file* exists and has its set-group-ID bit set.

'-k *file*'   True if *file* exists and has its *sticky* bit set.

'-r *file*'   True if *file* exists and read permission is granted.

'-u *file*'   True if *file* exists and has its set-user-ID bit set.

'-w *file*'   True if *file* exists and write permission is granted.

'-x *file*'   True if *file* exists and execute permission is granted (or search permission, if it is a directory).

'-O *file*'   True if *file* exists and is owned by the current effective user ID.

'-G *file*'   True if *file* exists and is owned by the current effective group ID.

16.3.3 File characteristic tests

These options test other file characteristics.

'-e *file*'   True if *file* exists.

'-s *file*'   True if *file* exists and has a size greater than zero.

'*file1* -nt *file2*'
> True if *file1* is newer (according to modification date) than *file2*, or if *file1* exists and *file2* does not.

'*file1* -ot *file2*'
> True if *file1* is older (according to modification date) than *file2*, or if *file2* exists and *file1* does not.

'*file1* -ef *file2*'
> True if *file1* and *file2* have the same device and inode numbers, i.e., if they are hard links to each other.

16.3.4 String tests

These options test string characteristics. You may need to quote *string* arguments for the shell. For example:

```
test -n "$V"
```

The quotes here prevent the wrong arguments from being passed to test if '$V' is empty or contains special characters.

'-z *string*'
> True if the length of *string* is zero.

'-n *string*'
'*string*'   True if the length of *string* is nonzero.

'*string1* = *string2*'
> True if the strings are equal.

'*string1* == *string2*'
> True if the strings are equal (synonym for =).

'*string1* != *string2*'
> True if the strings are not equal.

16.3.5 Numeric tests

Numeric relational operators. The arguments must be entirely numeric (possibly negative), or the special expression -l *string*, which evaluates to the length of *string*.

'*arg1* -eq *arg2*'
'*arg1* -ne *arg2*'
'*arg1* -lt *arg2*'
'*arg1* -le *arg2*'
'*arg1* -gt *arg2*'
'*arg1* -ge *arg2*'
> These arithmetic binary operators return true if *arg1* is equal, not-equal, less-than, less-than-or-equal, greater-than, or greater-than-or-equal than *arg2*, respectively.

> For example:
> ```
> test -1 -gt -2 && echo yes
> ⇒ yes
> test -l abc -gt 1 && echo yes
> ⇒ yes
> test 0x100 -eq 1
> ```
> error test: integer expression expected before -eq

16.3.6 Connectives for test

The usual logical connectives.

'! *expr*'   True if *expr* is false.

'*expr1* -a *expr2*'
> True if both *expr1* and *expr2* are true.

'*expr1* -o *expr2*'
> True if either *expr1* or *expr2* is true.

16.4 expr: Evaluate expressions

expr evaluates an expression and writes the result on standard output. Each token of the expression must be a separate argument.

Operands are either integers or strings. Integers consist of one or more decimal digits, with an optional leading '-'. expr converts anything appearing in an operand position to an integer or a string depending on the operation being applied to it.

Strings are not quoted for expr itself, though you may need to quote them to protect characters with special meaning to the shell, e.g., spaces. However, regardless of whether it is quoted, a string operand should not be a parenthesis or any of expr's operators like +, so you cannot safely pass an arbitrary string $str to expr merely by quoting it to the shell. One way to work around this is to use the GNU extension +, (e.g., + "$str" = foo); a more portable way is to use " $str" and to adjust the rest of the expression to take the leading space into account (e.g., " $str" = " foo").

You should not pass a negative integer or a string with leading '-' as expr's first argument, as it might be misinterpreted as an option; this can be avoided by parenthesization. Also, portable scripts should not use a string operand that happens to take the form of an integer; this can be worked around by inserting leading spaces as mentioned above.

Operators may be given as infix symbols or prefix keywords. Parentheses may be used for grouping in the usual manner. You must quote parentheses and many operators to avoid the shell evaluating them, however.

When built with support for the GNU MP library, expr uses arbitrary-precision arithmetic; otherwise, it uses native arithmetic types and may fail due to arithmetic overflow.

The only options are --help and --version. See Chapter 2 [Common options], page 2. Options must precede operands.

Exit status:

> 0 if the expression is neither null nor 0,
> 1 if the expression is null or 0,
> 2 if the expression is invalid,
> 3 if an internal error occurred (e.g., arithmetic overflow).

16.4.1 String expressions

expr supports pattern matching and other string operators. These have higher precedence than both the numeric and relational operators (in the next sections).

'string : regex'

> Perform pattern matching. The arguments are converted to strings and the second is considered to be a (basic, a la GNU grep) regular expression, with a ^ implicitly prepended. The first argument is then matched against this regular expression.
>
> If the match succeeds and regex uses '\(' and '\)', the : expression returns the part of string that matched the subexpression; otherwise, it returns the number of characters matched.
>
> If the match fails, the : operator returns the null string if '\(' and '\)' are used in regex, otherwise 0.
>
> Only the first '\(... \)' pair is relevant to the return value; additional pairs are meaningful only for grouping the regular expression operators.
>
> In the regular expression, \+, \?, and \| are operators which respectively match one or more, zero or one, or separate alternatives. SunOS and other expr's treat these as regular characters. (POSIX allows either behavior.) See Section "Regular Expression Library" in Regex, for details of regular expression syntax. Some examples are in Section 16.4.4 [Examples of expr], page 153.

'match string regex'

> An alternative way to do pattern matching. This is the same as 'string : regex'.

'`substr` *string position length*'

> Returns the substring of *string* beginning at *position* with length at most *length*. If either *position* or *length* is negative, zero, or non-numeric, returns the null string.

'`index` *string charset*'

> Returns the first position in *string* where the first character in *charset* was found. If no character in *charset* is found in *string*, return 0.

'`length` *string*'

> Returns the length of *string*.

'`+` *token*'   Interpret *token* as a string, even if it is a keyword like *match* or an operator like `/`. This makes it possible to test `expr length + "$x"` or `expr + "$x"` : '.*/\(.\)' and have it do the right thing even if the value of *$x* happens to be (for example) `/` or `index`. This operator is a GNU extension. Portable shell scripts should use `" $token"` : `' \(.*\)'` instead of `+ "$token"`.

To make `expr` interpret keywords as strings, you must use the `quote` operator.

16.4.2 Numeric expressions

`expr` supports the usual numeric operators, in order of increasing precedence. These numeric operators have lower precedence than the string operators described in the previous section, and higher precedence than the connectives (next section).

'`+ -`'   Addition and subtraction. Both arguments are converted to integers; an error occurs if this cannot be done.

'`* / %`'   Multiplication, division, remainder. Both arguments are converted to integers; an error occurs if this cannot be done.

16.4.3 Relations for `expr`

`expr` supports the usual logical connectives and relations. These have lower precedence than the string and numeric operators (previous sections). Here is the list, lowest-precedence operator first.

'`|`'   Returns its first argument if that is neither null nor zero, otherwise its second argument if it is neither null nor zero, otherwise 0. It does not evaluate its second argument if its first argument is neither null nor zero.

'`&`'   Return its first argument if neither argument is null or zero, otherwise 0. It does not evaluate its second argument if its first argument is null or zero.

'`< <= = == != >= >`'

> Compare the arguments and return 1 if the relation is true, 0 otherwise. `==` is a synonym for `=`. `expr` first tries to convert both arguments to integers and do a numeric comparison; if either conversion fails, it does a lexicographic comparison using the character collating sequence specified by the `LC_COLLATE` locale.

16.4.4 Examples of using `expr`

Here are a few examples, including quoting for shell metacharacters.

To add 1 to the shell variable `foo`, in Bourne-compatible shells:

```
foo=$(expr $foo + 1)
```

To print the non-directory part of the file name stored in `$fname`, which need not contain a `/`:

```
expr $fname : '.*/\(.*\)' '|' $fname
```

An example showing that `\+` is an operator:

```
expr aaa : 'a\+'
⇒ 3
expr abc : 'a\(.\)c'
⇒ b
expr index abcdef cz
⇒ 3
expr index index a
error  expr: syntax error
expr index + index a
⇒ 0
```

17 Redirection

Unix shells commonly provide several forms of *redirection*—ways to change the input source or output destination of a command. But one useful redirection is performed by a separate command, not by the shell; it's described here.

17.1 `tee`: Redirect output to multiple files or processes

The `tee` command copies standard input to standard output and also to any files given as arguments. This is useful when you want not only to send some data down a pipe, but also to save a copy. Synopsis:

    tee [option]... [file]...

If a file being written to does not already exist, it is created. If a file being written to already exists, the data it previously contained is overwritten unless the `-a` option is used.

In previous versions of GNU coreutils (v5.3.0 - v8.23), a *file* of '-' caused `tee` to send another copy of input to standard output. However, as the interleaved output was not very useful, `tee` now conforms to POSIX which explicitly mandates it to treat '-' as a file with such name.

The program accepts the following options. Also see Chapter 2 [Common options], page 2.

'`-a`'
'`--append`'
> Append standard input to the given files rather than overwriting them.

'`-i`'
'`--ignore-interrupts`'
> Ignore interrupt signals.

'`-p`'
'`--output-error[=mode]`'
> Select the behavior with errors on the outputs, where *mode* is one of the following:
>
> '`warn`'   Warn on error opening or writing any output, including pipes. Writing is continued to still open files/pipes. Exit status indicates failure if any output has an error.
>
> '`warn-nopipe`'
> > Warn on error opening or writing any output, except pipes. Writing is continued to still open files/pipes. Exit status indicates failure if any non pipe output had an error. This is the default *mode* when not specified.
>
> '`exit`'   Exit on error opening or writing any output, including pipes.
>
> '`exit-nopipe`'
> > Exit on error opening or writing any output, except pipes.

The `tee` command is useful when you happen to be transferring a large amount of data and also want to summarize that data without reading it a second time. For example, when you are downloading a DVD image, you often want to verify its signature or checksum right away. The inefficient way to do it is simply:

```
wget http://example.com/some.iso && sha1sum some.iso
```

One problem with the above is that it makes you wait for the download to complete before starting the time-consuming SHA1 computation. Perhaps even more importantly, the above requires reading the DVD image a second time (the first was from the network).

The efficient way to do it is to interleave the download and SHA1 computation. Then, you'll get the checksum for free, because the entire process parallelizes so well:

```
# slightly contrived, to demonstrate process substitution
wget -O - http://example.com/dvd.iso \
  | tee >(sha1sum > dvd.sha1) > dvd.iso
```

That makes **tee** write not just to the expected output file, but also to a pipe running **sha1sum** and saving the final checksum in a file named **dvd.sha1**.

Note, however, that this example relies on a feature of modern shells called *process substitution* (the '>(command)' syntax, above; See Section "Process Substitution" in *The Bash Reference Manual*.), so it works with zsh, bash, and ksh, but not with /bin/sh. So if you write code like this in a shell script, be sure to start the script with '#!/bin/bash'.

Since the above example writes to one file and one process, a more conventional and portable use of **tee** is even better:

```
wget -O - http://example.com/dvd.iso \
  | tee dvd.iso | sha1sum > dvd.sha1
```

You can extend this example to make **tee** write to two processes, computing MD5 and SHA1 checksums in parallel. In this case, process substitution is required:

```
wget -O - http://example.com/dvd.iso \
  | tee >(sha1sum > dvd.sha1) \
        >(md5sum > dvd.md5) \
  > dvd.iso
```

This technique is also useful when you want to make a *compressed* copy of the contents of a pipe. Consider a tool to graphically summarize disk usage data from 'du -ak'. For a large hierarchy, 'du -ak' can run for a long time, and can easily produce terabytes of data, so you won't want to rerun the command unnecessarily. Nor will you want to save the uncompressed output.

Doing it the inefficient way, you can't even start the GUI until after you've compressed all of the **du** output:

```
du -ak | gzip -9 > /tmp/du.gz
gzip -d /tmp/du.gz | xdiskusage -a
```

With **tee** and process substitution, you start the GUI right away and eliminate the decompression completely:

```
du -ak | tee >(gzip -9 > /tmp/du.gz) | xdiskusage -a
```

Finally, if you regularly create more than one type of compressed tarball at once, for example when **make dist** creates both **gzip**-compressed and **bzip2**-compressed tarballs, there may be a better way. Typical **automake**-generated **Makefile** rules create the two compressed tar archives with commands in sequence, like this (slightly simplified):

```
tardir=your-pkg-M.N
tar chof - "$tardir" | gzip  -9 -c > your-pkg-M.N.tar.gz
tar chof - "$tardir" | bzip2 -9 -c > your-pkg-M.N.tar.bz2
```

However, if the hierarchy you are archiving and compressing is larger than a couple megabytes, and especially if you are using a multi-processor system with plenty of memory, then you can do much better by reading the directory contents only once and running the compression programs in parallel:

```
tardir=your-pkg-M.N
tar chof - "$tardir" \
   | tee >(gzip -9 -c > your-pkg-M.N.tar.gz) \
   | bzip2 -9 -c > your-pkg-M.N.tar.bz2
```

An exit status of zero indicates success, and a nonzero value indicates failure.

18 File name manipulation

This section describes commands that manipulate file names.

18.1 basename: Strip directory and suffix from a file name

basename removes any leading directory components from *name*. Synopsis:

```
basename name [suffix]
basename option... name...
```

If *suffix* is specified and is identical to the end of *name*, it is removed from *name* as well. Note that since trailing slashes are removed prior to suffix matching, *suffix* will do nothing if it contains slashes. basename prints the result on standard output.

Together, basename and dirname are designed such that if 'ls "$name"' succeeds, then the command sequence 'cd "$(dirname "$name")"; ls "$(basename "$name")"' will, too. This works for everything except file names containing a trailing newline.

POSIX allows the implementation to define the results if *name* is empty or '//'. In the former case, GNU basename returns the empty string. In the latter case, the result is '//' on platforms where // is distinct from /, and '/' on platforms where there is no difference.

The program accepts the following options. Also see Chapter 2 [Common options], page 2. Options must precede operands.

'-a'
'--multiple'

> Support more than one argument. Treat every argument as a *name*. With this, an optional *suffix* must be specified using the -s option.

'-s suffix'
'--suffix=suffix'

> Remove a trailing *suffix*. This option implies the -a option.

'-z'
'--zero'   Output a zero byte (ASCII NUL) at the end of each line, rather than a newline. This option enables other programs to parse the output even when that output would contain data with embedded newlines.

An exit status of zero indicates success, and a nonzero value indicates failure.

Examples:

```
# Output "sort".
basename /usr/bin/sort

# Output "stdio".
basename include/stdio.h .h

# Output "stdio".
basename -s .h include/stdio.h

# Output "stdio" followed by "stdlib"
basename -a -s .h include/stdio.h include/stdlib.h
```

18.2 dirname: Strip last file name component

dirname prints all but the final slash-delimited component of each *name*. Slashes on either side of the final component are also removed. If the string contains no slash, dirname prints '.' (meaning the current directory). Synopsis:

    dirname [option] name...

name need not be a file name, but if it is, this operation effectively lists the directory that contains the final component, including the case when the final component is itself a directory.

Together, basename and dirname are designed such that if 'ls "$name"' succeeds, then the command sequence 'cd "$(dirname "$name")"; ls "$(basename "$name")"' will, too. This works for everything except file names containing a trailing newline.

POSIX allows the implementation to define the results if *name* is '//'. With GNU dirname, the result is '//' on platforms where // is distinct from /, and '/' on platforms where there is no difference.

The program accepts the following option. Also see Chapter 2 [Common options], page 2.

'-z'
'--zero'   Output a zero byte (ASCII NUL) at the end of each line, rather than a newline. This option enables other programs to parse the output even when that output would contain data with embedded newlines.

An exit status of zero indicates success, and a nonzero value indicates failure.

Examples:

    # Output "/usr/bin".
    dirname /usr/bin/sort
    dirname /usr/bin//.//

    # Output "dir1" followed by "dir2"
    dirname dir1/str dir2/str

    # Output ".".
    dirname stdio.h

18.3 pathchk: Check file name validity and portability

pathchk checks validity and portability of file names. Synopsis:

    pathchk [option]... name...

For each *name*, pathchk prints an error message if any of these conditions is true:

1. One of the existing directories in *name* does not have search (execute) permission,

2. The length of *name* is larger than the maximum supported by the operating system.

3. The length of one component of *name* is longer than its file system's maximum.

A nonexistent *name* is not an error, so long a file with that name could be created under the above conditions.

The program accepts the following options. Also see Chapter 2 [Common options], page 2. Options must precede operands.

'-p'   Instead of performing checks based on the underlying file system, print an error
                message if any of these conditions is true:

                1. A file name is empty.

                2. A file name contains a character outside the POSIX portable file name
                   character set, namely, the ASCII letters and digits, '.', '_', '-', and '/'.

                3. The length of a file name or one of its components exceeds the POSIX
                   minimum limits for portability.

'-P'   Print an error message if a file name is empty, or if it contains a component
                that begins with '-'.

'--portability'
                Print an error message if a file name is not portable to all POSIX hosts. This
                option is equivalent to '-p -P'.

      Exit status:

         0 if all specified file names passed all checks,
         1 otherwise.

18.4 mktemp: Create temporary file or directory

mktemp manages the creation of temporary files and directories. Synopsis:

         mktemp [option]... [template]

Safely create a temporary file or directory based on *template*, and print its name. If given,
template must include at least three consecutive 'X's in the last component. If omitted, the
template 'tmp.XXXXXXXXXX' is used, and option --tmpdir is implied. The final run of 'X's
in the *template* will be replaced by alpha-numeric characters; thus, on a case-sensitive file
system, and with a *template* including a run of n instances of 'X', there are '62**n' potential
file names.

Older scripts used to create temporary files by simply joining the name of the program
with the process id ('$$') as a suffix. However, that naming scheme is easily predictable,
and suffers from a race condition where the attacker can create an appropriately named
symbolic link, such that when the script then opens a handle to what it thought was an
unused file, it is instead modifying an existing file. Using the same scheme to create a
directory is slightly safer, since the mkdir will fail if the target already exists, but it is still
inferior because it allows for denial of service attacks. Therefore, modern scripts should use
the mktemp command to guarantee that the generated name will be unpredictable, and that
knowledge of the temporary file name implies that the file was created by the current script
and cannot be modified by other users.

When creating a file, the resulting file has read and write permissions for the current
user, but no permissions for the group or others; these permissions are reduced if the current
umask is more restrictive.

Here are some examples (although note that if you repeat them, you will most likely get
different file names):

• Create a temporary file in the current directory.

         $ mktemp file.XXXX
         file.H47c

- Create a temporary file with a known suffix.

  ```
  $ mktemp --suffix=.txt file-XXXX
  file-H08W.txt
  $ mktemp file-XXXX-XXXX.txt
  file-XXXX-eI9L.txt
  ```

- Create a secure fifo relative to the user's choice of TMPDIR, but falling back to the current directory rather than /tmp. Note that mktemp does not create fifos, but can create a secure directory in which the fifo can live. Exit the shell if the directory or fifo could not be created.

  ```
  $ dir=$(mktemp -p "${TMPDIR:-.}" -d dir-XXXX) || exit 1
  $ fifo=$dir/fifo
  $ mkfifo "$fifo" || { rmdir "$dir"; exit 1; }
  ```

- Create and use a temporary file if possible, but ignore failure. The file will reside in the directory named by TMPDIR, if specified, or else in /tmp.

  ```
  $ file=$(mktemp -q) && {
  >     # Safe to use $file only within this block.  Use quotes,
  >     # since $TMPDIR, and thus $file, may contain whitespace.
  >     echo ... > "$file"
  >     rm "$file"
  > }
  ```

- Act as a semi-random character generator (it is not fully random, since it is impacted by the contents of the current directory). To avoid security holes, do not use the resulting names to create a file.

  ```
  $ mktemp -u XXX
  Gb9
  $ mktemp -u XXX
  nzC
  ```

The program accepts the following options. Also see Chapter 2 [Common options], page 2.

'-d'
'--directory'
> Create a directory rather than a file. The directory will have read, write, and search permissions for the current user, but no permissions for the group or others; these permissions are reduced if the current umask is more restrictive.

'-q'
'--quiet' Suppress diagnostics about failure to create a file or directory. The exit status will still reflect whether a file was created.

'-u'
'--dry-run'
> Generate a temporary name that does not name an existing file, without changing the file system contents. Using the output of this command to create a new file is inherently unsafe, as there is a window of time between generating the name and using it where another process can create an object by the same name.

'-p *dir*'
'--tmpdir[=*dir*]'

> Treat *template* relative to the directory *dir*. If *dir* is not specified (only possible with the long option --tmpdir) or is the empty string, use the value of TMPDIR if available, otherwise use '/tmp'. If this is specified, *template* must not be absolute. However, *template* can still contain slashes, although intermediate directories must already exist.

'--suffix=*suffix*'

> Append *suffix* to the *template*. *suffix* must not contain slash. If --suffix is specified, *template* must end in 'X'; if it is not specified, then an appropriate --suffix is inferred by finding the last 'X' in *template*. This option exists for use with the default *template* and for the creation of a *suffix* that starts with 'X'.

'-t'

> Treat *template* as a single file relative to the value of TMPDIR if available, or to the directory specified by -p, otherwise to '/tmp'. *template* must not contain slashes. This option is deprecated; the use of -p without -t offers better defaults (by favoring the command line over TMPDIR) and more flexibility (by allowing intermediate directories).

Exit status:

> 0 if the file was created,
> 1 otherwise.

18.5 realpath: Print the resolved file name.

realpath expands all symbolic links and resolves references to './', '/../' and extra '/' characters. By default, all but the last component of the specified files must exist. Synopsis:

    realpath [*option*]... *file*...

The program accepts the following options. Also see Chapter 2 [Common options], page 2.

'-e'
'--canonicalize-existing'

> Ensure that all components of the specified file names exist. If any component is missing or unavailable, realpath will output a diagnostic unless the -q option is specified, and exit with a nonzero exit code. A trailing slash requires that the name resolve to a directory.

'-m'
'--canonicalize-missing'

> If any component of a specified file name is missing or unavailable, treat it as a directory.

'-L'
'--logical'

> Symbolic links are resolved in the specified file names, but they are resolved after any subsequent '..' components are processed.

'-p'

'--physical'

>   Symbolic links are resolved in the specified file names, and they are resolved
>   before any subsequent '..' components are processed. This is the default mode
>   of operation.

'-q'

'--quiet'   Suppress diagnostic messages for specified file names.

'--relative-to=*file*'

>   Print the resolved file names relative to the specified file. Note this option
>   honors the -m and -e options pertaining to file existence.

'--relative-base=*base*'

>   This option is valid when used with --relative-to, and will restrict the output
>   of --relative-to so that relative names are output, only when *files* are de-
>   scendants of *base*. Otherwise output the absolute file name. If --relative-to
>   was not specified, then the descendants of *base* are printed relative to *base*. If
>   --relative-to is specified, then that directory must be a descendant of *base*
>   for this option to have an effect. Note: this option honors the -m and -e options
>   pertaining to file existence. For example:

```
          realpath --relative-to=/usr /tmp /usr/bin
          ⇒ ../tmp
          ⇒ bin
          realpath --relative-base=/usr /tmp /usr/bin
          ⇒ /tmp
          ⇒ bin
```

'-s'

'--strip'

'--no-symlinks'

>   Do not resolve symbolic links. Only resolve references to '/./', '/../' and
>   remove extra '/' characters. When combined with the -m option, realpath
>   operates only on the file name, and does not touch any actual file.

'-z'

'--zero'   Output a zero byte (ASCII NUL) at the end of each line, rather than a newline.
>   This option enables other programs to parse the output even when that output
>   would contain data with embedded newlines.

Exit status:

>   0 if all file names were printed without issue.
>   1 otherwise.

19 Working context

This section describes commands that display or alter the context in which you are working: the current directory, the terminal settings, and so forth. See also the user-related commands in the next section.

19.1 `pwd`: Print working directory

`pwd` prints the name of the current directory. Synopsis:

    pwd [option]...

The program accepts the following options. Also see Chapter 2 [Common options], page 2.

'`-L`'
'`--logical`'

> If the contents of the environment variable `PWD` provide an absolute name of the current directory with no '.' or '..' components, but possibly with symbolic links, then output those contents. Otherwise, fall back to default `-P` handling.

'`-P`'
'`--physical`'

> Print a fully resolved name for the current directory. That is, all components of the printed name will be actual directory names—none will be symbolic links.

If `-L` and `-P` are both given, the last one takes precedence. If neither option is given, then this implementation uses `-P` as the default unless the `POSIXLY_CORRECT` environment variable is set.

Due to shell aliases and built-in `pwd` functions, using an unadorned `pwd` interactively or in a script may get you different functionality than that described here. Invoke it via `env` (i.e., `env pwd ...`) to avoid interference from the shell.

An exit status of zero indicates success, and a nonzero value indicates failure.

19.2 `stty`: Print or change terminal characteristics

`stty` prints or changes terminal characteristics, such as baud rate. Synopses:

    stty [option] [setting]...
    stty [option]

If given no line settings, `stty` prints the baud rate, line discipline number (on systems that support it), and line settings that have been changed from the values set by '`stty sane`'. By default, mode reading and setting are performed on the tty line connected to standard input, although this can be modified by the `--file` option.

`stty` accepts many non-option arguments that change aspects of the terminal line operation, as described below.

The program accepts the following options. Also see Chapter 2 [Common options], page 2.

'`-a`'
'`--all`'   Print all current settings in human-readable form. This option may not be used in combination with any line settings.

'`-F` *device*'
'`--file=`*device*'

> Set the line opened by the file name specified in *device* instead of the tty line connected to standard input. This option is necessary because opening a POSIX tty requires use of the `O_NONDELAY` flag to prevent a POSIX tty from blocking until the carrier detect line is high if the `clocal` flag is not set. Hence, it is not always possible to allow the shell to open the device in the traditional manner.

'`-g`'
'`--save`'   Print all current settings in a form that can be used as an argument to another `stty` command to restore the current settings. This option may not be used in combination with any line settings.

Many settings can be turned off by preceding them with a '`-`'. Such arguments are marked below with "May be negated" in their description. The descriptions themselves refer to the positive case, that is, when *not* negated (unless stated otherwise, of course).

Some settings are not available on all POSIX systems, since they use extensions. Such arguments are marked below with "Non-POSIX" in their description. On non-POSIX systems, those or other settings also may not be available, but it's not feasible to document all the variations: just try it and see.

`stty` is installed only on platforms with the POSIX terminal interface, so portable scripts should not rely on its existence on non-POSIX platforms.

An exit status of zero indicates success, and a nonzero value indicates failure.

19.2.1 Control settings

Control settings:

'`parenb`'   Generate parity bit in output and expect parity bit in input. May be negated.

'`parodd`'   Set odd parity (even if negated). May be negated.

'`cmspar`'   Use "stick" (mark/space) parity. If parodd is set, the parity bit is always 1; if parodd is not set, the parity bit is always zero. Non-POSIX. May be negated.

'`cs5`'
'`cs6`'
'`cs7`'
'`cs8`'   Set character size to 5, 6, 7, or 8 bits.

'`hup`'
'`hupcl`'   Send a hangup signal when the last process closes the tty. May be negated.

'`cstopb`'   Use two stop bits per character (one if negated). May be negated.

'`cread`'   Allow input to be received. May be negated.

'`clocal`'   Disable modem control signals. May be negated.

'`crtscts`'   Enable RTS/CTS flow control. Non-POSIX. May be negated.

'`cdtrdsr`'   Enable DTR/DSR flow control. Non-POSIX. May be negated.

19.2.2 Input settings

These settings control operations on data received from the terminal.

'ignbrk'   Ignore break characters. May be negated.

'brkint'   Make breaks cause an interrupt signal. May be negated.

'ignpar'   Ignore characters with parity errors. May be negated.

'parmrk'   Mark parity errors (with a 255 0-character sequence). May be negated.

'inpck'   Enable input parity checking. May be negated.

'istrip'   Clear high (8th) bit of input characters. May be negated.

'inlcr'   Translate newline to carriage return. May be negated.

'igncr'   Ignore carriage return. May be negated.

'icrnl'   Translate carriage return to newline. May be negated.

'iutf8'   Assume input characters are UTF-8 encoded. May be negated.

'ixon'   Enable XON/XOFF flow control (that is, *Ctrl-S*/*Ctrl-Q*). May be negated.

'ixoff'
'tandem'   Enable sending of **stop** character when the system input buffer is almost full, and **start** character when it becomes almost empty again. May be negated.

'iuclc'   Translate uppercase characters to lowercase. Non-POSIX. May be negated. Note ilcuc is not implemented, as one would not be able to issue almost any (lowercase) Unix command, after invoking it.

'ixany'   Allow any character to restart output (only the start character if negated). Non-POSIX. May be negated.

'imaxbel' Enable beeping and not flushing input buffer if a character arrives when the input buffer is full. Non-POSIX. May be negated.

19.2.3 Output settings

These settings control operations on data sent to the terminal.

'opost'   Postprocess output. May be negated.

'olcuc'   Translate lowercase characters to uppercase. Non-POSIX. May be negated. (Note ouclc is not currently implemented.)

'ocrnl'   Translate carriage return to newline. Non-POSIX. May be negated.

'onlcr'   Translate newline to carriage return-newline. Non-POSIX. May be negated.

'onocr'   Do not print carriage returns in the first column. Non-POSIX. May be negated.

'onlret'   Newline performs a carriage return. Non-POSIX. May be negated.

'ofill'   Use fill (padding) characters instead of timing for delays. Non-POSIX. May be negated.

'ofdel'   Use ASCII DEL characters for fill instead of ASCII NUL characters. Non-POSIX. May be negated.

'nl1'
'nl0'   Newline delay style. Non-POSIX.

'cr3'
'cr2'
'cr1'
'cr0'   Carriage return delay style. Non-POSIX.

'tab3'
'tab2'
'tab1'
'tab0'   Horizontal tab delay style. Non-POSIX.

'bs1'
'bs0'   Backspace delay style. Non-POSIX.

'vt1'
'vt0'   Vertical tab delay style. Non-POSIX.

'ff1'
'ff0'   Form feed delay style. Non-POSIX.

19.2.4 Local settings

'isig'   Enable `interrupt`, `quit`, and `suspend` special characters. May be negated.

'icanon'   Enable `erase`, `kill`, `werase`, and `rprnt` special characters. May be negated.

'iexten'   Enable non-POSIX special characters. May be negated.

'echo'   Echo input characters. May be negated.

'echoe'
'crterase'
               Echo `erase` characters as backspace-space-backspace. May be negated.

'echok'   Echo a newline after a `kill` character. May be negated.

'echonl'   Echo newline even if not echoing other characters. May be negated.

'noflsh'   Disable flushing after `interrupt` and `quit` special characters. May be negated.

'xcase'   Enable input and output of uppercase characters by preceding their lowercase
               equivalents with '\', when `icanon` is set. Non-POSIX. May be negated.

'tostop'   Stop background jobs that try to write to the terminal. Non-POSIX. May be
               negated.

'echoprt'
'prterase'
               Echo erased characters backward, between '\' and '/'. Non-POSIX. May be
               negated.

'echoctl'
'ctlecho'   Echo control characters in hat notation ('^c') instead of literally. Non-POSIX.
               May be negated.

'echoke'

'crtkill'   Echo the kill special character by erasing each character on the line as indi-
              cated by the echoprt and echoe settings, instead of by the echoctl and echok
              settings. Non-POSIX. May be negated.

'extproc'   Enable 'LINEMODE', which is used to avoid echoing each character over high
              latency links. See also Internet RFC 1116. Non-POSIX. May be negated.

19.2.5 Combination settings

Combination settings:

'evenp'

'parity'   Same as parenb -parodd cs7. May be negated. If negated, same as -parenb
              cs8.

'oddp'   Same as parenb parodd cs7. May be negated. If negated, same as -parenb
              cs8.

'nl'   Same as -icrnl -onlcr. May be negated. If negated, same as icrnl -inlcr
              -igncr onlcr -ocrnl -onlret.

'ek'   Reset the erase and kill special characters to their default values.

'sane'   Same as:

```
              cread -ignbrk brkint -inlcr -igncr icrnl
              icanon iexten echo echoe echok -echonl -noflsh
              -ixoff -iutf8 -iuclc -ixany imaxbel -xcase -olcuc -ocrnl
              opost -ofill onlcr -onocr -onlret nl0 cr0 tab0 bs0 vt0 ff0
              isig -tostop -ofdel -echoprt echoctl echoke -extproc
```

              and also sets all special characters to their default values.

'cooked'   Same as brkint ignpar istrip icrnl ixon opost isig icanon, plus sets the
              eof and eol characters to their default values if they are the same as the min
              and time characters. May be negated. If negated, same as raw.

'raw'   Same as:

```
              -ignbrk -brkint -ignpar -parmrk -inpck -istrip
              -inlcr -igncr -icrnl -ixon -ixoff -icanon -opost
              -isig -iuclc -ixany -imaxbel -xcase min 1 time 0
```

              May be negated. If negated, same as cooked.

'cbreak'   Same as -icanon. May be negated. If negated, same as icanon.

'pass8'   Same as -parenb -istrip cs8. May be negated. If negated, same as parenb
              istrip cs7.

'litout'   Same as -parenb -istrip -opost cs8. May be negated. If negated, same as
              parenb istrip opost cs7.

'decctlq'   Same as -ixany. Non-POSIX. May be negated.

'tabs'   Same as tab0. Non-POSIX. May be negated. If negated, same as tab3.

'lcase'

'LCASE'   Same as `xcase iuclc olcuc`. Non-POSIX. May be negated. (Used for termi-
               nals with uppercase characters only.)

'crt'   Same as `echoe echoctl echoke`.

'dec'   Same as `echoe echoctl echoke -ixany intr ^C erase ^? kill C-u`.

19.2.6 Special characters

The special characters' default values vary from system to system. They are set with the
syntax '`name value`', where the names are listed below and the value can be given either
literally, in hat notation ('`^c`'), or as an integer which may start with '`0x`' to indicate
hexadecimal, '`0`' to indicate octal, or any other digit to indicate decimal.

For GNU stty, giving a value of `^-` or `undef` disables that special character. (This is
incompatible with Ultrix `stty`, which uses a value of '`u`' to disable a special character. GNU
`stty` treats a value '`u`' like any other, namely to set that special character to `U`.)

'intr'   Send an interrupt signal.

'quit'   Send a quit signal.

'erase'   Erase the last character typed.

'kill'   Erase the current line.

'eof'   Send an end of file (terminate the input).

'eol'   End the line.

'eol2'   Alternate character to end the line. Non-POSIX.

'discard'   Alternate character to toggle discarding of output. Non-POSIX.

'swtch'   Switch to a different shell layer. Non-POSIX.

'status'   Send an info signal. Not currently supported on Linux. Non-POSIX.

'start'   Restart the output after stopping it.

'stop'   Stop the output.

'susp'   Send a terminal stop signal.

'dsusp'   Send a terminal stop signal after flushing the input. Non-POSIX.

'rprnt'   Redraw the current line. Non-POSIX.

'werase'   Erase the last word typed. Non-POSIX.

'lnext'   Enter the next character typed literally, even if it is a special character. Non-
               POSIX.

19.2.7 Special settings

'min n'   Set the minimum number of characters that will satisfy a read until the time
               value has expired, when `-icanon` is set.

'time n'   Set the number of tenths of a second before reads time out if the minimum
               number of characters have not been read, when `-icanon` is set.

'`ispeed `*`n`*' Set the input speed to *n*.

'`ospeed `*`n`*' Set the output speed to *n*.

'`rows `*`n`*'   Tell the tty kernel driver that the terminal has *n* rows. Non-POSIX.

'`cols `*`n`*'
'`columns `*`n`*'
               Tell the kernel that the terminal has *n* columns. Non-POSIX.

'`size`'   Print the number of rows and columns that the kernel thinks the terminal has. (Systems that don't support rows and columns in the kernel typically use the environment variables `LINES` and `COLUMNS` instead; however, GNU `stty` does not know anything about them.) Non-POSIX.

'`line `*`n`*'   Use line discipline *n*. Non-POSIX.

'`speed`'   Print the terminal speed.

'*`n`*'   Set the input and output speeds to *n*. *n* can be one of: 0 50 75 110 134 134.5 150 200 300 600 1200 1800 2400 4800 9600 19200 38400 `exta extb`. `exta` is the same as 19200; `extb` is the same as 38400. Many systems, including GNU/Linux, support higher speeds. The `stty` command includes support for speeds of 57600, 115200, 230400, 460800, 500000, 576000, 921600, 1000000, 1152000, 1500000, 2000000, 2500000, 3000000, 3500000, or 4000000 where the system supports these. 0 hangs up the line if `-clocal` is set.

19.3 `printenv`: Print all or some environment variables

`printenv` prints environment variable values. Synopsis:

>   printenv [*option*] [*variable*]...

If no *variable*s are specified, `printenv` prints the value of every environment variable. Otherwise, it prints the value of each *variable* that is set, and nothing for those that are not set.

The program accepts the following option. Also see Chapter 2 [Common options], page 2.

'`-0`'
'`--null`'   Output a zero byte (ASCII NUL) at the end of each line, rather than a newline. This option enables other programs to parse the output even when that output would contain data with embedded newlines.

Exit status:

>   0 if all variables specified were found
>   1 if at least one specified variable was not found
>   2 if a write error occurred

19.4 `tty`: Print file name of terminal on standard input

`tty` prints the file name of the terminal connected to its standard input. It prints '`not a tty`' if standard input is not a terminal. Synopsis:

>   tty [*option*]...

The program accepts the following option. Also see Chapter 2 [Common options], page 2.

'`-s`'
'`--silent`'
'`--quiet`' Print nothing; only return an exit status.

> Exit status:
>
> > 0 if standard input is a terminal
> > 1 if standard input is not a terminal
> > 2 if given incorrect arguments
> > 3 if a write error occurs

20 User information

This section describes commands that print user-related information: logins, groups, and so forth.

20.1 `id`: Print user identity

`id` prints information about the given user, or the process running it if no user is specified. Synopsis:

    id [option]... [user]

user can be either a user ID or a name, with name look-up taking precedence unless the ID is specified with a leading '+'. See Section 2.6 [Disambiguating names and IDs], page 7.

By default, it prints the real user ID, real group ID, effective user ID if different from the real user ID, effective group ID if different from the real group ID, and supplemental group IDs. In addition, if SELinux is enabled and the `POSIXLY_CORRECT` environment variable is not set, then print 'context=c', where *c* is the security context.

Each of these numeric values is preceded by an identifying string and followed by the corresponding user or group name in parentheses.

The options cause `id` to print only part of the above information. Also see Chapter 2 [Common options], page 2.

'-g'
'--group'   Print only the group ID.

'-G'
'--groups'
            Print only the group ID and the supplementary groups.

'-n'
'--name'   Print the user or group name instead of the ID number. Requires -u, -g, or -G.

'-r'
'--real'   Print the real, instead of effective, user or group ID. Requires -u, -g, or -G.

'-u'
'--user'   Print only the user ID.

'-Z'
'--context'
            Print only the security context of the process, which is generally the user's security context inherited from the parent process. If neither SELinux or SMACK is enabled then print a warning and set the exit status to 1.

'-z'
'--zero'   Delimit output items with NUL characters. This option is not permitted when using the default format.

            Example:

                $ id -Gn --zero
                users <NUL> devs <NUL>

Primary and supplementary groups for a process are normally inherited from its parent and are usually unchanged since login. This means that if you change the group database after logging in, `id` will not reflect your changes within your existing login session. Running `id` with a user argument causes the user and group database to be consulted afresh, and so will give a different result.

An exit status of zero indicates success, and a nonzero value indicates failure.

20.2 `logname`: Print current login name

`logname` prints the calling user's name, as found in a system-maintained file (often `/var/run/utmp` or `/etc/utmp`), and exits with a status of 0. If there is no entry for the calling process, `logname` prints an error message and exits with a status of 1.

The only options are `--help` and `--version`. See Chapter 2 [Common options], page 2.

An exit status of zero indicates success, and a nonzero value indicates failure.

20.3 `whoami`: Print effective user ID

`whoami` prints the user name associated with the current effective user ID. It is equivalent to the command '`id -un`'.

The only options are `--help` and `--version`. See Chapter 2 [Common options], page 2.

An exit status of zero indicates success, and a nonzero value indicates failure.

20.4 `groups`: Print group names a user is in

`groups` prints the names of the primary and any supplementary groups for each given *username*, or the current process if no names are given. If more than one name is given, the name of each user is printed before the list of that user's groups and the user name is separated from the group list by a colon. Synopsis:

```
groups [username]...
```

The group lists are equivalent to the output of the command '`id -Gn`'.

The only options are `--help` and `--version`. See Chapter 2 [Common options], page 2.

Primary and supplementary groups for a process are normally inherited from its parent and are usually unchanged since login. This means that if you change the group database after logging in, `groups` will not reflect your changes within your existing login session. Running `groups` with a list of users causes the user and group database to be consulted afresh, and so will give a different result.

An exit status of zero indicates success, and a nonzero value indicates failure.

20.5 `users`: Print login names of users currently logged in

`users` prints on a single line a blank-separated list of user names of users currently logged in to the current host. Each user name corresponds to a login session, so if a user has more than one login session, that user's name will appear the same number of times in the output. Synopsis:

```
users [file]
```

With no *file* argument, `users` extracts its information from a system-maintained file (often `/var/run/utmp` or `/etc/utmp`). If a file argument is given, `users` uses that file instead. A common choice is `/var/log/wtmp`.

The only options are `--help` and `--version`. See Chapter 2 [Common options], page 2.

The `users` command is installed only on platforms with the POSIX `<utmpx.h>` include file or equivalent, so portable scripts should not rely on its existence on non-POSIX platforms.

An exit status of zero indicates success, and a nonzero value indicates failure.

20.6 `who`: Print who is currently logged in

`who` prints information about users who are currently logged on. Synopsis:

```
who [option] [file] [am i]
```

If given no non-option arguments, `who` prints the following information for each user currently logged on: login name, terminal line, login time, and remote hostname or X display.

If given one non-option argument, `who` uses that instead of a default system-maintained file (often `/var/run/utmp` or `/etc/utmp`) as the name of the file containing the record of users logged on. `/var/log/wtmp` is commonly given as an argument to `who` to look at who has previously logged on.

If given two non-option arguments, `who` prints only the entry for the user running it (determined from its standard input), preceded by the hostname. Traditionally, the two arguments given are 'am i', as in 'who am i'.

Time stamps are listed according to the time zone rules specified by the `TZ` environment variable, or by the system default rules if `TZ` is not set. See Section "Specifying the Time Zone with TZ" in *The GNU C Library Reference Manual*.

The program accepts the following options. Also see Chapter 2 [Common options], page 2.

'-a'
'--all'   Same as '-b -d --login -p -r -t -T -u'.

'-b'
'--boot'   Print the date and time of last system boot.

'-d'
'--dead'   Print information corresponding to dead processes.

'-H'
'--heading'
             Print a line of column headings.

'-l'
'--login'   List only the entries that correspond to processes via which the system is waiting for a user to login. The user name is always 'LOGIN'.

'--lookup'
             Attempt to canonicalize hostnames found in utmp through a DNS lookup. This is not the default because it can cause significant delays on systems with automatic dial-up internet access.

'-m'   Same as 'who am i'.

'-p'
'--process'
          List active processes spawned by init.

'-q'
'--count'   Print only the login names and the number of users logged on. Overrides all
          other options.

'-r'
'--runlevel'
          Print the current (and maybe previous) run-level of the init process.

'-s'   Ignored; for compatibility with other versions of **who**.

'-t'
'--time'   Print last system clock change.

'-u'   After the login time, print the number of hours and minutes that the user has
          been idle. '.' means the user was active in the last minute. 'old' means the
          user has been idle for more than 24 hours.

'-w'
'-T'
'--mesg'
'--message'
'--writable'
          After each login name print a character indicating the user's message status:

                    '+' allowing **write** messages
                    '−' disallowing **write** messages
                    '?' cannot find terminal device

The **who** command is installed only on platforms with the POSIX `<utmpx.h>` include file
or equivalent, so portable scripts should not rely on its existence on non-POSIX platforms.

An exit status of zero indicates success, and a nonzero value indicates failure.

21 System context

This section describes commands that print or change system-wide information.

21.1 date: Print or set system date and time

Synopses:

```
date [option]... [+format]
date [-u|--utc|--universal] [ MMDDhhmm[[CC]YY][.ss] ]
```

Invoking **date** with no *format* argument is equivalent to invoking it with a default format that depends on the LC_TIME locale category. In the default C locale, this format is ''+%a %b %e %H:%M:%S %Z %Y'', so the output looks like 'Thu Mar 3 13:47:51 PST 2005'.

Normally, **date** uses the time zone rules indicated by the TZ environment variable, or the system default rules if TZ is not set. See Section "Specifying the Time Zone with TZ" in *The GNU C Library Reference Manual*.

If given an argument that starts with a '+', **date** prints the current date and time (or the date and time specified by the **--date** option, see below) in the format defined by that argument, which is similar to that of the **strftime** function. Except for conversion specifiers, which start with '%', characters in the format string are printed unchanged. The conversion specifiers are described below.

An exit status of zero indicates success, and a nonzero value indicates failure.

21.1.1 Time conversion specifiers

date conversion specifiers related to times.

'%H'   hour ('00'...'23')

'%I'   hour ('01'...'12')

'%k'   hour, space padded (' 0'...'23'); equivalent to '%_H'. This is a GNU extension.

'%l'   hour, space padded (' 1'...'12'); equivalent to '%_I'. This is a GNU extension.

'%M'   minute ('00'...'59')

'%N'   nanoseconds ('000000000'...'999999999'). This is a GNU extension.

'%p'   locale's equivalent of either 'AM' or 'PM'; blank in many locales. Noon is treated as 'PM' and midnight as 'AM'.

'%P'   like '%p', except lower case. This is a GNU extension.

'%r'   locale's 12-hour clock time (e.g., '11:11:04 PM')

'%R'   24-hour hour and minute. Same as '%H:%M'.

'%s'   seconds since the epoch, i.e., since 1970-01-01 00:00:00 UTC. Leap seconds are not counted unless leap second support is available. See [%s-examples], page 181, for examples. This is a GNU extension.

'%S'   second ('00'...'60'). This may be '60' if leap seconds are supported.

'%T'   24-hour hour, minute, and second. Same as '%H:%M:%S'.

'%X'   locale's time representation (e.g., '23:13:48')

'%z'   RFC 2822/ISO 8601 style numeric time zone (e.g., '-0600' or '+0530'), or noth-
              ing if no time zone is determinable. This value reflects the numeric time zone
              appropriate for the current time, using the time zone rules specified by the TZ
              environment variable. The time (and optionally, the time zone rules) can be
              overridden by the --date option.

'%:z'   RFC 3339/ISO 8601 style numeric time zone with ':' (e.g., '-06:00' or
              '+05:30'), or nothing if no time zone is determinable. This is a GNU extension.

'%::z'   Numeric time zone to the nearest second with ':' (e.g., '-06:00:00' or
              '+05:30:00'), or nothing if no time zone is determinable. This is a GNU
              extension.

'%:::z'   Numeric time zone with ':' using the minimum necessary precision (e.g., '-06',
              '+05:30', or '-04:56:02'), or nothing if no time zone is determinable. This is
              a GNU extension.

'%Z'   alphabetic time zone abbreviation (e.g., 'EDT'), or nothing if no time zone is
              determinable. See '%z' for how it is determined.

21.1.2 Date conversion specifiers

date conversion specifiers related to dates.

'%a'   locale's abbreviated weekday name (e.g., 'Sun')

'%A'   locale's full weekday name, variable length (e.g., 'Sunday')

'%b'   locale's abbreviated month name (e.g., 'Jan')

'%B'   locale's full month name, variable length (e.g., 'January')

'%c'   locale's date and time (e.g., 'Thu Mar 3 23:05:25 2005')

'%C'   century. This is like '%Y', except the last two digits are omitted. For example,
              it is '20' if '%Y' is '2000', and is '-0' if '%Y' is '-001'. It is normally at least two
              characters, but it may be more.

'%d'   day of month (e.g., '01')

'%D'   date; same as '%m/%d/%y'

'%e'   day of month, space padded; same as '%_d'

'%F'   full date in ISO 8601 format; same as '%Y-%m-%d'. This is a good choice for a
              date format, as it is standard and is easy to sort in the usual case where years
              are in the range 0000...9999.

'%g'   year corresponding to the ISO week number, but without the century (range
              '00' through '99'). This has the same format and value as '%y', except that if
              the ISO week number (see '%V') belongs to the previous or next year, that year
              is used instead.

'%G'   year corresponding to the ISO week number. This has the same format and
              value as '%Y', except that if the ISO week number (see '%V') belongs to the

previous or next year, that year is used instead. It is normally useful only if '%V' is also used; for example, the format '%G-%m-%d' is probably a mistake, since it combines the ISO week number year with the conventional month and day.

'%h'   same as '%b'

'%j'   day of year ('001'...'366')

'%m'   month ('01'...'12')

'%u'   day of week ('1'...'7') with '1' corresponding to Monday

'%U'   week number of year, with Sunday as the first day of the week ('00'...'53'). Days in a new year preceding the first Sunday are in week zero.

'%V'   ISO week number, that is, the week number of year, with Monday as the first day of the week ('01'...'53'). If the week containing January 1 has four or more days in the new year, then it is considered week 1; otherwise, it is week 53 of the previous year, and the next week is week 1. (See the ISO 8601 standard.)

'%w'   day of week ('0'...'6') with 0 corresponding to Sunday

'%W'   week number of year, with Monday as first day of week ('00'...'53'). Days in a new year preceding the first Monday are in week zero.

'%x'   locale's date representation (e.g., '12/31/99')

'%y'   last two digits of year ('00'...'99')

'%Y'   year. This is normally at least four characters, but it may be more. Year '0000' precedes year '0001', and year '-001' precedes year '0000'.

21.1.3 Literal conversion specifiers

date conversion specifiers that produce literal strings.

'%%'   a literal %

'%n'   a newline

'%t'   a horizontal tab

21.1.4 Padding and other flags

Unless otherwise specified, date normally pads numeric fields with zeros, so that, for example, numeric months are always output as two digits. Seconds since the epoch are not padded, though, since there is no natural width for them.

As a GNU extension, date recognizes any of the following optional flags after the '%':

'-'   (hyphen) Do not pad the field; useful if the output is intended for human consumption.

'_'   (underscore) Pad with spaces; useful if you need a fixed number of characters in the output, but zeros are too distracting.

'0'   (zero) Pad with zeros even if the conversion specifier would normally pad with spaces.

'^'   Use upper case characters if possible.

'#'   Use opposite case characters if possible. A field that is normally upper case
             becomes lower case, and vice versa.

Here are some examples of padding:

```
date +%d/%m -d "Feb 1"
⇒ 01/02
date +%-d/%-m -d "Feb 1"
⇒ 1/2
date +%_d/%_m -d "Feb 1"
⇒  1/ 2
```

As a GNU extension, you can specify the field width (after any flag, if present) as a
decimal number. If the natural size of the output of the field has less than the specified
number of characters, the result is written right adjusted and padded to the given size. For
example, '%9B' prints the right adjusted month name in a field of width 9.

An optional modifier can follow the optional flag and width specification. The modifiers
are:

'E'   Use the locale's alternate representation for date and time. This modifier applies
             to the '%c', '%C', '%x', '%X', '%y' and '%Y' conversion specifiers. In a Japanese
             locale, for example, '%Ex' might yield a date format based on the Japanese
             Emperors' reigns.

'O'   Use the locale's alternate numeric symbols for numbers. This modifier applies
             only to numeric conversion specifiers.

If the format supports the modifier but no alternate representation is available, it is
ignored.

21.1.5 Setting the time

If given an argument that does not start with '+', date sets the system clock to the date and
time specified by that argument (as described below). You must have appropriate privileges
to set the system clock. Note for changes to persist across a reboot, the hardware clock
may need to be updated from the system clock, which might not happen automatically on
your system.

The argument must consist entirely of digits, which have the following meaning:

'MM'   month

'DD'   day within month

'hh'   hour

'mm'   minute

'CC'   first two digits of year (optional)

'YY'   last two digits of year (optional)

'ss'   second (optional)

Note, the `--date` and `--set` options may not be used with an argument in the above format. The `--universal` option may be used with such an argument to indicate that the specified date and time are relative to Coordinated Universal Time rather than to the local time zone.

21.1.6 Options for `date`

The program accepts the following options. Also see Chapter 2 [Common options], page 2.

'`-d datestr`'
'`--date=datestr`'

> Display the date and time specified in *datestr* instead of the current date and time. *datestr* can be in almost any common format. It can contain month names, time zones, 'am' and 'pm', 'yesterday', etc. For example, `--date="2004-02-27 14:19:13.489392193 +0530"` specifies the instant of time that is 489,392,193 nanoseconds after February 27, 2004 at 2:19:13 PM in a time zone that is 5 hours and 30 minutes east of UTC.
>
> Note: input currently must be in locale independent format. E.g., the LC_TIME=C below is needed to print back the correct date in many locales:
>
> > `date -d "$(LC_TIME=C date)"`
>
> See Chapter 28 [Date input formats], page 214.

'`-f datefile`'
'`--file=datefile`'

> Parse each line in *datefile* as with `-d` and display the resulting date and time. If *datefile* is '-', use standard input. This is useful when you have many dates to process, because the system overhead of starting up the `date` executable many times can be considerable.

'`-I[timespec]`'
'`--iso-8601[=timespec]`'

> Display the date using the ISO 8601 format, '%Y-%m-%d'.
>
> The argument *timespec* specifies the number of additional terms of the time to include. It can be one of the following:
>
> 'auto'   Print just the date. This is the default if *timespec* is omitted.
>
> 'hours'   Append the hour of the day to the date.
>
> 'minutes'   Append the hours and minutes.
>
> 'seconds'   Append the hours, minutes and seconds.
>
> 'ns'   Append the hours, minutes, seconds and nanoseconds.
>
> If showing any time terms, then include the time zone using the format '%z'.

'`-r file`'
'`--reference=file`'

> Display the date and time of the last modification of *file*, instead of the current date and time.

'`-R`'
'`--rfc-822`'
'`--rfc-2822`'

> Display the date and time using the format '`%a, %d %b %Y %H:%M:%S %z`', evaluated in the C locale so abbreviations are always in English. For example:
>
>   Fri, 09 Sep 2005 13:51:39 -0700
>
> This format conforms to Internet RFCs 2822 and 822, the current and previous standards for Internet email.

'`--rfc-3339=timespec`'

> Display the date using a format specified by Internet RFC 3339. This is a subset of the ISO 8601 format, except that it also permits applications to use a space rather than a 'T' to separate dates from times. Unlike the other standard formats, RFC 3339 format is always suitable as input for the `--date` (`-d`) and `--file` (`-f`) options, regardless of the current locale.
>
> The argument *timespec* specifies how much of the time to include. It can be one of the following:

> '`date`'   Print just the full-date, e.g., '`2005-09-14`'. This is equivalent to the format '`%Y-%m-%d`'.

> '`seconds`'   Print the full-date and full-time separated by a space, e.g., '`2005-09-14 00:56:06+05:30`'. The output ends with a numeric time-offset; here the '`+05:30`' means that local time is five hours and thirty minutes east of UTC. This is equivalent to the format '`%Y-%m-%d %H:%M:%S%:z`'.

> '`ns`'   Like '`seconds`', but also print nanoseconds, e.g., '`2005-09-14 00:56:06.998458565+05:30`'. This is equivalent to the format '`%Y-%m-%d %H:%M:%S.%N%:z`'.

'`-s datestr`'
'`--set=datestr`'

> Set the date and time to *datestr*. See `-d` above. See also Section 21.1.5 [Setting the time], page 178.

'`-u`'
'`--utc`'
'`--universal`'

> Use Coordinated Universal Time (UTC) by operating as if the `TZ` environment variable were set to the string '`UTC0`'. Coordinated Universal Time is often called "Greenwich Mean Time" (GMT) for historical reasons. Typically, systems ignore leap seconds and thus implement an approximation to UTC rather than true UTC.

21.1.7 Examples of `date`

Here are a few examples. Also see the documentation for the `-d` option in the previous section.

- To print the date of the day before yesterday:

```
date --date='2 days ago'
```

- To print the date of the day three months and one day hence:

  ```
  date --date='3 months 1 day'
  ```

- To print the day of year of Christmas in the current year:

  ```
  date --date='25 Dec' +%j
  ```

- To print the current full month name and the day of the month:

  ```
  date '+%B %d'
  ```

  But this may not be what you want because for the first nine days of the month, the '%d' expands to a zero-padded two-digit field, for example 'date -d 1may '+%B %d'' will print 'May 01'.

- To print a date without the leading zero for one-digit days of the month, you can use the (GNU extension) '-' flag to suppress the padding altogether:

  ```
  date -d 1may '+%B %-d
  ```

- To print the current date and time in the format required by many non-GNU versions of `date` when setting the system clock:

  ```
  date +%m%d%H%M%Y.%S
  ```

- To set the system clock forward by two minutes:

  ```
  date --set='+2 minutes'
  ```

- To print the date in RFC 2822 format, use 'date --rfc-2822'. Here is some example output:

  ```
  Fri, 09 Sep 2005 13:51:39 -0700
  ```

- To convert a date string to the number of seconds since the epoch (which is 1970-01-01 00:00:00 UTC), use the `--date` option with the '%s' format. That can be useful in sorting and/or graphing and/or comparing data by date. The following command outputs the number of the seconds since the epoch for the time two minutes after the epoch:

  ```
  date --date='1970-01-01 00:02:00 +0000' +%s
  120
  ```

If you do not specify time zone information in the date string, `date` uses your computer's idea of the time zone when interpreting the string. For example, if your computer's time zone is that of Cambridge, Massachusetts, which was then 5 hours (i.e., 18,000 seconds) behind UTC:

```
# local time zone used
date --date='1970-01-01 00:02:00' +%s
18120
```

- If you're sorting or graphing dated data, your raw date values may be represented as seconds since the epoch. But few people can look at the date '946684800' and casually note "Oh, that's the first second of the year 2000 in Greenwich, England."

  ```
  date --date='2000-01-01 UTC' +%s
  946684800
  ```

An alternative is to use the `--utc` (-u) option. Then you may omit 'UTC' from the date string. Although this produces the same result for '%s' and many other format sequences, with a time zone offset different from zero, it would give a different result for zone-dependent formats like '%z'.

```
date -u --date=2000-01-01 +%s
946684800
```

To convert such an unwieldy number of seconds back to a more readable form, use a command like this:

```
# local time zone used
date -d '1970-01-01 UTC 946684800 seconds' +"%Y-%m-%d %T %z"
1999-12-31 19:00:00 -0500
```

Or if you do not mind depending on the '@' feature present since coreutils 5.3.0, you could shorten this to:

```
date -d @946684800 +"%F %T %z"
1999-12-31 19:00:00 -0500
```

Often it is better to output UTC-relative date and time:

```
date -u -d '1970-01-01 946684800 seconds' +"%Y-%m-%d %T %z"
2000-01-01 00:00:00 +0000
```

• Typically the seconds count omits leap seconds, but some systems are exceptions. Because leap seconds are not predictable, the mapping between the seconds count and a future timestamp is not reliable on the atypical systems that include leap seconds in their counts.

Here is how the two kinds of systems handle the leap second at 2012-06-30 23:59:60 UTC:

```
# Typical systems ignore leap seconds:
date --date='2012-06-30 23:59:59 +0000' +%s
1341100799
date --date='2012-06-30 23:59:60 +0000' +%s
date: invalid date '2012-06-30 23:59:60 +0000'
date --date='2012-07-01 00:00:00 +0000' +%s
1341100800

# Atypical systems count leap seconds:
date --date='2012-06-30 23:59:59 +0000' +%s
1341100823
date --date='2012-06-30 23:59:60 +0000' +%s
1341100824
date --date='2012-07-01 00:00:00 +0000' +%s
1341100825
```

21.2 arch: Print machine hardware name

arch prints the machine hardware name, and is equivalent to 'uname -m'. Synopsis:

```
arch [option]
```

The program accepts the Chapter 2 [Common options], page 2 only.

arch is not installed by default, so portable scripts should not rely on its existence.

An exit status of zero indicates success, and a nonzero value indicates failure.

21.3 nproc: Print the number of available processors

Print the number of processing units available to the current process, which may be less than the number of online processors. If this information is not accessible, then print the number of processors installed. If the `OMP_NUM_THREADS` environment variable is set, then it will determine the returned value. The result is guaranteed to be greater than zero. Synopsis:

```
nproc [option]
```

The program accepts the following options. Also see Chapter 2 [Common options], page 2.

'`--all`'   Print the number of installed processors on the system, which may be greater than the number online or available to the current process. The `OMP_NUM_THREADS` environment variable is not honored in this case.

'`--ignore=number`'
          If possible, exclude this *number* of processing units.

An exit status of zero indicates success, and a nonzero value indicates failure.

21.4 uname: Print system information

`uname` prints information about the machine and operating system it is run on. If no options are given, `uname` acts as if the `-s` option were given. Synopsis:

```
uname [option]...
```

If multiple options or `-a` are given, the selected information is printed in this order:

```
kernel-name nodename kernel-release kernel-version
machine processor hardware-platform operating-system
```

The information may contain internal spaces, so such output cannot be parsed reliably. In the following example, *release* is '`2.2.18ss.e820-bda652a #4 SMP Tue Jun 5 11:24:08 PDT 2001`':

```
uname -a
⇒ Linux dumdum 2.2.18 #4 SMP Tue Jun 5 11:24:08 PDT 2001 i686 unknown unknown GNU/Linux
```

The program accepts the following options. Also see Chapter 2 [Common options], page 2.

'`-a`'
'`--all`'   Print all of the below information, except omit the processor type and the hardware platform name if they are unknown.

'`-i`'
'`--hardware-platform`'
          Print the hardware platform name (sometimes called the hardware implementation). Print '`unknown`' if the kernel does not make this information easily available, as is the case with Linux kernels.

'`-m`'
'`--machine`'
          Print the machine hardware name (sometimes called the hardware class or hardware type).

'`-n`'
'`--nodename`'
> Print the network node hostname.

'`-p`'
'`--processor`'
> Print the processor type (sometimes called the instruction set architecture or ISA). Print '`unknown`' if the kernel does not make this information easily available, as is the case with Linux kernels.

'`-o`'
'`--operating-system`'
> Print the name of the operating system.

'`-r`'
'`--kernel-release`'
> Print the kernel release.

'`-s`'
'`--kernel-name`'
> Print the kernel name. POSIX 1003.1-2001 (see Section 2.13 [Standards conformance], page 11) calls this "the implementation of the operating system", because the POSIX specification itself has no notion of "kernel". The kernel name might be the same as the operating system name printed by the `-o` or `--operating-system` option, but it might differ. Some operating systems (e.g., FreeBSD, HP-UX) have the same name as their underlying kernels; others (e.g., GNU/Linux, Solaris) do not.

'`-v`'
'`--kernel-version`'
> Print the kernel version.

An exit status of zero indicates success, and a nonzero value indicates failure.

21.5 `hostname`: **Print or set system name**

With no arguments, `hostname` prints the name of the current host system. With one argument, it sets the current host name to the specified string. You must have appropriate privileges to set the host name. Synopsis:

> `hostname [name]`

The only options are `--help` and `--version`. See Chapter 2 [Common options], page 2.

`hostname` is not installed by default, and other packages also supply a `hostname` command, so portable scripts should not rely on its existence or on the exact behavior documented above.

An exit status of zero indicates success, and a nonzero value indicates failure.

21.6 `hostid`: **Print numeric host identifier**

`hostid` prints the numeric identifier of the current host in hexadecimal. This command accepts no arguments. The only options are `--help` and `--version`. See Chapter 2 [Common options], page 2.

For example, here's what it prints on one system I use:

```
$ hostid
1bac013d
```

On that system, the 32-bit quantity happens to be closely related to the system's Internet address, but that isn't always the case.

hostid is installed only on systems that have the gethostid function, so portable scripts should not rely on its existence.

An exit status of zero indicates success, and a nonzero value indicates failure.

21.7 uptime: Print system uptime and load

uptime prints the current time, the system's uptime, the number of logged-in users and the current load average.

If an argument is specified, it is used as the file to be read to discover how many users are logged in. If no argument is specified, a system default is used (uptime --help indicates the default setting).

The only options are --help and --version. See Chapter 2 [Common options], page 2.

For example, here's what it prints right now on one system I use:

```
$ uptime
 14:07  up   3:35,  3 users,  load average: 1.39, 1.15, 1.04
```

The precise method of calculation of load average varies somewhat between systems. Some systems calculate it as the average number of runnable processes over the last 1, 5 and 15 minutes, but some systems also include processes in the uninterruptible sleep state (that is, those processes which are waiting for disk I/O). The Linux kernel includes uninterruptible processes.

uptime is installed only on platforms with infrastructure for obtaining the boot time, and other packages also supply an uptime command, so portable scripts should not rely on its existence or on the exact behavior documented above.

An exit status of zero indicates success, and a nonzero value indicates failure.

22 SELinux context

This section describes commands for operations with SELinux contexts.

22.1 `chcon`: Change SELinux context of file

`chcon` changes the SELinux security context of the selected files. Synopses:

```
chcon [option]... context file...
chcon [option]... [-u user] [-r role] [-l range] [-t type] file...
chcon [option]... --reference=rfile file...
```

Change the SELinux security context of each *file* to *context*. With `--reference`, change the security context of each *file* to that of *rfile*.

The program accepts the following options. Also see Chapter 2 [Common options], page 2.

'`--dereference`'

> Do not affect symbolic links but what they refer to; this is the default.

'`-h`'
'`--no-dereference`'

> Affect the symbolic links themselves instead of any referenced file.

'`--reference=rfile`'

> Use *rfile*'s security context rather than specifying a *context* value.

'`-R`'
'`--recursive`'

> Operate on files and directories recursively.

'`--preserve-root`'

> Refuse to operate recursively on the root directory, /, when used together with the `--recursive` option. See Section 2.11 [Treating / specially], page 10.

'`--no-preserve-root`'

> Do not treat the root directory, /, specially when operating recursively; this is the default. See Section 2.11 [Treating / specially], page 10.

'`-H`'   If `--recursive` (`-R`) is specified and a command line argument is a symbolic link to a directory, traverse it.See Section 2.10 [Traversing symlinks], page 9.

'`-L`'   In a recursive traversal, traverse every symbolic link to a directory that is encountered.See Section 2.10 [Traversing symlinks], page 9.

'`-P`'   Do not traverse any symbolic links. This is the default if none of `-H`, `-L`, or `-P` is specified.See Section 2.10 [Traversing symlinks], page 9.

'`-v`'
'`--verbose`'

> Output a diagnostic for every file processed.

'`-u user`'
'`--user=user`'

> Set user *user* in the target security context.

'-r *role*'
'--role=*role*'

> Set role *role* in the target security context.

'-t *type*'
'--type=*type*'

> Set type *type* in the target security context.

'-l *range*'
'--range=*range*'

> Set range *range* in the target security context.

An exit status of zero indicates success, and a nonzero value indicates failure.

22.2 runcon: Run a command in specified SELinux context

runcon runs file in specified SELinux security context.

> Synopses:
>
> ```
> runcon context command [args]
> runcon [ -c ] [-u user] [-r role] [-t type] [-l range] command [args]
> ```

Run *command* with completely-specified *context*, or with current or transitioned security context modified by one or more of *level*, *role*, *type* and *user*.

If none of -c, -t, -u, -r, or -l is specified, the first argument is used as the complete context. Any additional arguments after *command* are interpreted as arguments to the command.

With neither *context* nor *command*, print the current security context.

The program accepts the following options. Also see Chapter 2 [Common options], page 2.

'-c'
'--compute'

> Compute process transition context before modifying.

'-u *user*'
'--user=*user*'

> Set user *user* in the target security context.

'-r *role*'
'--role=*role*'

> Set role *role* in the target security context.

'-t *type*'
'--type=*type*'

> Set type *type* in the target security context.

'-l *range*'
'--range=*range*'

> Set range *range* in the target security context.

> Exit status:
>
> > 126 if *command* is found but cannot be invoked
> > 127 if runcon itself fails or if *command* cannot be found
> > the exit status of *command* otherwise

23 Modified command invocation

This section describes commands that run other commands in some context different than the current one: a modified environment, as a different user, etc.

23.1 `chroot`: Run a command with a different root directory

`chroot` runs a command with a specified root directory. On many systems, only the super-user can do this.[1]. Synopses:

```
chroot option newroot [command [args]...]
chroot option
```

Ordinarily, file names are looked up starting at the root of the directory structure, i.e., `/`. `chroot` changes the root to the directory *newroot* (which must exist), then changes the working directory to `/`, and finally runs *command* with optional *args*. If *command* is not specified, the default is the value of the `SHELL` environment variable or `/bin/sh` if not set, invoked with the `-i` option. *command* must not be a special built-in utility (see Section 2.12 [Special built-in utilities], page 10).

The program accepts the following options. Also see Chapter 2 [Common options], page 2. Options must precede operands.

'`--groups=groups`'

> Use this option to override the supplementary *groups* to be used by the new process. The items in the list (names or numeric IDs) must be separated by commas. Use '`--groups=''`' to disable the supplementary group look-up implicit in the `--userspec` option.

'`--userspec=user[:group]`'

> By default, *command* is run with the same credentials as the invoking process. Use this option to run it as a different *user* and/or with a different primary *group*. If a *user* is specified then the supplementary groups are set according to the system defined list for that user, unless overridden with the `--groups` option.

'`--skip-chdir`'

> Use this option to not change the working directory to `/` after changing the root directory to *newroot*, i.e., inside the chroot. This option is only permitted when *newroot* is the old `/` directory, and therefore is mostly useful together with the `--groups` and `--userspec` options to retain the previous working directory.

The user and group name look-up performed by the `--userspec` and `--groups` options, is done both outside and inside the chroot, with successful look-ups inside the chroot taking precedence. If the specified user or group items are intended to represent a numeric ID, then a name to ID resolving step is avoided by specifying a leading '`+`'. See Section 2.6 [Disambiguating names and IDs], page 7.

---

[1] However, some systems (e.g., FreeBSD) can be configured to allow certain regular users to use the `chroot` system call, and hence to run this program. Also, on Cygwin, anyone can run the `chroot` command, because the underlying function is non-privileged due to lack of support in MS-Windows. Furthermore, the `chroot` command avoids the `chroot` system call when *newroot* is identical to the old `/` directory for consistency with systems where this is allowed for non-privileged users.

Here are a few tips to help avoid common problems in using chroot. To start with a simple example, make *command* refer to a statically linked binary. If you were to use a dynamically linked executable, then you'd have to arrange to have the shared libraries in the right place under your new root directory.

For example, if you create a statically linked `ls` executable, and put it in `/tmp/empty`, you can run this command as root:

```
$ chroot /tmp/empty /ls -R1 /
```

Then you'll see output like this:

```
/:
total 1023
-rwxr-xr-x 1 0 0 1041745 Aug 16 11:17 ls
```

If you want to use a dynamically linked executable, say `bash`, then first run 'ldd bash' to see what shared objects it needs. Then, in addition to copying the actual binary, also copy the listed files to the required positions under your intended new root directory. Finally, if the executable requires any other files (e.g., data, state, device files), copy them into place, too.

`chroot` is installed only on systems that have the `chroot` function, so portable scripts should not rely on its existence.

Exit status:

125 if `chroot` itself fails
126 if *command* is found but cannot be invoked
127 if *command* cannot be found
the exit status of *command* otherwise

23.2 env: Run a command in a modified environment

`env` runs a command with a modified environment. Synopses:

```
env [option]... [name=value]... [command [args]...]
env
```

Operands of the form '`variable=value`' set the environment variable *variable* to value *value*. *value* may be empty ('`variable=`'). Setting a variable to an empty value is different from unsetting it. These operands are evaluated left-to-right, so if two operands mention the same variable the earlier is ignored.

Environment variable names can be empty, and can contain any characters other than '=' and ASCII NUL. However, it is wise to limit yourself to names that consist solely of underscores, digits, and ASCII letters, and that begin with a non-digit, as applications like the shell do not work well with other names.

The first operand that does not contain the character '=' specifies the program to invoke; it is searched for according to the `PATH` environment variable. Any remaining arguments are passed as arguments to that program. The program should not be a special built-in utility (see Section 2.12 [Special built-in utilities], page 10).

Modifications to `PATH` take effect prior to searching for *command*. Use caution when reducing `PATH`; behavior is not portable when `PATH` is undefined or omits key directories such as `/bin`.

In the rare case that a utility contains a '=' in the name, the only way to disambiguate it from a variable assignment is to use an intermediate command for *command*, and pass the problematic program name via *args*. For example, if ./prog= is an executable in the current PATH:

```
env prog= true # runs 'true', with prog= in environment
env ./prog= true # runs 'true', with ./prog= in environment
env -- prog= true # runs 'true', with prog= in environment
env sh -c '\prog= true' # runs 'prog=' with argument 'true'
env sh -c 'exec "$@"' sh prog= true # also runs 'prog='
```

If no command name is specified following the environment specifications, the resulting environment is printed. This is like specifying the printenv program.

For some examples, suppose the environment passed to env contains 'LOGNAME=rms', 'EDITOR=emacs', and 'PATH=.:/gnubin:/hacks':

- Output the current environment.

    ```
    $ env | LC_ALL=C sort
    EDITOR=emacs
    LOGNAME=rms
    PATH=.:/gnubin:/hacks
    ```

- Run foo with a reduced environment, preserving only the original PATH to avoid problems in locating foo.

    ```
    env - PATH="$PATH" foo
    ```

- Run foo with the environment containing 'LOGNAME=rms', 'EDITOR=emacs', and 'PATH=.:/gnubin:/hacks', and guarantees that foo was found in the file system rather than as a shell built-in.

    ```
    env foo
    ```

- Run nemacs with the environment containing 'LOGNAME=foo', 'EDITOR=emacs', 'PATH=.:/gnubin:/hacks', and 'DISPLAY=gnu:0'.

    ```
    env DISPLAY=gnu:0 LOGNAME=foo nemacs
    ```

- Attempt to run the program /energy/-- (as that is the only possible path search result); if the command exists, the environment will contain 'LOGNAME=rms' and 'PATH=/energy', and the arguments will be 'e=mc2', 'bar', and 'baz'.

    ```
    env -u EDITOR PATH=/energy -- e=mc2 bar baz
    ```

The program accepts the following options. Also see Chapter 2 [Common options], page 2. Options must precede operands.

'-0'
'--null'   Output a zero byte (ASCII NUL) at the end of each line, rather than a newline. This option enables other programs to parse the output even when that output would contain data with embedded newlines.

'-u *name*'
'--unset=*name*'
            Remove variable *name* from the environment, if it was in the environment.

'_'
'-i'
'--ignore-environment'
>   Start with an empty environment, ignoring the inherited environment.

Exit status:

>   0   if no *command* is specified and the environment is output
>   125 if env itself fails
>   126 if *command* is found but cannot be invoked
>   127 if *command* cannot be found
>   the exit status of *command* otherwise

23.3 nice: Run a command with modified niceness

nice prints a process's *niceness*, or runs a command with modified niceness. *niceness* affects how favorably the process is scheduled in the system. Synopsis:

>   nice [*option*]... [*command* [*arg*]...]

If no arguments are given, nice prints the current niceness. Otherwise, nice runs the given *command* with its niceness adjusted. By default, its niceness is incremented by 10.

Niceness values range at least from −20 (process has high priority and gets more resources, thus slowing down other processes) through 19 (process has lower priority and runs slowly itself, but has less impact on the speed of other running processes). Some systems may have a wider range of niceness values; conversely, other systems may enforce more restrictive limits. An attempt to set the niceness outside the supported range is treated as an attempt to use the minimum or maximum supported value.

A niceness should not be confused with a scheduling priority, which lets applications determine the order in which threads are scheduled to run. Unlike a priority, a niceness is merely advice to the scheduler, which the scheduler is free to ignore. Also, as a point of terminology, POSIX defines the behavior of nice in terms of a *nice value*, which is the non-negative difference between a niceness and the minimum niceness. Though nice conforms to POSIX, its documentation and diagnostics use the term "niceness" for compatibility with historical practice.

command must not be a special built-in utility (see Section 2.12 [Special built-in utilities], page 10).

Due to shell aliases and built-in nice functions, using an unadorned nice interactively or in a script may get you different functionality than that described here. Invoke it via env (i.e., env nice ...) to avoid interference from the shell.

Note to change the *niceness* of an existing process, one needs to use the **renice** command.

The program accepts the following option. Also see Chapter 2 [Common options], page 2. Options must precede operands.

'-n *adjustment*'
'--adjustment=*adjustment*'
>   Add *adjustment* instead of 10 to the command's niceness. If *adjustment* is negative and you lack appropriate privileges, nice issues a warning but otherwise acts as if you specified a zero adjustment.

For compatibility `nice` also supports an obsolete option syntax `-adjustment`. New scripts should use `-n adjustment` instead.

`nice` is installed only on systems that have the POSIX `setpriority` function, so portable scripts should not rely on its existence on non-POSIX platforms.

Exit status:

0   if no *command* is specified and the niceness is output
125 if `nice` itself fails
126 if *command* is found but cannot be invoked
127 if *command* cannot be found
the exit status of *command* otherwise

It is sometimes useful to run a non-interactive program with reduced niceness.

```
$ nice factor 4611686018427387903
```

Since `nice` prints the current niceness, you can invoke it through itself to demonstrate how it works.

The default behavior is to increase the niceness by '10':

```
$ nice
0
$ nice nice
10
$ nice -n 10 nice
10
```

The *adjustment* is relative to the current niceness. In the next example, the first `nice` invocation runs the second one with niceness 10, and it in turn runs the final one with a niceness that is 3 more:

```
$ nice nice -n 3 nice
13
```

Specifying a niceness larger than the supported range is the same as specifying the maximum supported value:

```
$ nice -n 10000000000 nice
19
```

Only a privileged user may run a process with lower niceness:

```
$ nice -n -1 nice
nice: cannot set niceness: Permission denied
0
$ sudo nice -n -1 nice
-1
```

23.4 nohup: Run a command immune to hangups

`nohup` runs the given *command* with hangup signals ignored, so that the command can continue running in the background after you log out. Synopsis:

```
nohup command [arg]...
```

If standard input is a terminal, redirect it so that terminal sessions do not mistakenly consider the terminal to be used by the command. Make the substitute file descriptor unreadable, so that commands that mistakenly attempt to read from standard input can report an error. This redirection is a GNU extension; programs intended to be portable to non-GNU hosts can use 'nohup *command* [*arg*]... 0>/dev/null' instead.

If standard output is a terminal, the command's standard output is appended to the file nohup.out; if that cannot be written to, it is appended to the file $HOME/nohup.out; and if that cannot be written to, the command is not run. Any nohup.out or $HOME/nohup.out file created by nohup is made readable and writable only to the user, regardless of the current umask settings.

If standard error is a terminal, it is normally redirected to the same file descriptor as the (possibly-redirected) standard output. However, if standard output is closed, standard error terminal output is instead appended to the file nohup.out or $HOME/nohup.out as above.

To capture the command's output to a file other than nohup.out you can redirect it. For example, to capture the output of make:

```
nohup make > make.log
```

nohup does not automatically put the command it runs in the background; you must do that explicitly, by ending the command line with an '&'. Also, nohup does not alter the niceness of *command*; use nice for that, e.g., 'nohup nice *command*'.

command must not be a special built-in utility (see Section 2.12 [Special built-in utilities], page 10).

The only options are --help and --version. See Chapter 2 [Common options], page 2. Options must precede operands.

Exit status:

> 125 if nohup itself fails, and POSIXLY_CORRECT is not set
> 126 if *command* is found but cannot be invoked
> 127 if *command* cannot be found
> the exit status of *command* otherwise

If POSIXLY_CORRECT is set, internal failures give status 127 instead of 125.

23.5 stdbuf: Run a command with modified I/O stream buffering

stdbuf allows one to modify the buffering operations of the three standard I/O streams associated with a program. Synopsis:

```
stdbuf option... command
```

command must start with the name of a program that

1. uses the ISO C FILE streams for input/output (note the programs dd and cat don't do that),

2. does not adjust the buffering of its standard streams (note the program tee is not in this category).

Any additional *args* are passed as additional arguments to the *command*.

The program accepts the following options. Also see Chapter 2 [Common options], page 2.

'-i *mode*'
'--input=*mode*'
>   Adjust the standard input stream buffering.

'-o *mode*'
'--output=*mode*'
>   Adjust the standard output stream buffering.

'-e *mode*'
'--error=*mode*'
>   Adjust the standard error stream buffering.

The *mode* can be specified as follows:

'L'   Set the stream to line buffered mode. In this mode data is coalesced until a newline is output or input is read from any stream attached to a terminal device. This option is invalid with standard input.

'0'   Disable buffering of the selected stream. In this mode, data is output immediately and only the amount of data requested is read from input. Note the difference in function for input and output. Disabling buffering for input will not influence the responsiveness or blocking behavior of the stream input functions. For example `fread` will still block until `EOF` or error, even if the underlying `read` returns less data than requested.

'*size*'   Specify the size of the buffer to use in fully buffered mode. *size* may be, or may be an integer optionally followed by, one of the following multiplicative suffixes:

>   'KB' => 1000 (KiloBytes)
>   'K' => 1024 (KibiBytes)
>   'MB' => 1000*1000 (MegaBytes)
>   'M' => 1024*1024 (MebiBytes)
>   'GB' => 1000*1000*1000 (GigaBytes)
>   'G' => 1024*1024*1024 (GibiBytes)

>   and so on for 'T', 'P', 'E', 'Z', and 'Y'.

stdbuf is installed only on platforms that use the Executable and Linkable Format (ELF) and support the `constructor` attribute, so portable scripts should not rely on its existence.

Exit status:

>   125 if stdbuf itself fails
>   126 if *command* is found but cannot be invoked
>   127 if *command* cannot be found
>   the exit status of *command* otherwise

23.6 `timeout`: Run a command with a time limit

timeout runs the given *command* and kills it if it is still running after the specified time interval. Synopsis:

>   timeout [*option*] *duration command* [*arg*]...

command must not be a special built-in utility (see Section 2.12 [Special built-in utilities], page 10).

The program accepts the following options. Also see Chapter 2 [Common options], page 2. Options must precede operands.

'`--preserve-status`'

> Return the exit status of the managed *command* on timeout, rather than a specific exit status indicating a timeout. This is useful if the managed *command* supports running for an indeterminate amount of time.

'`--foreground`'

> Don't create a separate background program group, so that the managed *command* can use the foreground TTY normally. This is needed to support timing out commands not started directly from an interactive shell, in two situations.
>
> 1. *command* is interactive and needs to read from the terminal for example
> 2. the user wants to support sending signals directly to *command* from the terminal (like Ctrl-C for example)
>
> Note in this mode of operation, any children of *command* will not be timed out. Also SIGCONT will not be sent to *command*, as it's generally not needed with foreground processes, and can cause intermittent signal delivery issues with programs that are monitors themselves (like GDB for example).

'`-k duration`'
'`--kill-after=duration`'

> Ensure the monitored *command* is killed by also sending a '`KILL`' signal, after the specified *duration*. Without this option, if the selected signal proves not to be fatal, `timeout` does not kill the *command*.

'`-s signal`'
'`--signal=signal`'

> Send this *signal* to *command* on timeout, rather than the default '`TERM`' signal. *signal* may be a name like '`HUP`' or a number. See Section 2.5 [Signal specifications], page 6.

duration is a floating point number followed by an optional unit:

'`s`' for seconds (the default)
'`m`' for minutes
'`h`' for hours
'`d`' for days

A duration of 0 disables the associated timeout. Note that the actual timeout duration is dependent on system conditions, which should be especially considered when specifying sub-second timeouts.

Exit status:

124 if *command* times out
125 if `timeout` itself fails
126 if *command* is found but cannot be invoked
127 if *command* cannot be found
137 if *command* is sent the KILL(9) signal (128+9)
the exit status of *command* otherwise

24 Process control

24.1 `kill`: Send a signal to processes

The `kill` command sends a signal to processes, causing them to terminate or otherwise act upon receiving the signal in some way. Alternatively, it lists information about signals. Synopses:

```
kill [-s signal | --signal signal | -signal] pid...
kill [-l | --list | -t | --table] [signal]...
```

Due to shell aliases and built-in `kill` functions, using an unadorned `kill` interactively or in a script may get you different functionality than that described here. Invoke it via `env` (i.e., `env kill ...`) to avoid interference from the shell.

The first form of the `kill` command sends a signal to all *pid* arguments. The default signal to send if none is specified is 'TERM'. The special signal number '0' does not denote a valid signal, but can be used to test whether the *pid* arguments specify processes to which a signal could be sent.

If *pid* is positive, the signal is sent to the process with the process ID *pid*. If *pid* is zero, the signal is sent to all processes in the process group of the current process. If *pid* is −1, the signal is sent to all processes for which the user has permission to send a signal. If *pid* is less than −1, the signal is sent to all processes in the process group that equals the absolute value of *pid*.

If *pid* is not positive, a system-dependent set of system processes is excluded from the list of processes to which the signal is sent.

If a negative *pid* argument is desired as the first one, it should be preceded by `--`. However, as a common extension to POSIX, `--` is not required with '`kill -signal -pid`'. The following commands are equivalent:

```
kill -15 -1
kill -TERM -1
kill -s TERM -- -1
kill -- -1
```

The first form of the `kill` command succeeds if every *pid* argument specifies at least one process that the signal was sent to.

The second form of the `kill` command lists signal information. Either the `-l` or `--list` option, or the `-t` or `--table` option must be specified. Without any *signal* argument, all supported signals are listed. The output of `-l` or `--list` is a list of the signal names, one per line; if *signal* is already a name, the signal number is printed instead. The output of `-t` or `--table` is a table of signal numbers, names, and descriptions. This form of the `kill` command succeeds if all *signal* arguments are valid and if there is no output error.

The `kill` command also supports the `--help` and `--version` options. See Chapter 2 [Common options], page 2.

A *signal* may be a signal name like 'HUP', or a signal number like '1', or an exit status of a process terminated by the signal. A signal name can be given in canonical form or prefixed by 'SIG'. The case of the letters is ignored, except for the `-signal` option which must use upper case to avoid ambiguity with lower case option letters. See Section 2.5 [Signal specifications], page 6, for a list of supported signal names and numbers.

25 Delaying

25.1 `sleep`: Delay for a specified time

`sleep` pauses for an amount of time specified by the sum of the values of the command line arguments. Synopsis:

```
sleep number[smhd]...
```

Each argument is a number followed by an optional unit; the default is seconds. The units are:

'`s`'   seconds

'`m`'   minutes

'`h`'   hours

'`d`'   days

Historical implementations of `sleep` have required that *number* be an integer, and only accepted a single argument without a suffix. However, GNU `sleep` accepts arbitrary floating point numbers. See Section 2.4 [Floating point], page 5.

The only options are `--help` and `--version`. See Chapter 2 [Common options], page 2.

Due to shell aliases and built-in `sleep` functions, using an unadorned `sleep` interactively or in a script may get you different functionality than that described here. Invoke it via `env` (i.e., `env sleep ...`) to avoid interference from the shell.

An exit status of zero indicates success, and a nonzero value indicates failure.

26 Numeric operations

These programs do numerically-related operations.

26.1 `factor`: Print prime factors

`factor` prints prime factors. Synopses:

```
factor [number]...
factor option
```

If no *number* is specified on the command line, `factor` reads numbers from standard input, delimited by newlines, tabs, or spaces.

The `factor` command supports only a small number of options:

'`--help`'   Print a short help on standard output, then exit without further processing.

'`--version`'
Print the program version on standard output, then exit without further processing.

Factoring the product of the eighth and ninth Mersenne primes takes about 30 milliseconds of CPU time on a 2.2 GHz Athlon.

```
M8=$(echo 2^31-1|bc)
M9=$(echo 2^61-1|bc)
n=$(echo "$M8 * $M9" | bc)
/usr/bin/time -f %U factor $n
4951760154835678088235319297: 2147483647 2305843009213693951
0.03
```

Similarly, factoring the eighth Fermat number $2^{256} + 1$ takes about 20 seconds on the same machine.

Factoring large numbers is, in general, hard. The Pollard Rho algorithm used by `factor` is particularly effective for numbers with relatively small factors. If you wish to factor large numbers which do not have small factors (for example, numbers which are the product of two large primes), other methods are far better.

If `factor` is built without using GNU MP, only single-precision arithmetic is available, and so large numbers (typically 2^{64} and above) will not be supported. The single-precision code uses an algorithm which is designed for factoring smaller numbers.

An exit status of zero indicates success, and a nonzero value indicates failure.

26.2 `numfmt`: Reformat numbers

`numfmt` reads numbers in various representations and reformats them as requested. The most common usage is converting numbers to/from *human* representation (e.g. '`4G`' $\mapsto$ '`4,000,000,000`').

```
numfmt [option]... [number]
```

`numfmt` converts each *number* on the command-line according to the specified options (see below). If no *number*s are given, it reads numbers from standard input. `numfmt` can optionally extract numbers from specific columns, maintaining proper line padding and alignment.

An exit status of zero indicates success, and a nonzero value indicates failure.

See `--invalid` for additional information regarding exit status.

26.2.1 General options

The program accepts the following options. Also see Chapter 2 [Common options], page 2.

'`--debug`'   Print (to standard error) warning messages about possible erroneous usage.

'`-d d`'
'`--delimiter=d`'

> Use the character d as input field separator (default: whitespace). *Note*: Using non-default delimiter turns off automatic padding.

'`--field=fields`'

> Convert the number in input field *fields* (default: 1). *fields* supports `cut` style field ranges:

```
N     N'th field, counted from 1
N-    from N'th field, to end of line
N-M   from N'th to M'th field (inclusive)
-M    from first to M'th field (inclusive)
-     all fields
```

'`--format=format`'

> Use printf-style floating FORMAT string. The *format* string must contain one '`%f`' directive, optionally with '' ', '`-`', '`0`', width or precision modifiers. The '' ' modifier will enable `--grouping`, the '`-`' modifier will enable left-aligned `--padding` and the width modifier will enable right-aligned `--padding`. The '`0`' width modifier (without the '`-`' modifier) will generate leading zeros on the number, up to the specified width. A precision specification like '`%.1f`' will override the precision determined from the input data or set due to `--to` option auto scaling.

'`--from=unit`'

> Auto-scales input numbers according to *unit*. See UNITS below. The default is no scaling, meaning suffixes (e.g. '`M`', '`G`') will trigger an error.

'`--from-unit=n`'

> Specify the input unit size (instead of the default 1). Use this option when the input numbers represent other units (e.g. if the input number '`10`' represents 10 units of 512 bytes, use '`--from-unit=512`'). Suffixes are handled as with '`--from=auto`'.

'`--grouping`'

> Group digits in output numbers according to the current locale's grouping rules (e.g *Thousands Separator* character, commonly '`.`' (dot) or '`,`' comma). This option has no effect in '`POSIX/C`' locale.

'`--header[=n]`'

> Print the first n (default: 1) lines without any conversion.

'--invalid=*mode*'

>   The default action on input errors is to exit immediately with status code 2.
>   --invalid='abort' explicitly specifies this default mode. With a *mode* of
>   'fail', print a warning for *each* conversion error, and exit with status 2. With
>   a *mode* of 'warn', exit with status 0, even in the presence of conversion errors,
>   and with a *mode* of 'ignore' do not even print diagnostics.

'--padding=*n*'

>   Pad the output numbers to *n* characters, by adding spaces. If *n* is a positive
>   number, numbers will be right-aligned. If *n* is a negative number, numbers will
>   be left-aligned. By default, numbers are automatically aligned based on the
>   input line's width (only with the default delimiter).

'--round=*method*'

>   When converting number representations, round the number according to
>   *method*, which can be 'up', 'down', 'from-zero' (the default), 'towards-zero',
>   'nearest'.

'--suffix=*suffix*'

>   Add 'SUFFIX' to the output numbers, and accept optional 'SUFFIX' in input
>   numbers.

'--to=*unit*'

>   Auto-scales output numbers according to *unit*. See *Units* below. The default
>   is no scaling, meaning all the digits of the number are printed.

'--to-unit=*n*'

>   Specify the output unit size (instead of the default 1). Use this option when the
>   output numbers represent other units (e.g. to represent '4,000,000' bytes in
>   blocks of 1KB, use '--to=si --to-unit=1000'). Suffixes are handled as with
>   '--from=auto'.

26.2.2 Possible *units*:

The following are the possible *unit* options with --from=UNITS and --to=UNITS:

none   No scaling is performed. For input numbers, no suffixes are accepted, and
             any trailing characters following the number will trigger an error. For output
             numbers, all digits of the numbers will be printed.

si   Auto-scale numbers according to the *International System of Units (SI)* stan-
             dard. For input numbers, accept one of the following suffixes. For output
             numbers, values larger than 1000 will be rounded, and printed with one of the
             following suffixes:

$$
\begin{array}{llll}
\text{`K'} & \Rightarrow & 1000^1 = 10^3 & \text{(Kilo)} \\
\text{`M'} & \Rightarrow & 1000^2 = 10^6 & \text{(Mega)} \\
\text{`G'} & \Rightarrow & 1000^3 = 10^9 & \text{(Giga)} \\
\text{`T'} & \Rightarrow & 1000^4 = 10^{12} & \text{(Tera)} \\
\text{`P'} & \Rightarrow & 1000^5 = 10^{15} & \text{(Peta)} \\
\text{`E'} & \Rightarrow & 1000^6 = 10^{18} & \text{(Exa)} \\
\text{`Z'} & \Rightarrow & 1000^7 = 10^{21} & \text{(Zetta)} \\
\text{`Y'} & \Rightarrow & 1000^8 = 10^{24} & \text{(Yotta)}
\end{array}
$$

iec   Auto-scale numbers according to the *International Electrotechnical Commission (IEC)* standard. For input numbers, accept one of the following suffixes. For output numbers, values larger than 1024 will be rounded, and printed with one of the following suffixes:

$$\begin{array}{lllll}
\text{`K'} & => & 1024^1 & = & 2^{10} \ (\texttt{Kibi}) \\
\text{`M'} & => & 1024^2 & = & 2^{20} \ (\texttt{Mebi}) \\
\text{`G'} & => & 1024^3 & = & 2^{30} \ (\texttt{Gibi}) \\
\text{`T'} & => & 1024^4 & = & 2^{40} \ (\texttt{Tebi}) \\
\text{`P'} & => & 1024^5 & = & 2^{50} \ (\texttt{Pebi}) \\
\text{`E'} & => & 1024^6 & = & 2^{60} \ (\texttt{Exbi}) \\
\text{`Z'} & => & 1024^7 & = & 2^{70} \ (\texttt{Zebi}) \\
\text{`Y'} & => & 1024^8 & = & 2^{80} \ (\texttt{Yobi}) \\
\end{array}$$

The `iec` option uses a single letter suffix (e.g. 'G'), which is not fully standard, as the *iec* standard recommends a two-letter symbol (e.g 'Gi') - but in practice, this method common. Compare with the `iec-i` option.

iec-i   Auto-scale numbers according to the *International Electrotechnical Commission (IEC)* standard. For input numbers, accept one of the following suffixes. For output numbers, values larger than 1024 will be rounded, and printed with one of the following suffixes:

$$\begin{array}{lllll}
\text{`Ki'} & => & 1024^1 & = & 2^{10} \ (\texttt{Kibi}) \\
\text{`Mi'} & => & 1024^2 & = & 2^{20} \ (\texttt{Mebi}) \\
\text{`Gi'} & => & 1024^3 & = & 2^{30} \ (\texttt{Gibi}) \\
\text{`Ti'} & => & 1024^4 & = & 2^{40} \ (\texttt{Tebi}) \\
\text{`Pi'} & => & 1024^5 & = & 2^{50} \ (\texttt{Pebi}) \\
\text{`Ei'} & => & 1024^6 & = & 2^{60} \ (\texttt{Exbi}) \\
\text{`Zi'} & => & 1024^7 & = & 2^{70} \ (\texttt{Zebi}) \\
\text{`Yi'} & => & 1024^8 & = & 2^{80} \ (\texttt{Yobi}) \\
\end{array}$$

The `iec-i` option uses a two-letter suffix symbol (e.g. 'Gi'), as the *iec* standard recommends, but this is not always common in practice. Compare with the `iec` option.

auto   'auto' can only be used with `--from`. With this method, numbers with 'K','M','G','T','P','E','Z','Y' suffixes are interpreted as *SI* values, and numbers with 'Ki', 'Mi','Gi','Ti','Pi','Ei','Zi','Yi' suffixes are interpreted as *IEC* values.

26.2.3 Examples of using `numfmt`

Converting a single number from/to *human* representation:

```
$ numfmt --to=si 500000
500K
```

```
$ numfmt --to=iec 500000
489K
```

```
$ numfmt --to=iec-i 500000
489Ki
```

```
$ numfmt --from=si 1M
1000000

$ numfmt --from=iec 1M
1048576

# with '--from=auto', M=Mega, Mi=Mebi
$ numfmt --from=auto 1M
1000000
$ numfmt --from=auto 1Mi
1048576
```

Converting from 'SI' to 'IEC' scales (e.g. when a harddisk capacity is advertised as '1TB', while checking the drive's capacity gives lower values):

```
$ numfmt --from=si --to=iec 1T
932G
```

Converting a single field from an input file / piped input (these contrived examples are for demonstration purposes only, as both `ls` and `df` support the `--human-readable` option to output sizes in human-readable format):

```
# Third field (file size) will be shown in SI representation
$ ls -log | numfmt --field 3 --header --to=si | head -n4
-rw-r--r--  1     94K Aug 23  2011 ABOUT-NLS
-rw-r--r--  1    3.7K Jan  7 16:15 AUTHORS
-rw-r--r--  1     36K Jun  1  2011 COPYING
-rw-r--r--  1       0 Jan  7 15:15 ChangeLog


# Second field (size) will be shown in IEC representation
$ df --block-size=1 | numfmt --field 2 --header --to=iec | head -n4
File system    1B-blocks       Used  Available Use% Mounted on
rootfs              132G  104741408   26554036  80% /
tmpfs               794M       7580     804960   1% /run/shm
/dev/sdb1           694G  651424756   46074696  94% /home
```

Output can be tweaked using `--padding` or `--format`:

```
# Pad to 10 characters, right-aligned
$ du -s * | numfmt --to=si --padding=10
      2.5K config.log
       108 config.status
      1.7K configure
        20 configure.ac


# Pad to 10 characters, left-aligned
$ du -s * | numfmt --to=si --padding=-10
2.5K       config.log
108        config.status
1.7K       configure
20         configure.ac
```

```
# Pad to 10 characters, left-aligned, using 'format'
$ du -s * | numfmt --to=si --format="%10f"
      2.5K config.log
       108 config.status
      1.7K configure
        20 configure.ac


# Pad to 10 characters, left-aligned, using 'format'
$ du -s * | numfmt --to=si --padding="%-10f"
2.5K       config.log
108        config.status
1.7K       configure
20         configure.ac
```

With locales that support grouping digits, using `--grouping` or `--format` enables grouping. In 'POSIX' locale, grouping is silently ignored:

```
$ LC_ALL=C numfmt --from=iec --grouping 2G
2147483648


$ LC_ALL=en_US.utf8 numfmt --from=iec --grouping 2G
2,147,483,648


$ LC_ALL=ta_IN numfmt --from=iec --grouping 2G
2,14,74,83,648


$ LC_ALL=C ./src/numfmt --from=iec --format="==%'15f==" 2G
==     2147483648==


$ LC_ALL=en_US.utf8 ./src/numfmt --from=iec --format="==%'15f==" 2G
==   2,147,483,648==


$ LC_ALL=en_US.utf8 ./src/numfmt --from=iec --format="==%'-15f==" 2G
==2,147,483,648   ==


$ LC_ALL=ta_IN ./src/numfmt --from=iec --format="==%'15f==" 2G
==   2,14,74,83,648==
```

26.3 seq: Print numeric sequences

seq prints a sequence of numbers to standard output. Synopses:

```
seq [option]... last
seq [option]... first last
seq [option]... first increment last
```

seq prints the numbers from *first* to *last* by *increment*. By default, each number is printed on a separate line. When *increment* is not specified, it defaults to '1', even when *first* is larger than *last*. *first* also defaults to '1'. So seq 1 prints '1', but seq 0 and seq 10 5 produce no output. The sequence of numbers ends when the sum of the current number and *increment* would become greater than *last*, so `seq 1 10 10` only produces '1'. Floating-point numbers may be specified. See Section 2.4 [Floating point], page 5.

The program accepts the following options. Also see Chapter 2 [Common options], page 2. Options must precede operands.

'-f *format*'
'--format=*format*'

> Print all numbers using *format*. *format* must contain exactly one of the 'printf'-style floating point conversion specifications '%a', '%e', '%f', '%g', '%A', '%E', '%F', '%G'. The '%' may be followed by zero or more flags taken from the set '-+#0 '', then an optional width containing one or more digits, then an optional precision consisting of a '.' followed by zero or more digits. *format* may also contain any number of '%%' conversion specifications. All conversion specifications have the same meaning as with 'printf'.
>
> The default format is derived from *first*, *step*, and *last*. If these all use a fixed point decimal representation, the default format is '%.*p*f', where *p* is the minimum precision that can represent the output numbers exactly. Otherwise, the default format is '%g'.

'-s *string*'
'--separator=*string*'

> Separate numbers with *string*; default is a newline. The output always terminates with a newline.

'-w'
'--equal-width'

> Print all numbers with the same width, by padding with leading zeros. *first*, *step*, and *last* should all use a fixed point decimal representation. (To have other kinds of padding, use --format).

You can get finer-grained control over output with -f:

```
$ seq -f '(%9.2E)' -9e5 1.1e6 1.3e6
(-9.00E+05)
( 2.00E+05)
( 1.30E+06)
```

If you want hexadecimal integer output, you can use printf to perform the conversion:

```
$ printf '%x\n' $(seq 1048575 1024 1050623)
fffff
1003ff
1007ff
```

For very long lists of numbers, use xargs to avoid system limitations on the length of an argument list:

```
$ seq 1000000 | xargs printf '%x\n' | tail -n 3
f423e
f423f
f4240
```

To generate octal output, use the printf %o format instead of %x.

On most systems, seq can produce whole-number output for values up to at least 2^{53}. Larger integers are approximated. The details differ depending on your floating-point implementation. See Section 2.4 [Floating point], page 5. A common case is that **seq** works with integers through 2^{64}, and larger integers may not be numerically correct:

```
$ seq 50000000000000000000 2 50000000000000000004
50000000000000000000
50000000000000000000
50000000000000000004
```

However, note that when limited to non-negative whole numbers, an increment of 1 and no format-specifying option, seq can print arbitrarily large numbers.

Be careful when using **seq** with outlandish values: otherwise you may see surprising results, as **seq** uses floating point internally. For example, on the x86 platform, where the internal representation uses a 64-bit fraction, the command:

```
seq 1 0.0000000000000000001 1.0000000000000000009
```

outputs 1.0000000000000000007 twice and skips 1.0000000000000000008.

An exit status of zero indicates success, and a nonzero value indicates failure.

27 File permissions

Each file has a set of *file mode bits* that control the kinds of access that users have to that file. They can be represented either in symbolic form or as an octal number.

27.1 Structure of File Mode Bits

The file mode bits have two parts: the *file permission bits*, which control ordinary access to the file, and *special mode bits*, which affect only some files.

There are three kinds of permissions that a user can have for a file:

1. permission to read the file. For directories, this means permission to list the contents of the directory.

2. permission to write to (change) the file. For directories, this means permission to create and remove files in the directory.

3. permission to execute the file (run it as a program). For directories, this means permission to access files in the directory.

There are three categories of users who may have different permissions to perform any of the above operations on a file:

1. the file's owner;

2. other users who are in the file's group;

3. everyone else.

Files are given an owner and group when they are created. Usually the owner is the current user and the group is the group of the directory the file is in, but this varies with the operating system, the file system the file is created on, and the way the file is created. You can change the owner and group of a file by using the **chown** and **chgrp** commands.

In addition to the three sets of three permissions listed above, the file mode bits have three special components, which affect only executable files (programs) and, on most systems, directories:

1. Set the process's effective user ID to that of the file upon execution (called the *set-user-ID bit*, or sometimes the *setuid bit*). For directories on a few systems, give files created in the directory the same owner as the directory, no matter who creates them, and set the set-user-ID bit of newly-created subdirectories.

2. Set the process's effective group ID to that of the file upon execution (called the *set-group-ID bit*, or sometimes the *setgid bit*). For directories on most systems, give files created in the directory the same group as the directory, no matter what group the user who creates them is in, and set the set-group-ID bit of newly-created subdirectories.

3. Prevent unprivileged users from removing or renaming a file in a directory unless they own the file or the directory; this is called the *restricted deletion flag* for the directory, and is commonly found on world-writable directories like **/tmp**.

   For regular files on some older systems, save the program's text image on the swap device so it will load more quickly when run; this is called the *sticky bit*.

In addition to the file mode bits listed above, there may be file attributes specific to the file system, e.g., access control lists (ACLs), whether a file is compressed, whether a file can be modified (immutability), and whether a file can be dumped. These are usually set using programs specific to the file system. For example:

ext2   On GNU and GNU/Linux the file attributes specific to the ext2 file system are set using `chattr`.

FFS   On FreeBSD the file flags specific to the FFS file system are set using `chflags`.

Even if a file's mode bits allow an operation on that file, that operation may still fail, because:

- the file-system-specific attributes or flags do not permit it; or
- the file system is mounted as read-only.

For example, if the immutable attribute is set on a file, it cannot be modified, regardless of the fact that you may have just run `chmod a+w FILE`.

27.2 Symbolic Modes

Symbolic modes represent changes to files' mode bits as operations on single-character symbols. They allow you to modify either all or selected parts of files' mode bits, optionally based on their previous values, and perhaps on the current `umask` as well (see Section 27.2.6 [Umask and Protection], page 210).

The format of symbolic modes is:

[ugoa...][-+=]perms...[,...]

where *perms* is either zero or more letters from the set '`rwxXst`', or a single letter from the set '`ugo`'.

The following sections describe the operators and other details of symbolic modes.

27.2.1 Setting Permissions

The basic symbolic operations on a file's permissions are adding, removing, and setting the permission that certain users have to read, write, and execute or search the file. These operations have the following format:

users operation permissions

The spaces between the three parts above are shown for readability only; symbolic modes cannot contain spaces.

The *users* part tells which users' access to the file is changed. It consists of one or more of the following letters (or it can be empty; see Section 27.2.6 [Umask and Protection], page 210, for a description of what happens then). When more than one of these letters is given, the order that they are in does not matter.

u   the user who owns the file;

g   other users who are in the file's group;

o   all other users;

a   all users; the same as '`ugo`'.

The *operation* part tells how to change the affected users' access to the file, and is one of the following symbols:

+   to add the *permissions* to whatever permissions the *users* already have for the
               file;

–   to remove the *permissions* from whatever permissions the *users* already have
               for the file;

=   to make the *permissions* the only permissions that the *users* have for the file.

The *permissions* part tells what kind of access to the file should be changed; it is normally
zero or more of the following letters. As with the *users* part, the order does not matter
when more than one letter is given. Omitting the *permissions* part is useful only with the
'=' operation, where it gives the specified *users* no access at all to the file.

r   the permission the *users* have to read the file;

w   the permission the *users* have to write to the file;

x   the permission the *users* have to execute the file, or search it if it is a directory.

For example, to give everyone permission to read and write a regular file, but not to
execute it, use:

        a=rw

To remove write permission for all users other than the file's owner, use:

        go-w

The above command does not affect the access that the owner of the file has to it, nor does
it affect whether other users can read or execute the file.

To give everyone except a file's owner no permission to do anything with that file, use
the mode below. Other users could still remove the file, if they have write permission on
the directory it is in.

        go=

Another way to specify the same thing is:

        og-rwx

27.2.2 Copying Existing Permissions

You can base a file's permissions on its existing permissions. To do this, instead of using
a series of 'r', 'w', or 'x' letters after the operator, you use the letter 'u', 'g', or 'o'. For
example, the mode

        o+g

adds the permissions for users who are in a file's group to the permissions that other
users have for the file. Thus, if the file started out as mode 664 ('rw-rw-r--'), the above
mode would change it to mode 666 ('rw-rw-rw-'). If the file had started out as mode 741
('rwxr----x'), the above mode would change it to mode 745 ('rwxr--r-x'). The '-' and
'=' operations work analogously.

27.2.3 Changing Special Mode Bits

In addition to changing a file's read, write, and execute/search permissions, you can change
its special mode bits. See Section 27.1 [Mode Structure], page 206, for a summary of these
special mode bits.

To change the file mode bits to set the user ID on execution, use 'u' in the *users* part of the symbolic mode and 's' in the *permissions* part.

To change the file mode bits to set the group ID on execution, use 'g' in the *users* part of the symbolic mode and 's' in the *permissions* part.

To set both user and group ID on execution, omit the *users* part of the symbolic mode (or use 'a') and use 's' in the *permissions* part.

To change the file mode bits to set the restricted deletion flag or sticky bit, omit the *users* part of the symbolic mode (or use 'a') and use 't' in the *permissions* part.

For example, to set the set-user-ID mode bit of a program, you can use the mode:

```
u+s
```

To remove both set-user-ID and set-group-ID mode bits from it, you can use the mode:

```
a-s
```

To set the restricted deletion flag or sticky bit, you can use the mode:

```
+t
```

The combination 'o+s' has no effect. On GNU systems the combinations 'u+t' and 'g+t' have no effect, and 'o+t' acts like plain '+t'.

The '=' operator is not very useful with special mode bits. For example, the mode:

```
o=t
```

does set the restricted deletion flag or sticky bit, but it also removes all read, write, and execute/search permissions that users not in the file's group might have had for it.

See Section 27.5 [Directory Setuid and Setgid], page 212, for additional rules concerning set-user-ID and set-group-ID bits and directories.

27.2.4 Conditional Executability

There is one more special type of symbolic permission: if you use 'X' instead of 'x', execute/search permission is affected only if the file is a directory or already had execute permission.

For example, this mode:

```
a+X
```

gives all users permission to search directories, or to execute files if anyone could execute them before.

27.2.5 Making Multiple Changes

The format of symbolic modes is actually more complex than described above (see Section 27.2.1 [Setting Permissions], page 207). It provides two ways to make multiple changes to files' mode bits.

The first way is to specify multiple *operation* and *permissions* parts after a *users* part in the symbolic mode.

For example, the mode:

```
og+rX-w
```

gives users other than the owner of the file read permission and, if it is a directory or if someone already had execute permission to it, gives them execute/search permission; and it also denies them write permission to the file. It does not affect the permission that the owner of the file has for it. The above mode is equivalent to the two modes:

```
og+rX
og-w
```

The second way to make multiple changes is to specify more than one simple symbolic mode, separated by commas. For example, the mode:

```
a+r,go-w
```

gives everyone permission to read the file and removes write permission on it for all users except its owner. Another example:

```
u=rwx,g=rx,o=
```

sets all of the permission bits for the file explicitly. (It gives users who are not in the file's group no permission at all for it.)

The two methods can be combined. The mode:

```
a+r,g+x-w
```

gives all users permission to read the file, and gives users who are in the file's group permission to execute/search it as well, but not permission to write to it. The above mode could be written in several different ways; another is:

```
u+r,g+rx,o+r,g-w
```

27.2.6 The Umask and Protection

If the *users* part of a symbolic mode is omitted, it defaults to 'a' (affect all users), except that any permissions that are *set* in the system variable **umask** are *not affected*. The value of **umask** can be set using the **umask** command. Its default value varies from system to system.

Omitting the *users* part of a symbolic mode is generally not useful with operations other than '+'. It is useful with '+' because it allows you to use **umask** as an easily customizable protection against giving away more permission to files than you intended to.

As an example, if **umask** has the value 2, which removes write permission for users who are not in the file's group, then the mode:

```
+w
```

adds permission to write to the file to its owner and to other users who are in the file's group, but *not* to other users. In contrast, the mode:

```
a+w
```

ignores **umask**, and *does* give write permission for the file to all users.

27.3 Numeric Modes

As an alternative to giving a symbolic mode, you can give an octal (base 8) number that represents the mode. This number is always interpreted in octal; you do not have to add a leading '0', as you do in C. Mode '0055' is the same as mode '55'. (However, modes of five digits or more, such as '00055', are sometimes special. See Section 27.5 [Directory Setuid and Setgid], page 212.)

A numeric mode is usually shorter than the corresponding symbolic mode, but it is limited in that normally it cannot take into account the previous file mode bits; it can only set them absolutely. The set-user-ID and set-group-ID bits of directories are an exception to this general limitation. See Section 27.5 [Directory Setuid and Setgid], page 212. Also, operator numeric modes can take previous file mode bits into account. See Section 27.4 [Operator Numeric Modes], page 211.

The permissions granted to the user, to other users in the file's group, and to other users not in the file's group each require three bits, which are represented as one octal digit. The three special mode bits also require one bit each, and they are as a group represented as another octal digit. Here is how the bits are arranged, starting with the lowest valued bit:

```
Value in   Corresponding
Mode       Mode Bit


           Other users not in the file's group:
    1      Execute/search
    2      Write
    4      Read


           Other users in the file's group:
   10      Execute/search
   20      Write
   40      Read


           The file's owner:
  100      Execute/search
  200      Write
  400      Read


           Special mode bits:
 1000      Restricted deletion flag or sticky bit
 2000      Set group ID on execution
 4000      Set user ID on execution
```

For example, numeric mode '4755' corresponds to symbolic mode 'u=rwxs,go=rx', and numeric mode '664' corresponds to symbolic mode 'ug=rw,o=r'. Numeric mode '0' corresponds to symbolic mode 'a='.

27.4 Operator Numeric Modes

An operator numeric mode is a numeric mode that is prefixed by a '-', '+', or '=' operator, which has the same interpretation as in symbolic modes. For example, '+440' enables read permission for the file's owner and group, '-1' disables execute permission for other users, and '=600' clears all permissions except for enabling read-write permissions for the file's owner. Operator numeric modes can be combined with symbolic modes by separating them with a comma; for example, '=0,u+r' clears all permissions except for enabling read permission for the file's owner.

The commands 'chmod =755 dir' and 'chmod 755 dir' differ in that the former clears the directory dir's setuid and setgid bits, whereas the latter preserves them. See Section 27.5 [Directory Setuid and Setgid], page 212.

Operator numeric modes are a GNU extension.

27.5 Directories and the Set-User-ID and Set-Group-ID Bits

On most systems, if a directory's set-group-ID bit is set, newly created subfiles inherit the same group as the directory, and newly created subdirectories inherit the set-group-ID bit of the parent directory. On a few systems, a directory's set-user-ID bit has a similar effect on the ownership of new subfiles and the set-user-ID bits of new subdirectories. These mechanisms let users share files more easily, by lessening the need to use chmod or chown to share new files.

These convenience mechanisms rely on the set-user-ID and set-group-ID bits of directories. If commands like chmod and mkdir routinely cleared these bits on directories, the mechanisms would be less convenient and it would be harder to share files. Therefore, a command like chmod does not affect the set-user-ID or set-group-ID bits of a directory unless the user specifically mentions them in a symbolic mode, or uses an operator numeric mode such as '=755', or sets them in a numeric mode, or clears them in a numeric mode that has five or more octal digits. For example, on systems that support set-group-ID inheritance:

```
# These commands leave the set-user-ID and
# set-group-ID bits of the subdirectories alone,
# so that they retain their default values.
mkdir A B C
chmod 755 A
chmod 0755 B
chmod u=rwx,go=rx C
mkdir -m 755 D
mkdir -m 0755 E
mkdir -m u=rwx,go=rx F
```

If you want to try to set these bits, you must mention them explicitly in the symbolic or numeric modes, e.g.:

```
# These commands try to set the set-user-ID
# and set-group-ID bits of the subdirectories.
mkdir G
chmod 6755 G
chmod +6000 G
chmod u=rwx,go=rx,a+s G
mkdir -m 6755 H
mkdir -m +6000 I
mkdir -m u=rwx,go=rx,a+s J
```

If you want to try to clear these bits, you must mention them explicitly in a symbolic mode, or use an operator numeric mode, or specify a numeric mode with five or more octal digits, e.g.:

```
# These commands try to clear the set-user-ID
# and set-group-ID bits of the directory D.
chmod a-s D
chmod -6000 D
chmod =755 D
```

```
chmod 00755 D
```

This behavior is a GNU extension. Portable scripts should not rely on requests to set or clear these bits on directories, as POSIX allows implementations to ignore these requests. The GNU behavior with numeric modes of four or fewer digits is intended for scripts portable to systems that preserve these bits; the behavior with numeric modes of five or more digits is for scripts portable to systems that do not preserve the bits.

28 Date input formats

First, a quote:

> Our units of temporal measurement, from seconds on up to months, are so complicated, asymmetrical and disjunctive so as to make coherent mental reckoning in time all but impossible. Indeed, had some tyrannical god contrived to enslave our minds to time, to make it all but impossible for us to escape subjection to sodden routines and unpleasant surprises, he could hardly have done better than handing down our present system. It is like a set of trapezoidal building blocks, with no vertical or horizontal surfaces, like a language in which the simplest thought demands ornate constructions, useless particles and lengthy circumlocutions. Unlike the more successful patterns of language and science, which enable us to face experience boldly or at least level-headedly, our system of temporal calculation silently and persistently encourages our terror of time.
>
> ... It is as though architects had to measure length in feet, width in meters and height in ells; as though basic instruction manuals demanded a knowledge of five different languages. It is no wonder then that we often look into our own immediate past or future, last Tuesday or a week from Sunday, with feelings of helpless confusion. ...
>
> —Robert Grudin, *Time and the Art of Living*.

This section describes the textual date representations that GNU programs accept. These are the strings you, as a user, can supply as arguments to the various programs. The C interface (via the `parse_datetime` function) is not described here.

28.1 General date syntax

A *date* is a string, possibly empty, containing many items separated by whitespace. The whitespace may be omitted when no ambiguity arises. The empty string means the beginning of today (i.e., midnight). Order of the items is immaterial. A date string may contain many flavors of items:

- calendar date items
- time of day items
- time zone items
- combined date and time of day items
- day of the week items
- relative items
- pure numbers.

We describe each of these item types in turn, below.

A few ordinal numbers may be written out in words in some contexts. This is most useful for specifying day of the week items or relative items (see below). Among the most commonly used ordinal numbers, the word 'last' stands for −1, 'this' stands for 0, and 'first' and 'next' both stand for 1. Because the word 'second' stands for the unit of time there is no way to write the ordinal number 2, but for convenience 'third' stands for 3, 'fourth' for 4, 'fifth' for 5, 'sixth' for 6, 'seventh' for 7, 'eighth' for 8, 'ninth' for 9, 'tenth' for 10, 'eleventh' for 11 and 'twelfth' for 12.

When a month is written this way, it is still considered to be written numerically, instead of being "spelled in full"; this changes the allowed strings.

In the current implementation, only English is supported for words and abbreviations like 'AM', 'DST', 'EST', 'first', 'January', 'Sunday', 'tomorrow', and 'year'.

The output of the date command is not always acceptable as a date string, not only because of the language problem, but also because there is no standard meaning for time zone items like 'IST'. When using date to generate a date string intended to be parsed later, specify a date format that is independent of language and that does not use time zone items other than 'UTC' and 'Z'. Here are some ways to do this:

```
$ LC_ALL=C TZ=UTC0 date
Mon Mar  1 00:21:42 UTC 2004
$ TZ=UTC0 date +'%Y-%m-%d %H:%M:%SZ'
2004-03-01 00:21:42Z
$ date --rfc-3339=ns  # --rfc-3339 is a GNU extension.
2004-02-29 16:21:42.692722128-08:00
$ date --rfc-2822  # a GNU extension
Sun, 29 Feb 2004 16:21:42 -0800
$ date +'%Y-%m-%d %H:%M:%S %z'  # %z is a GNU extension.
2004-02-29 16:21:42 -0800
$ date +'@%s.%N'  # %s and %N are GNU extensions.
@1078100502.692722128
```

Alphabetic case is completely ignored in dates. Comments may be introduced between round parentheses, as long as included parentheses are properly nested. Hyphens not followed by a digit are currently ignored. Leading zeros on numbers are ignored.

Invalid dates like '2005-02-29' or times like '24:00' are rejected. In the typical case of a host that does not support leap seconds, a time like '23:59:60' is rejected even if it corresponds to a valid leap second.

28.2 Calendar date items

A *calendar date item* specifies a day of the year. It is specified differently, depending on whether the month is specified numerically or literally. All these strings specify the same calendar date:

```
1972-09-24      # ISO 8601.
72-9-24         # Assume 19xx for 69 through 99,
                # 20xx for 00 through 68.
72-09-24        # Leading zeros are ignored.
9/24/72         # Common U.S. writing.
24 September 1972
24 Sept 72      # September has a special abbreviation.
24 Sep 72       # Three-letter abbreviations always allowed.
Sep 24, 1972
24-sep-72
24sep72
```

The year can also be omitted. In this case, the last specified year is used, or the current year if none. For example:

```
9/24
sep 24
```

Here are the rules.

For numeric months, the ISO 8601 format '*year-month-day*' is allowed, where *year* is any positive number, *month* is a number between 01 and 12, and *day* is a number between 01 and 31. A leading zero must be present if a number is less than ten. If *year* is 68 or smaller, then 2000 is added to it; otherwise, if *year* is less than 100, then 1900 is added to it. The construct '*month/day/year*', popular in the United States, is accepted. Also '*month/day*', omitting the year.

Literal months may be spelled out in full: 'January', 'February', 'March', 'April', 'May', 'June', 'July', 'August', 'September', 'October', 'November' or 'December'. Literal months may be abbreviated to their first three letters, possibly followed by an abbreviating dot. It is also permitted to write 'Sept' instead of 'September'.

When months are written literally, the calendar date may be given as any of the following:

```
day month year
day month
month day year
day-month-year
```

Or, omitting the year:

```
month day
```

28.3 Time of day items

A *time of day item* in date strings specifies the time on a given day. Here are some examples, all of which represent the same time:

```
20:02:00.000000
20:02
8:02pm
20:02-0500      # In EST (U.S. Eastern Standard Time).
```

More generally, the time of day may be given as '*hour:minute:second*', where *hour* is a number between 0 and 23, *minute* is a number between 0 and 59, and *second* is a number between 0 and 59 possibly followed by '.' or ',' and a fraction containing one or more digits. Alternatively, ':*second*' can be omitted, in which case it is taken to be zero. On the rare hosts that support leap seconds, *second* may be 60.

If the time is followed by 'am' or 'pm' (or 'a.m.' or 'p.m.'), *hour* is restricted to run from 1 to 12, and ':*minute*' may be omitted (taken to be zero). 'am' indicates the first half of the day, 'pm' indicates the second half of the day. In this notation, 12 is the predecessor of 1: midnight is '12am' while noon is '12pm'. (This is the zero-oriented interpretation of '12am' and '12pm', as opposed to the old tradition derived from Latin which uses '12m' for noon and '12pm' for midnight.)

The time may alternatively be followed by a time zone correction, expressed as '*shhmm*', where *s* is '+' or '-', *hh* is a number of zone hours and *mm* is a number of zone minutes. The zone minutes term, *mm*, may be omitted, in which case the one- or two-digit correction is interpreted as a number of hours. You can also separate *hh* from *mm* with a colon. When a time zone correction is given this way, it forces interpretation of the time relative to Coordinated Universal Time (UTC), overriding any previous specification for the time zone or the local time zone. For example, '+0530' and '+05:30' both stand for the time zone 5.5 hours ahead of UTC (e.g., India). This is the best way to specify a time zone correction by fractional parts of an hour. The maximum zone correction is 24 hours.

Either 'am'/'pm' or a time zone correction may be specified, but not both.

28.4 Time zone items

A *time zone item* specifies an international time zone, indicated by a small set of letters, e.g., 'UTC' or 'Z' for Coordinated Universal Time. Any included periods are ignored. By following a non-daylight-saving time zone by the string 'DST' in a separate word (that is, separated by some white space), the corresponding daylight saving time zone may be specified. Alternatively, a non-daylight-saving time zone can be followed by a time zone correction, to add the two values. This is normally done only for 'UTC'; for example, 'UTC+05:30' is equivalent to '+05:30'.

Time zone items other than 'UTC' and 'Z' are obsolescent and are not recommended, because they are ambiguous; for example, 'EST' has a different meaning in Australia than in the United States. Instead, it's better to use unambiguous numeric time zone corrections like '-0500', as described in the previous section.

If neither a time zone item nor a time zone correction is supplied, time stamps are interpreted using the rules of the default time zone (see Section 28.10 [Specifying time zone rules], page 219).

28.5 Combined date and time of day items

The ISO 8601 date and time of day extended format consists of an ISO 8601 date, a 'T' character separator, and an ISO 8601 time of day. This format is also recognized if the 'T' is replaced by a space.

In this format, the time of day should use 24-hour notation. Fractional seconds are allowed, with either comma or period preceding the fraction. ISO 8601 fractional minutes and hours are not supported. Typically, hosts support nanosecond timestamp resolution; excess precision is silently discarded.

Here are some examples:

```
2012-09-24T20:02:00.052-0500
2012-12-31T23:59:59,999999999+1100
1970-01-01 00:00Z
```

28.6 Day of week items

The explicit mention of a day of the week will forward the date (only if necessary) to reach that day of the week in the future.

Days of the week may be spelled out in full: 'Sunday', 'Monday', 'Tuesday', 'Wednesday', 'Thursday', 'Friday' or 'Saturday'. Days may be abbreviated to their first three letters, optionally followed by a period. The special abbreviations 'Tues' for 'Tuesday', 'Wednes' for 'Wednesday' and 'Thur' or 'Thurs' for 'Thursday' are also allowed.

A number may precede a day of the week item to move forward supplementary weeks. It is best used in expression like 'third monday'. In this context, 'last *day*' or 'next *day*' is also acceptable; they move one week before or after the day that *day* by itself would represent.

A comma following a day of the week item is ignored.

28.7 Relative items in date strings

Relative items adjust a date (or the current date if none) forward or backward. The effects of relative items accumulate. Here are some examples:

```
1 year
1 year ago
3 years
2 days
```

The unit of time displacement may be selected by the string 'year' or 'month' for moving by whole years or months. These are fuzzy units, as years and months are not all of equal duration. More precise units are 'fortnight' which is worth 14 days, 'week' worth 7 days, 'day' worth 24 hours, 'hour' worth 60 minutes, 'minute' or 'min' worth 60 seconds, and 'second' or 'sec' worth one second. An 's' suffix on these units is accepted and ignored.

The unit of time may be preceded by a multiplier, given as an optionally signed number. Unsigned numbers are taken as positively signed. No number at all implies 1 for a multiplier. Following a relative item by the string 'ago' is equivalent to preceding the unit by a multiplier with value −1.

The string 'tomorrow' is worth one day in the future (equivalent to 'day'), the string 'yesterday' is worth one day in the past (equivalent to 'day ago').

The strings 'now' or 'today' are relative items corresponding to zero-valued time displacement, these strings come from the fact a zero-valued time displacement represents the current time when not otherwise changed by previous items. They may be used to stress other items, like in '12:00 today'. The string 'this' also has the meaning of a zero-valued time displacement, but is preferred in date strings like 'this thursday'.

When a relative item causes the resulting date to cross a boundary where the clocks were adjusted, typically for daylight saving time, the resulting date and time are adjusted accordingly.

The fuzz in units can cause problems with relative items. For example, '2003-07-31 -1 month' might evaluate to 2003-07-01, because 2003-06-31 is an invalid date. To determine the previous month more reliably, you can ask for the month before the 15th of the current month. For example:

```
$ date -R
Thu, 31 Jul 2003 13:02:39 -0700
$ date --date='-1 month' +'Last month was %B?'
Last month was July?
$ date --date="$(date +%Y-%m-15) -1 month" +'Last month was %B!'
Last month was June!
```

Also, take care when manipulating dates around clock changes such as daylight saving leaps. In a few cases these have added or subtracted as much as 24 hours from the clock, so it is often wise to adopt universal time by setting the TZ environment variable to 'UTC0' before embarking on calendrical calculations.

28.8 Pure numbers in date strings

The precise interpretation of a pure decimal number depends on the context in the date string.

If the decimal number is of the form *yyyymmdd* and no other calendar date item (see Section 28.2 [Calendar date items], page 215) appears before it in the date string, then *yyyy* is read as the year, *mm* as the month number and *dd* as the day of the month, for the specified calendar date.

If the decimal number is of the form *hhmm* and no other time of day item appears before it in the date string, then *hh* is read as the hour of the day and *mm* as the minute of the hour, for the specified time of day. *mm* can also be omitted.

If both a calendar date and a time of day appear to the left of a number in the date string, but no relative item, then the number overrides the year.

28.9 Seconds since the Epoch

If you precede a number with '@', it represents an internal time stamp as a count of seconds. The number can contain an internal decimal point (either '.' or ','); any excess precision not supported by the internal representation is truncated toward minus infinity. Such a number cannot be combined with any other date item, as it specifies a complete time stamp.

Internally, computer times are represented as a count of seconds since an epoch—a well-defined point of time. On GNU and POSIX systems, the epoch is 1970-01-01 00:00:00 UTC, so '@0' represents this time, '@1' represents 1970-01-01 00:00:01 UTC, and so forth. GNU and most other POSIX-compliant systems support such times as an extension to POSIX, using negative counts, so that '@-1' represents 1969-12-31 23:59:59 UTC.

Traditional Unix systems count seconds with 32-bit two's-complement integers and can represent times from 1901-12-13 20:45:52 through 2038-01-19 03:14:07 UTC. More modern systems use 64-bit counts of seconds with nanosecond subcounts, and can represent all the times in the known lifetime of the universe to a resolution of 1 nanosecond.

On most hosts, these counts ignore the presence of leap seconds. For example, on most hosts '@915148799' represents 1998-12-31 23:59:59 UTC, '@915148800' represents 1999-01-01 00:00:00 UTC, and there is no way to represent the intervening leap second 1998-12-31 23:59:60 UTC.

28.10 Specifying time zone rules

Normally, dates are interpreted using the rules of the current time zone, which in turn are specified by the TZ environment variable, or by a system default if TZ is not set. To specify a different set of default time zone rules that apply just to one date, start the date with a string of the form 'TZ="rule"'. The two quote characters ('"') must be present in the date, and any quotes or backslashes within *rule* must be escaped by a backslash.

For example, with the GNU date command you can answer the question "What time is it in New York when a Paris clock shows 6:30am on October 31, 2004?" by using a date beginning with 'TZ="Europe/Paris"' as shown in the following shell transcript:

```
$ export TZ="America/New_York"
$ date --date='TZ="Europe/Paris" 2004-10-31 06:30'
Sun Oct 31 01:30:00 EDT 2004
```

In this example, the `--date` operand begins with its own `TZ` setting, so the rest of that operand is processed according to 'Europe/Paris' rules, treating the string '2004-10-31 06:30' as if it were in Paris. However, since the output of the `date` command is processed according to the overall time zone rules, it uses New York time. (Paris was normally six hours ahead of New York in 2004, but this example refers to a brief Halloween period when the gap was five hours.)

A `TZ` value is a rule that typically names a location in the 'tz' database. A recent catalog of location names appears in the TWiki Date and Time Gateway. A few non-GNU hosts require a colon before a location name in a `TZ` setting, e.g., 'TZ=":America/New_York"'.

The 'tz' database includes a wide variety of locations ranging from 'Arctic/Longyearbyen' to 'Antarctica/South_Pole', but if you are at sea and have your own private time zone, or if you are using a non-GNU host that does not support the 'tz' database, you may need to use a POSIX rule instead. Simple POSIX rules like 'UTC0' specify a time zone without daylight saving time; other rules can specify simple daylight saving regimes. See Section "Specifying the Time Zone with TZ" in *The GNU C Library*.

28.11 Authors of `parse_datetime`

`parse_datetime` started life as `getdate`, as originally implemented by Steven M. Bellovin (smb@research.att.com) while at the University of North Carolina at Chapel Hill. The code was later tweaked by a couple of people on Usenet, then completely overhauled by Rich $alz (rsalz@bbn.com) and Jim Berets (jberets@bbn.com) in August, 1990. Various revisions for the GNU system were made by David MacKenzie, Jim Meyering, Paul Eggert and others, including renaming it to `get_date` to avoid a conflict with the alternative Posix function `getdate`, and a later rename to `parse_datetime`. The Posix function `getdate` can parse more locale-specific dates using `strptime`, but relies on an environment variable and external file, and lacks the thread-safety of `parse_datetime`.

This chapter was originally produced by François Pinard (pinard@iro.umontreal.ca) from the `parse_datetime.y` source code, and then edited by K. Berry (kb@cs.umb.edu).

29 Opening the Software Toolbox

An earlier version of this chapter appeared in the *What's GNU?* column of the June 1994 *Linux Journal*. It was written by Arnold Robbins.

Toolbox Introduction

This month's column is only peripherally related to the GNU Project, in that it describes a number of the GNU tools on your GNU/Linux system and how they might be used. What it's really about is the "Software Tools" philosophy of program development and usage.

The software tools philosophy was an important and integral concept in the initial design and development of Unix (of which Linux and GNU are essentially clones). Unfortunately, in the modern day press of Internetworking and flashy GUIs, it seems to have fallen by the wayside. This is a shame, since it provides a powerful mental model for solving many kinds of problems.

Many people carry a Swiss Army knife around in their pants pockets (or purse). A Swiss Army knife is a handy tool to have: it has several knife blades, a screwdriver, tweezers, toothpick, nail file, corkscrew, and perhaps a number of other things on it. For the everyday, small miscellaneous jobs where you need a simple, general purpose tool, it's just the thing.

On the other hand, an experienced carpenter doesn't build a house using a Swiss Army knife. Instead, he has a toolbox chock full of specialized tools—a saw, a hammer, a screwdriver, a plane, and so on. And he knows exactly when and where to use each tool; you won't catch him hammering nails with the handle of his screwdriver.

The Unix developers at Bell Labs were all professional programmers and trained computer scientists. They had found that while a one-size-fits-all program might appeal to a user because there's only one program to use, in practice such programs are

a. difficult to write,

b. difficult to maintain and debug, and

c. difficult to extend to meet new situations.

Instead, they felt that programs should be specialized tools. In short, each program "should do one thing well." No more and no less. Such programs are simpler to design, write, and get right—they only do one thing.

Furthermore, they found that with the right machinery for hooking programs together, that the whole was greater than the sum of the parts. By combining several special purpose programs, you could accomplish a specific task that none of the programs was designed for, and accomplish it much more quickly and easily than if you had to write a special purpose program. We will see some (classic) examples of this further on in the column. (An important additional point was that, if necessary, take a detour and build any software tools you may need first, if you don't already have something appropriate in the toolbox.)

I/O Redirection

Hopefully, you are familiar with the basics of I/O redirection in the shell, in particular the concepts of "standard input," "standard output," and "standard error". Briefly, "standard input" is a data source, where data comes from. A program should not need to either know or care if the data source is a disk file, a keyboard, a magnetic tape, or even a punched card reader. Similarly, "standard output" is a data sink, where data goes to. The program should neither know nor care where this might be. Programs that only read their standard input, do something to the data, and then send it on, are called *filters*, by analogy to filters in a water pipeline.

With the Unix shell, it's very easy to set up data pipelines:

```
program_to_create_data | filter1 | ... | filterN > final.pretty.data
```

We start out by creating the raw data; each filter applies some successive transformation to the data, until by the time it comes out of the pipeline, it is in the desired form.

This is fine and good for standard input and standard output. Where does the standard error come in to play? Well, think about `filter1` in the pipeline above. What happens if it encounters an error in the data it sees? If it writes an error message to standard output, it will just disappear down the pipeline into `filter2`'s input, and the user will probably never see it. So programs need a place where they can send error messages so that the user will notice them. This is standard error, and it is usually connected to your console or window, even if you have redirected standard output of your program away from your screen.

For filter programs to work together, the format of the data has to be agreed upon. The most straightforward and easiest format to use is simply lines of text. Unix data files are generally just streams of bytes, with lines delimited by the ASCII LF (Line Feed) character, conventionally called a "newline" in the Unix literature. (This is '\n' if you're a C programmer.) This is the format used by all the traditional filtering programs. (Many earlier operating systems had elaborate facilities and special purpose programs for managing binary data. Unix has always shied away from such things, under the philosophy that it's easiest to simply be able to view and edit your data with a text editor.)

OK, enough introduction. Let's take a look at some of the tools, and then we'll see how to hook them together in interesting ways. In the following discussion, we will only present those command line options that interest us. As you should always do, double check your system documentation for the full story.

The `who` Command

The first program is the `who` command. By itself, it generates a list of the users who are currently logged in. Although I'm writing this on a single-user system, we'll pretend that several people are logged in:

```
$ who
⊣ arnold    console Jan 22 19:57
⊣ miriam    ttyp0   Jan 23 14:19(:0.0)
⊣ bill      ttyp1   Jan 21 09:32(:0.0)
⊣ arnold    ttyp2   Jan 23 20:48(:0.0)
```

Here, the '$' is the usual shell prompt, at which I typed 'who'. There are three people logged in, and I am logged in twice. On traditional Unix systems, user names are never more than eight characters long. This little bit of trivia will be useful later. The output of `who` is nice, but the data is not all that exciting.

The cut Command

The next program we'll look at is the cut command. This program cuts out columns or fields of input data. For example, we can tell it to print just the login name and full name from the /etc/passwd file. The /etc/passwd file has seven fields, separated by colons:

```
arnold:xyzzy:2076:10:Arnold D. Robbins:/home/arnold:/bin/bash
```

To get the first and fifth fields, we would use cut like this:

```
$ cut -d: -f1,5 /etc/passwd
⊣ root:Operator
...
⊣ arnold:Arnold D. Robbins
⊣ miriam:Miriam A. Robbins
...
```

With the -c option, cut will cut out specific characters (i.e., columns) in the input lines. This is useful for input data that has fixed width fields, and does not have a field separator. For example, list the Monday dates for the current month:

```
$ cal | cut -c 3-5
⊣Mo
⊣
⊣  6
⊣ 13
⊣ 20
⊣ 27
```

The sort Command

Next we'll look at the sort command. This is one of the most powerful commands on a Unix-style system; one that you will often find yourself using when setting up fancy data plumbing.

The sort command reads and sorts each file named on the command line. It then merges the sorted data and writes it to standard output. It will read standard input if no files are given on the command line (thus making it into a filter). The sort is based on the character collating sequence or based on user-supplied ordering criteria.

The uniq Command

Finally (at least for now), we'll look at the uniq program. When sorting data, you will often end up with duplicate lines, lines that are identical. Usually, all you need is one instance of each line. This is where uniq comes in. The uniq program reads its standard input. It prints only one copy of each repeated line. It does have several options. Later on, we'll use the -c option, which prints each unique line, preceded by a count of the number of times that line occurred in the input.

Putting the Tools Together

Now, let's suppose this is a large ISP server system with dozens of users logged in. The management wants the system administrator to write a program that will generate a sorted list of logged in users. Furthermore, even if a user is logged in multiple times, his or her name should only show up in the output once.

The administrator could sit down with the system documentation and write a C program that did this. It would take perhaps a couple of hundred lines of code and about two hours to write it, test it, and debug it. However, knowing the software toolbox, the administrator can instead start out by generating just a list of logged on users:

```
$ who | cut -c1-8
⊣ arnold
⊣ miriam
⊣ bill
⊣ arnold
```

Next, sort the list:

```
$ who | cut -c1-8 | sort
⊣ arnold
⊣ arnold
⊣ bill
⊣ miriam
```

Finally, run the sorted list through **uniq**, to weed out duplicates:

```
$ who | cut -c1-8 | sort | uniq
⊣ arnold
⊣ bill
⊣ miriam
```

The **sort** command actually has a -u option that does what **uniq** does. However, **uniq** has other uses for which one cannot substitute 'sort -u'.

The administrator puts this pipeline into a shell script, and makes it available for all the users on the system ('#' is the system administrator, or **root**, prompt):

```
# cat > /usr/local/bin/listusers
who | cut -c1-8 | sort | uniq
^D
# chmod +x /usr/local/bin/listusers
```

There are four major points to note here. First, with just four programs, on one command line, the administrator was able to save about two hours worth of work. Furthermore, the shell pipeline is just about as efficient as the C program would be, and it is much more efficient in terms of programmer time. People time is much more expensive than computer time, and in our modern "there's never enough time to do everything" society, saving two hours of programmer time is no mean feat.

Second, it is also important to emphasize that with the *combination* of the tools, it is possible to do a special purpose job never imagined by the authors of the individual programs.

Third, it is also valuable to build up your pipeline in stages, as we did here. This allows you to view the data at each stage in the pipeline, which helps you acquire the confidence that you are indeed using these tools correctly.

Finally, by bundling the pipeline in a shell script, other users can use your command, without having to remember the fancy plumbing you set up for them. In terms of how you run them, shell scripts and compiled programs are indistinguishable.

After the previous warm-up exercise, we'll look at two additional, more complicated pipelines. For them, we need to introduce two more tools.

The first is the `tr` command, which stands for "transliterate." The `tr` command works on a character-by-character basis, changing characters. Normally it is used for things like mapping upper case to lower case:

```
$ echo ThIs ExAmPlE HaS MIXED case! | tr '[:upper:]' '[:lower:]'
⊣ this example has mixed case!
```

There are several options of interest:

-c   work on the complement of the listed characters, i.e., operations apply to characters not in the given set

-d   delete characters in the first set from the output

-s   squeeze repeated characters in the output into just one character.

We will be using all three options in a moment.

The other command we'll look at is `comm`. The `comm` command takes two sorted input files as input data, and prints out the files' lines in three columns. The output columns are the data lines unique to the first file, the data lines unique to the second file, and the data lines that are common to both. The -1, -2, and -3 command line options *omit* the respective columns. (This is non-intuitive and takes a little getting used to.) For example:

```
$ cat f1
⊣ 11111
⊣ 22222
⊣ 33333
⊣ 44444
$ cat f2
⊣ 00000
⊣ 22222
⊣ 33333
⊣ 55555
$ comm f1 f2
⊣           00000
⊣ 11111
⊣                     22222
⊣                     33333
⊣ 44444
⊣           55555
```

The file name - tells `comm` to read standard input instead of a regular file.

Now we're ready to build a fancy pipeline. The first application is a word frequency counter. This helps an author determine if he or she is over-using certain words.

The first step is to change the case of all the letters in our input file to one case. "The" and "the" are the same word when doing counting.

```
$ tr '[:upper:]' '[:lower:]' < whats.gnu | ...
```

The next step is to get rid of punctuation. Quoted words and unquoted words should be treated identically; it's easiest to just get the punctuation out of the way.

```
$ tr '[:upper:]' '[:lower:]' < whats.gnu | tr -cd '[:alnum:]_ \n' | ...
```

The second **tr** command operates on the complement of the listed characters, which are all the letters, the digits, the underscore, and the blank. The '\n' represents the newline character; it has to be left alone. (The ASCII tab character should also be included for good measure in a production script.)

At this point, we have data consisting of words separated by blank space. The words only contain alphanumeric characters (and the underscore). The next step is break the data apart so that we have one word per line. This makes the counting operation much easier, as we will see shortly.

```
$ tr '[:upper:]' '[:lower:]' < whats.gnu | tr -cd '[:alnum:]_ \n' |
> tr -s ' ' '\n' | ...
```

This command turns blanks into newlines. The **-s** option squeezes multiple newline characters in the output into just one. This helps us avoid blank lines. (The '>' is the shell's "secondary prompt." This is what the shell prints when it notices you haven't finished typing in all of a command.)

We now have data consisting of one word per line, no punctuation, all one case. We're ready to count each word:

```
$ tr '[:upper:]' '[:lower:]' < whats.gnu | tr -cd '[:alnum:]_ \n' |
> tr -s ' ' '\n' | sort | uniq -c | ...
```

At this point, the data might look something like this:

```
60 a
 2 able
 6 about
 1 above
 2 accomplish
 1 acquire
 1 actually
 2 additional
```

The output is sorted by word, not by count! What we want is the most frequently used words first. Fortunately, this is easy to accomplish, with the help of two more **sort** options:

-n   do a numeric sort, not a textual one

-r   reverse the order of the sort

The final pipeline looks like this:

```
$ tr '[:upper:]' '[:lower:]' < whats.gnu | tr -cd '[:alnum:]_ \n' |
> tr -s ' ' '\n' | sort | uniq -c | sort -n -r
⊣    156 the
⊣     60 a
⊣     58 to
⊣     51 of
⊣     51 and
...
```

Whew! That's a lot to digest. Yet, the same principles apply. With six commands, on two lines (really one long one split for convenience), we've created a program that does something interesting and useful, in much less time than we could have written a C program to do the same thing.

A minor modification to the above pipeline can give us a simple spelling checker! To determine if you've spelled a word correctly, all you have to do is look it up in a dictionary. If it is not there, then chances are that your spelling is incorrect. So, we need a dictionary. The conventional location for a dictionary is **/usr/dict/words**. On my GNU/Linux system,[1] this is a sorted, 45,402 word dictionary.

Now, how to compare our file with the dictionary? As before, we generate a sorted list of words, one per line:

```
$ tr '[:upper:]' '[:lower:]' < whats.gnu | tr -cd '[:alnum:]_ \n' |
> tr -s ' ' '\n' | sort -u | ...
```

Now, all we need is a list of words that are *not* in the dictionary. Here is where the `comm` command comes in.

```
$ tr '[:upper:]' '[:lower:]' < whats.gnu | tr -cd '[:alnum:]_ \n' |
> tr -s ' ' '\n' | sort -u |
> comm -23 - /usr/dict/words
```

The `-2` and `-3` options eliminate lines that are only in the dictionary (the second file), and lines that are in both files. Lines only in the first file (standard input, our stream of words), are words that are not in the dictionary. These are likely candidates for spelling errors. This pipeline was the first cut at a production spelling checker on Unix.

There are some other tools that deserve brief mention.

grep   search files for text that matches a regular expression

wc   count lines, words, characters

tee   a T-fitting for data pipes, copies data to files and to standard output

sed   the stream editor, an advanced tool

awk   a data manipulation language, another advanced tool

The software tools philosophy also espoused the following bit of advice: "Let someone else do the hard part." This means, take something that gives you most of what you need, and then massage it the rest of the way until it's in the form that you want.

To summarize:

1. Each program should do one thing well. No more, no less.

2. Combining programs with appropriate plumbing leads to results where the whole is greater than the sum of the parts. It also leads to novel uses of programs that the authors might never have imagined.

3. Programs should never print extraneous header or trailer data, since these could get sent on down a pipeline. (A point we didn't mention earlier.)

4. Let someone else do the hard part.

5. Know your toolbox! Use each program appropriately. If you don't have an appropriate tool, build one.

As of this writing, all the programs discussed are available from http://ftp.gnu.org/old-gnu/textutils/textutils-1.22.tar.gz, with more recent versions available from http://ftp.gnu.org/gnu/coreutils.

---

[1] Redhat Linux 6.1, for the November 2000 revision of this article.

None of what I have presented in this column is new. The Software Tools philosophy was first introduced in the book *Software Tools*, by Brian Kernighan and P.J. Plauger (Addison-Wesley, ISBN 0-201-03669-X). This book showed how to write and use software tools. It was written in 1976, using a preprocessor for FORTRAN named `ratfor` (RATional FORtran). At the time, C was not as ubiquitous as it is now; FORTRAN was. The last chapter presented a `ratfor` to FORTRAN processor, written in `ratfor`. `ratfor` looks an awful lot like C; if you know C, you won't have any problem following the code.

In 1981, the book was updated and made available as *Software Tools in Pascal* (Addison-Wesley, ISBN 0-201-10342-7). Both books are still in print and are well worth reading if you're a programmer. They certainly made a major change in how I view programming.

The programs in both books are available from Brian Kernighan's home page. For a number of years, there was an active Software Tools Users Group, whose members had ported the original `ratfor` programs to essentially every computer system with a FOR-TRAN compiler. The popularity of the group waned in the middle 1980s as Unix began to spread beyond universities.

With the current proliferation of GNU code and other clones of Unix programs, these programs now receive little attention; modern C versions are much more efficient and do more than these programs do. Nevertheless, as exposition of good programming style, and evangelism for a still-valuable philosophy, these books are unparalleled, and I recommend them highly.

Acknowledgment: I would like to express my gratitude to Brian Kernighan of Bell Labs, the original Software Toolsmith, for reviewing this column.

Appendix A GNU Free Documentation License

Version 1.3, 3 November 2008

Copyright © 2000, 2001, 2002, 2007, 2008 Free Software Foundation, Inc.
http://fsf.org/

0. PREAMBLE

The purpose of this License is to make a manual, textbook, or other functional and useful document *free* in the sense of freedom: to assure everyone the effective freedom to copy and redistribute it, with or without modifying it, either commercially or non-commercially. Secondarily, this License preserves for the author and publisher a way to get credit for their work, while not being considered responsible for modifications made by others.

This License is a kind of "copyleft", which means that derivative works of the document must themselves be free in the same sense. It complements the GNU General Public License, which is a copyleft license designed for free software.

We have designed this License in order to use it for manuals for free software, because free software needs free documentation: a free program should come with manuals providing the same freedoms that the software does. But this License is not limited to software manuals; it can be used for any textual work, regardless of subject matter or whether it is published as a printed book. We recommend this License principally for works whose purpose is instruction or reference.

1. APPLICABILITY AND DEFINITIONS

This License applies to any manual or other work, in any medium, that contains a notice placed by the copyright holder saying it can be distributed under the terms of this License. Such a notice grants a world-wide, royalty-free license, unlimited in duration, to use that work under the conditions stated herein. The "Document", below, refers to any such manual or work. Any member of the public is a licensee, and is addressed as "you". You accept the license if you copy, modify or distribute the work in a way requiring permission under copyright law.

A "Modified Version" of the Document means any work containing the Document or a portion of it, either copied verbatim, or with modifications and/or translated into another language.

A "Secondary Section" is a named appendix or a front-matter section of the Document that deals exclusively with the relationship of the publishers or authors of the Document to the Document's overall subject (or to related matters) and contains nothing that could fall directly within that overall subject. (Thus, if the Document is in part a textbook of mathematics, a Secondary Section may not explain any mathematics.) The relationship could be a matter of historical connection with the subject or with related matters, or of legal, commercial, philosophical, ethical or political position regarding them.

The "Invariant Sections" are certain Secondary Sections whose titles are designated, as being those of Invariant Sections, in the notice that says that the Document is released under this License. If a section does not fit the above definition of Secondary then it is not allowed to be designated as Invariant. The Document may contain zero Invariant Sections. If the Document does not identify any Invariant Sections then there are none.

The "Cover Texts" are certain short passages of text that are listed, as Front-Cover Texts or Back-Cover Texts, in the notice that says that the Document is released under this License. A Front-Cover Text may be at most 5 words, and a Back-Cover Text may be at most 25 words.

A "Transparent" copy of the Document means a machine-readable copy, represented in a format whose specification is available to the general public, that is suitable for revising the document straightforwardly with generic text editors or (for images composed of pixels) generic paint programs or (for drawings) some widely available drawing editor, and that is suitable for input to text formatters or for automatic translation to a variety of formats suitable for input to text formatters. A copy made in an otherwise Transparent file format whose markup, or absence of markup, has been arranged to thwart or discourage subsequent modification by readers is not Transparent. An image format is not Transparent if used for any substantial amount of text. A copy that is not "Transparent" is called "Opaque".

Examples of suitable formats for Transparent copies include plain ASCII without markup, Texinfo input format, LaTeX input format, SGML or XML using a publicly available DTD, and standard-conforming simple HTML, PostScript or PDF designed for human modification. Examples of transparent image formats include PNG, XCF and JPG. Opaque formats include proprietary formats that can be read and edited only by proprietary word processors, SGML or XML for which the DTD and/or processing tools are not generally available, and the machine-generated HTML, PostScript or PDF produced by some word processors for output purposes only.

The "Title Page" means, for a printed book, the title page itself, plus such following pages as are needed to hold, legibly, the material this License requires to appear in the title page. For works in formats which do not have any title page as such, "Title Page" means the text near the most prominent appearance of the work's title, preceding the beginning of the body of the text.

The "publisher" means any person or entity that distributes copies of the Document to the public.

A section "Entitled XYZ" means a named subunit of the Document whose title either is precisely XYZ or contains XYZ in parentheses following text that translates XYZ in another language. (Here XYZ stands for a specific section name mentioned below, such as "Acknowledgements", "Dedications", "Endorsements", or "History".) To "Preserve the Title" of such a section when you modify the Document means that it remains a section "Entitled XYZ" according to this definition.

The Document may include Warranty Disclaimers next to the notice which states that this License applies to the Document. These Warranty Disclaimers are considered to be included by reference in this License, but only as regards disclaiming warranties: any other implication that these Warranty Disclaimers may have is void and has no effect on the meaning of this License.

2. VERBATIM COPYING

You may copy and distribute the Document in any medium, either commercially or noncommercially, provided that this License, the copyright notices, and the license notice saying this License applies to the Document are reproduced in all copies, and that you add no other conditions whatsoever to those of this License. You may not use technical measures to obstruct or control the reading or further copying of the copies you make or distribute. However, you may accept compensation in exchange for copies. If you distribute a large enough number of copies you must also follow the conditions in section 3.

You may also lend copies, under the same conditions stated above, and you may publicly display copies.

3. COPYING IN QUANTITY

If you publish printed copies (or copies in media that commonly have printed covers) of the Document, numbering more than 100, and the Document's license notice requires Cover Texts, you must enclose the copies in covers that carry, clearly and legibly, all these Cover Texts: Front-Cover Texts on the front cover, and Back-Cover Texts on the back cover. Both covers must also clearly and legibly identify you as the publisher of these copies. The front cover must present the full title with all words of the title equally prominent and visible. You may add other material on the covers in addition. Copying with changes limited to the covers, as long as they preserve the title of the Document and satisfy these conditions, can be treated as verbatim copying in other respects.

If the required texts for either cover are too voluminous to fit legibly, you should put the first ones listed (as many as fit reasonably) on the actual cover, and continue the rest onto adjacent pages.

If you publish or distribute Opaque copies of the Document numbering more than 100, you must either include a machine-readable Transparent copy along with each Opaque copy, or state in or with each Opaque copy a computer-network location from which the general network-using public has access to download using public-standard network protocols a complete Transparent copy of the Document, free of added material. If you use the latter option, you must take reasonably prudent steps, when you begin distribution of Opaque copies in quantity, to ensure that this Transparent copy will remain thus accessible at the stated location until at least one year after the last time you distribute an Opaque copy (directly or through your agents or retailers) of that edition to the public.

It is requested, but not required, that you contact the authors of the Document well before redistributing any large number of copies, to give them a chance to provide you with an updated version of the Document.

4. MODIFICATIONS

You may copy and distribute a Modified Version of the Document under the conditions of sections 2 and 3 above, provided that you release the Modified Version under precisely this License, with the Modified Version filling the role of the Document, thus licensing distribution and modification of the Modified Version to whoever possesses a copy of it. In addition, you must do these things in the Modified Version:

A. Use in the Title Page (and on the covers, if any) a title distinct from that of the Document, and from those of previous versions (which should, if there were any, be listed in the History section of the Document). You may use the same title as a previous version if the original publisher of that version gives permission.

B. List on the Title Page, as authors, one or more persons or entities responsible for authorship of the modifications in the Modified Version, together with at least five of the principal authors of the Document (all of its principal authors, if it has fewer than five), unless they release you from this requirement.

C. State on the Title page the name of the publisher of the Modified Version, as the publisher.

D. Preserve all the copyright notices of the Document.

E. Add an appropriate copyright notice for your modifications adjacent to the other copyright notices.

F. Include, immediately after the copyright notices, a license notice giving the public permission to use the Modified Version under the terms of this License, in the form shown in the Addendum below.

G. Preserve in that license notice the full lists of Invariant Sections and required Cover Texts given in the Document's license notice.

H. Include an unaltered copy of this License.

I. Preserve the section Entitled "History", Preserve its Title, and add to it an item stating at least the title, year, new authors, and publisher of the Modified Version as given on the Title Page. If there is no section Entitled "History" in the Document, create one stating the title, year, authors, and publisher of the Document as given on its Title Page, then add an item describing the Modified Version as stated in the previous sentence.

J. Preserve the network location, if any, given in the Document for public access to a Transparent copy of the Document, and likewise the network locations given in the Document for previous versions it was based on. These may be placed in the "History" section. You may omit a network location for a work that was published at least four years before the Document itself, or if the original publisher of the version it refers to gives permission.

K. For any section Entitled "Acknowledgements" or "Dedications", Preserve the Title of the section, and preserve in the section all the substance and tone of each of the contributor acknowledgements and/or dedications given therein.

L. Preserve all the Invariant Sections of the Document, unaltered in their text and in their titles. Section numbers or the equivalent are not considered part of the section titles.

M. Delete any section Entitled "Endorsements". Such a section may not be included in the Modified Version.

N. Do not retitle any existing section to be Entitled "Endorsements" or to conflict in title with any Invariant Section.

O. Preserve any Warranty Disclaimers.

If the Modified Version includes new front-matter sections or appendices that qualify as Secondary Sections and contain no material copied from the Document, you may at your option designate some or all of these sections as invariant. To do this, add their titles to the list of Invariant Sections in the Modified Version's license notice. These titles must be distinct from any other section titles.

You may add a section Entitled "Endorsements", provided it contains nothing but endorsements of your Modified Version by various parties—for example, statements of peer review or that the text has been approved by an organization as the authoritative definition of a standard.

You may add a passage of up to five words as a Front-Cover Text, and a passage of up to 25 words as a Back-Cover Text, to the end of the list of Cover Texts in the Modified Version. Only one passage of Front-Cover Text and one of Back-Cover Text may be added by (or through arrangements made by) any one entity. If the Document already includes a cover text for the same cover, previously added by you or by arrangement made by the same entity you are acting on behalf of, you may not add another; but you may replace the old one, on explicit permission from the previous publisher that added the old one.

The author(s) and publisher(s) of the Document do not by this License give permission to use their names for publicity for or to assert or imply endorsement of any Modified Version.

5. COMBINING DOCUMENTS

You may combine the Document with other documents released under this License, under the terms defined in section 4 above for modified versions, provided that you include in the combination all of the Invariant Sections of all of the original documents, unmodified, and list them all as Invariant Sections of your combined work in its license notice, and that you preserve all their Warranty Disclaimers.

The combined work need only contain one copy of this License, and multiple identical Invariant Sections may be replaced with a single copy. If there are multiple Invariant Sections with the same name but different contents, make the title of each such section unique by adding at the end of it, in parentheses, the name of the original author or publisher of that section if known, or else a unique number. Make the same adjustment to the section titles in the list of Invariant Sections in the license notice of the combined work.

In the combination, you must combine any sections Entitled "History" in the various original documents, forming one section Entitled "History"; likewise combine any sections Entitled "Acknowledgements", and any sections Entitled "Dedications". You must delete all sections Entitled "Endorsements."

6. COLLECTIONS OF DOCUMENTS

You may make a collection consisting of the Document and other documents released under this License, and replace the individual copies of this License in the various documents with a single copy that is included in the collection, provided that you follow the rules of this License for verbatim copying of each of the documents in all other respects.

You may extract a single document from such a collection, and distribute it individually under this License, provided you insert a copy of this License into the extracted document, and follow this License in all other respects regarding verbatim copying of that document.

7. AGGREGATION WITH INDEPENDENT WORKS

A compilation of the Document or its derivatives with other separate and independent documents or works, in or on a volume of a storage or distribution medium, is called an "aggregate" if the copyright resulting from the compilation is not used to limit the legal rights of the compilation's users beyond what the individual works permit. When the Document is included in an aggregate, this License does not apply to the other works in the aggregate which are not themselves derivative works of the Document.

If the Cover Text requirement of section 3 is applicable to these copies of the Document, then if the Document is less than one half of the entire aggregate, the Document's Cover Texts may be placed on covers that bracket the Document within the aggregate, or the electronic equivalent of covers if the Document is in electronic form. Otherwise they must appear on printed covers that bracket the whole aggregate.

8. TRANSLATION

Translation is considered a kind of modification, so you may distribute translations of the Document under the terms of section 4. Replacing Invariant Sections with translations requires special permission from their copyright holders, but you may include translations of some or all Invariant Sections in addition to the original versions of these Invariant Sections. You may include a translation of this License, and all the license notices in the Document, and any Warranty Disclaimers, provided that you also include the original English version of this License and the original versions of those notices and disclaimers. In case of a disagreement between the translation and the original version of this License or a notice or disclaimer, the original version will prevail.

If a section in the Document is Entitled "Acknowledgements", "Dedications", or "History", the requirement (section 4) to Preserve its Title (section 1) will typically require changing the actual title.

9. TERMINATION

You may not copy, modify, sublicense, or distribute the Document except as expressly provided under this License. Any attempt otherwise to copy, modify, sublicense, or distribute it is void, and will automatically terminate your rights under this License.

However, if you cease all violation of this License, then your license from a particular copyright holder is reinstated (a) provisionally, unless and until the copyright holder explicitly and finally terminates your license, and (b) permanently, if the copyright holder fails to notify you of the violation by some reasonable means prior to 60 days after the cessation.

Moreover, your license from a particular copyright holder is reinstated permanently if the copyright holder notifies you of the violation by some reasonable means, this is the first time you have received notice of violation of this License (for any work) from that copyright holder, and you cure the violation prior to 30 days after your receipt of the notice.

Termination of your rights under this section does not terminate the licenses of parties who have received copies or rights from you under this License. If your rights have been terminated and not permanently reinstated, receipt of a copy of some or all of the same material does not give you any rights to use it.

10. FUTURE REVISIONS OF THIS LICENSE

The Free Software Foundation may publish new, revised versions of the GNU Free Documentation License from time to time. Such new versions will be similar in spirit to the present version, but may differ in detail to address new problems or concerns. See http://www.gnu.org/copyleft/.

Each version of the License is given a distinguishing version number. If the Document specifies that a particular numbered version of this License "or any later version" applies to it, you have the option of following the terms and conditions either of that specified version or of any later version that has been published (not as a draft) by the Free Software Foundation. If the Document does not specify a version number of this License, you may choose any version ever published (not as a draft) by the Free Software Foundation. If the Document specifies that a proxy can decide which future versions of this License can be used, that proxy's public statement of acceptance of a version permanently authorizes you to choose that version for the Document.

11. RELICENSING

"Massive Multiauthor Collaboration Site" (or "MMC Site") means any World Wide Web server that publishes copyrightable works and also provides prominent facilities for anybody to edit those works. A public wiki that anybody can edit is an example of such a server. A "Massive Multiauthor Collaboration" (or "MMC") contained in the site means any set of copyrightable works thus published on the MMC site.

"CC-BY-SA" means the Creative Commons Attribution-Share Alike 3.0 license published by Creative Commons Corporation, a not-for-profit corporation with a principal place of business in San Francisco, California, as well as future copyleft versions of that license published by that same organization.

"Incorporate" means to publish or republish a Document, in whole or in part, as part of another Document.

An MMC is "eligible for relicensing" if it is licensed under this License, and if all works that were first published under this License somewhere other than this MMC, and subsequently incorporated in whole or in part into the MMC, (1) had no cover texts or invariant sections, and (2) were thus incorporated prior to November 1, 2008.

The operator of an MMC Site may republish an MMC contained in the site under CC-BY-SA on the same site at any time before August 1, 2009, provided the MMC is eligible for relicensing.

ADDENDUM: How to use this License for your documents

To use this License in a document you have written, include a copy of the License in the document and put the following copyright and license notices just after the title page:

```
Copyright (C)  year  your name.
Permission is granted to copy, distribute and/or modify this document
under the terms of the GNU Free Documentation License, Version 1.3
or any later version published by the Free Software Foundation;
with no Invariant Sections, no Front-Cover Texts, and no Back-Cover
Texts.  A copy of the license is included in the section entitled ''GNU
Free Documentation License''.
```

If you have Invariant Sections, Front-Cover Texts and Back-Cover Texts, replace the "with...Texts." line with this:

```
with the Invariant Sections being list their titles, with
the Front-Cover Texts being list, and with the Back-Cover Texts
being list.
```

If you have Invariant Sections without Cover Texts, or some other combination of the three, merge those two alternatives to suit the situation.

If your document contains nontrivial examples of program code, we recommend releasing these examples in parallel under your choice of free software license, such as the GNU General Public License, to permit their use in free software.

Index

C

D

M

N

O

P

Q

R

www.ingramcontent.com/pod-product-compliance
Lightning Source LLC
LaVergne TN
LVHW060138070326
832902LV00018B/2844